Aloha China
COOKBOOK

# COOKBOOK

**THE HEALTH AND FITNESS WAY OF COOKING**

**By MASTER CHEF—**

TITUS CHAN

---

ORIENTAL COOKBOOK
PUBLISHERS

Chan, Titus.
Aloha China cookbook.

Includes index.
1. Cookery, Chinese. I. Title.
TX724.5.C5C4626 1985 641.5951 85-383
ISBN 0-916630-46-3


Manufactured at Kingsport Press, Kingsport Tennessee, USA.
Book produced by Jane Wilkins Pultz.
Typeset by Stats 'n Graphics, Honolulu, Hawaii.
Available from: Oriental Cookbook Publishers, P.O. Box 8297,
Honolulu, Hawaii 96815

Many recipes in this book are from the television series ALOHA CHINA produced by the Mississippi Authority for Educational Television.

# *Dedication Page*



This book is dedicated to:

Mississippi Educational Television for its cooperation in co-producing with me, 26 half-hour Chinese cooking shows filmed in Hawaii.

The filming crew: Chris Rogers, Chris McGuire, Glenroy Smith, Eddie Bunkley and Stanley Graham, headed by Executive Producer Mr. Ed Van Cleef, for their competency and dedication to the task undertaken.

George Page, Executive Producer at WNET/13, New York and Frank Little of PBS Headquarters in Washington, D.C., who were the catalysts that started my television career in 1974.

KHET, Channel 11, Honolulu, and all the stations across the nation that have been, and are, carrying our shows now and in the past years.

The Public Broadcasting Service, which has been carrying my shows to educate the American public in Chinese culture and how to enjoy Chinese cuisine.

Hal and Thais Bothwell for their fabulous cooperation in not only offering their home to be turned into a Chinese kitchen for filming, but also for their patience in offering us complete privacy during our 12-14 hours of shooting each day.

# *TABLE OF CONTENTS*

*Acknowledgements* . . . . . *viii*
*Introduction* . . . . . *ix*
Titus Chan's China . . . . . 1
Appetizers . . . . . 9
Soups . . . . . 25
Salads . . . . . 33
For Vegetarians . . . . . 39
Recipes from Famous Honolulu Restaurants . . . . . 55
Seafood . . . . . 65
Poultry . . . . . 89
Peking Duck . . . . . 115
Pork . . . . . 133
Beef . . . . . 151
Tofu . . . . . 161
Microwave . . . . . 169
Vegetables . . . . . 183
Noodles . . . . . 195
Desserts . . . . . 203
Dips and Sauces . . . . . 213
Menus . . . . . 219
Cooking Tips . . . . . 245
*Index* . . . . . 273

# Acknowledgements

The author wishes to thank Mississippi Educational Television for co-producing the 26 shows titled *Aloha China,* for their professionalism, competency, and understanding.

Gary Pietsch for his outstanding photography in this book.

Chris McGuire, a producer at Mississippi ETV, who also contributed outstanding photos during the cooking sessions.

Hal and Thais Bothwell of Honolulu for their loving, sharing spirit in allowing their home to be converted into a Chinese setting for the taping of the *Aloha China* TV series. Thais also tested several microwave recipes for us.

John Dominis Restaurant of Honolulu for contributing some of its secret seafood recipes for which it is famous, and for providing the beautiful ocean-front restaurant setting for photographs.

Yen King Restaurant of Honolulu for providing a few of its famous secret recipes to be used as references and for its cooperation in a photo-taking session.

Pacific Beach and Outrigger Prince Kuhio hotels for their accommodations and fine food in their beautiful, well-operated establishments.

Patti's Chinese Kitchen for its generosity and cooperation.

Fred and Milly Singletary for sharing the privacy of their home in the preparation of this manuscript. Milly Singletary is a well-known Honolulu author who has written and published many books on Hawaii, including *Hawaii Bus and Travel Guide, Restaurant Encyclopedia of Hawaii, Honolulu's Best New Restaurants, Punchbowl, Hawaiian Quilting made Easy, Hilo Hattie's Official Biography,* and *The Party Planner,* to name a few. Her spirit of sharing her talents and time towards preparation of this book is greatly appreciated.

Attorney Ron Leong of the law firm of Kobayashi, Watanabe, Sugita and Kawashima, for years of patience and sound legal advice.

The cookie and cake recipes are the contribution of Ailene Carlos, an outstanding home economics teacher and a former student of the author.

# *Introduction*

Writing a good cookbook is one of the most frustrating experiences for a chef. Just think of all the tasty food that I will have had a "hand" in helping you to prepare, without the pleasure of sitting down with you to taste your creations.

On the other hand, I am pleased that you will have my book as a lasting resource for many enjoyable meals. If the mood strikes you, won't you please drop me a line and share with me some of your experiences. I am anxious to learn from you, as, hopefully, you will have learned from me.

All too often, cookbooks are looked upon as the "final word" when one wishes to prepare a particular dish. I hope to change this notion because, for me, a recipe is a carefully prepared point-of-departure for continued adventures in good eating. I recommend that you use the *Aloha China Cookbook* as a working resource.

First, try the recipes of your choice with as few modifications as possible. Get to know how I think each dish should taste. Then, before putting the book away, take the time to make some notes in the space provided to customize the recipes to suit your own taste. Of course, you may find that the recipes are very much to your liking. In that case, note that also. This will save you time in the future when you are trying to figure out an answer to the perennial question, "What's for dinner?"

Since cooking is becoming more and more popular as a pastime for both men and women, your own notes will help you to keep track of those recipes that are sure to become your favorites. Besides, whoever said that you shouldn't write in books, except, perhaps, your third grade teacher?

Cookbooks are meant to be used, and by that I mean, you should feel free to make notes in the *Aloha China Cookbook.* Just think, you are going to be my co-author, so to speak, and your copy of my book will become a valuable heirloom, to be shared and passed on as a treasure for generations to come.

The organization of this book is simplicity itself. Like most cookbooks on the market today, I have divided the subject matter into logical chapters. The recipes are designed to help you to create many tasty and healthy meals for your family and friends. Please feel free to consult other cookbooks if you do not want to prepare only Chinese food. After all, you must be pleased with your efforts, or why bother . . . just send out for pizza! Like everything else, mixing and matching are the order of the day, and why not? What tastes best to you is what you should eat.

Most of the "great" cuisines of the world share many underlying principles: principles such as freshness, using seasonal foods, balance, and variety. In these respects most great cuisines are compatible. Therefore, go ahead and combine recipes from various sources. Just remember, the goal is to enjoy whatever it is you cook. You may not "live to eat," but you most certainly can get a greater measure of enjoyment by eating creatively.

Nutrition and health are becoming increasingly important as we all strive to improve the quality of life that we enjoy. Just look around at the astonishing number of people who are engaged in recreational sports and exercise. After working out, whether it be aerobics, jogging, playing tennis, swimming or training at a gym, your appetite may be diminished, but at the same time, each of us is ready to treat ourself to tasty, nutritious food. Cooking the Titus Chan way is just what the body ordered. Eating Chinese food may be the simplest way to good health and longevity.

With these brief remarks, I want to introduce you to my brand of good cooking, and encourage you to experiment with the recipes in my cookbook. This is your passport to freshness, seasonal foods, balance and variety. Join me, won't you, and know that your efforts will be rewarded, not by gains in weight, but by the delighted smiles from your family and friends as you share in preparing and consuming your own good food.

I begin this book with an armchair tour of some of the famous sights and restaurants of today's China. I feel that the variety and diversity of Chinese cooking is easier to understand when you have a picture of the land and its people because, just as here in North America, China is a country of distinct regions. Regional climate, terrain, livestock and native vegetation help to define and shape cooking styles. Just think about Southern Fried Chicken for a minute, and you will see what I mean.

Modern cooks like you have less and less time these days to spend on meal preparation; yet, as we become more and more sophisticated, we demand greater and greater taste experiences. This seeming paradox is addressed in my chapter on *Cooking Tips;* it is a chapter filled with time-saving ideas, and a review of cooking techniques as well as hints on using the latest labor-saving kitchen appliances in order to shorten preparation time. Additionally, because we share a concern for good health and nutrition, I also discuss some flavorful options and ingredients that you may not have associated with Chinese cooking. As you will discover, one of the most interesting alternatives to meat of any kind is tofu, a vegetable product that can be used in dishes from soup to dessert.

Join me now, as we begin our chef's tour of China, and enter the taste realm of Chinese cooking. Let me be your guide and teacher the first time through, but be ready to strike out on your own. Remember, each of you is going to be my co-author, so make this book your own. May you derive as much pleasure from preparing these recipes as I did in setting them down for you. ENJOY!

Honolulu, Hawaii 1985.

*Titus Chan's China*

# Titus Chan's China

The China of my boyhood was not the China of today. I guess that can be said by anyone of his or her childhood and youth, but in my case, images of my China reside only in my memory. Like many other Chinese, or Han, as we sometimes call ourselves, I am proud of my language, culture and history and wish to share some of this heritage with each of you through the cooking of Chinese food.

It was not long after the establishment of the first unified Chinese state that members of the Imperial household, government officials, and scholars began to turn their attention to the enjoyment of food. With each change in government and the rise and fall of dynasties, the Han peoples were forced to adapt to new cultural, political and religious influences. While each new dynasty had an immediate impact on the country, it was the Han who ultimatey changed the conquering hordes, and brought them into the mainstream of Chinese life.

China is not one nation, but rather a rich and diverse mosaic of cultures and people, all of whom share the same written language while maintaining their own regional identities. Politics and political affiliations have always been viewed as useful coping behaviors, and though governments come and go, Chinese cooking continues to evolve as a focus for understanding the Han and their history.

Chinese cooking is as varied as the talent of each chef. Tastes and smells that I fondly recall may not be to your liking, but it is upon those remembrances that I base my recipes, as well as, of course, the experiences that I personally managed to collect as I learned to cook professionally. While I may eat certain things that some of you might find repulsive, there is within the broad spectrum of foods a common meeting ground from which all of us can develop an understanding of, and mutual respect for, each other's food preferences and different cooking styles.

The China to which I will be taking you in the following pages is one that is dear to the hearts of gourmets, whatever their nationalities. It is a China filled with exciting places and wonderful stories. Most importantly, it is a China that, in recalling its past glories, is not tied to the past, but rather is forward-looking and progressive.

During my many travels, I have been very fortunate to be able to visit many world-renowned restaurants in different places around the globe. On my most recent trip, I was able to sample specialties at some of the finest restaurants in the People's Republic of China. It has been many years that Americans have not been able to travel to China, but with the recent "thaw" in relations between the United States and China, Americans are once again able to go there and sample some of the finest foods in the world.

BEIJING (Peking): China's capital is known for a most famous dish, Peking Duck, and the most famous restaurant that features this exceptional delicacy is called *Quanjade,* Wong Ping Mon, (phone 338-031). *Quanjade* means "Gathering friends together to enjoy fine food is a virtue." This restaurant, in one form or another, has been serving patrons Peking Duck for more than 100 years! Most recently, the Chinese spent a considerable sum of money to build a new multi-story *Quanjade* that serves Peking Duck exclusively, and that can seat more than 2,000 people at once. This establishment is always busy, because, Peking Duck has become such a national culinary treasure. The government has produced a thick manual that describes the whole process for producing Peking Duck, from the hatching of the egg and raising of the duckling to its final presentation for dinner. Each duck is carefully raised and force-fed for the last two to three weeks of its 65-day life. It is this final force-feeding that produces the deliciously plump duck.

Peking Duck, notwithstanding, the capital of China is the nation's main political, economic, cultural and communications center. Beijing is a city with a long history.

Early in the 10th Century, it was the secondary capital of the Liao Kingdom, and subsequently the capital of the Jin, Yuan, Ming and Ching Dynasties. Today, Beijing is one of the country's major industrial cities. Agricultural production in the suburbs has gone up considerably. The city is also known for its traditional arts and crafts, which include sculpture, jade carving, cloisonne, and carpet manufacturing. Majestic Tien An Mon (Gate of Heavenly Peace) stands in the center of the city at the north of Tian An Mon Square. In urban Beijing, there are a wealth of ancient sites and exquisite gardens. Likewise, the restaurants and varieties of regional cuisines available are other resources to be explored. *Quanjade* is one of the best restaurants, and its Peking Duck is without peer.

KWANGCHOW (Canton): Kwangchow, or Canton, as it was known previously, is the provincial capital of Kwantung Province. It is located at the northern edge of the Pearl River Delta. Kwangchow is an ancient city, its initial construction dating back to the 8th century B.C. It is not only the political, economic and cultural center of Kwantung Province, but also one of the ports for Chinese export and foreign trade.

The Chinese Export Commodities Fair is held in Canton each spring and autumn. The fair plays a very useful part in promoting trade and friendly contacts with other countries and regions of the world.

Kwangchow is a city rich in revolutionary traditions. There are memorials to the revolution, such as the National Institute of Martyrs in Kwangchow Uprisings, and the Mausoleum of the 72 Martyrs at Huang Huangang.

Kwangchow is home to some of the most adventurous people in the world.

The Cantonese have historically been great travelers and have been responsible for more than 90 percent of the Chinese restaurants throughout the world. In fact, to most people, Cantonese and Chinese cooking are synonymous.

The *Bon Kai Restaurant,* located in the Bon Tong area of Kwangchow City, 151 Heung Yo Road #1, (phone 856-55), is one of the finest restaurants in Kwangchow, and is called by many "The Pearl of Lichee Bay Lake." The chefs here are famous for using fresh lotus root, water chestnuts, bamboo shoots and a rich variety of local ingredients to create tasty dishes.

The restaurant is in a natural setting that is breathtaking in its diversity. More than 30 dining rooms overlook the shoreline amidst ponds and rocky outcroppings. The interior decor is reflective of the Sung Dynasty.

For fine dining, *The Bon Kai Restaurant* is unequalled in its Dim Sum or Tea Lunch menu because the 50 to 60 modern-day chefs there carry on the tradition begun by Chef Lo Quan, who was known as "The King of Dim Sum" in China. Today, the menu at *The Bon Kai Restaurant* features 400-500 different Cantonese dishes and the chefs routinely prepare 1,000 different kinds of cakes, pastries and Dim Sum for the more than 30,000 patrons that often crowd the 1,700 to 1,800 seats in this extraordinary restaurant.

The marvelous food and exquisite surroundings prompt visitors and local residents alike to return again and again to dine in their favorite settings. This is a world-class restaurant worthy of visiting, in the heart of the adventurer's China.

SHANGHAI: In this cosmopolitan seaport and trading center, citizens and visitors alike have enjoyed lamb firepot cooking at *The Hong Cheong Hing Lamb Restaurant* since 1913, although it has been fashionable to eat lamb firepot since the mid-1700s. *The Hong Cheong Hing Lamb Restaurant* is located at Lin Won Road #6, (phone 538-0520).

Shanghai is a city that is under the direct jurisdiction of the central government of China. Shanghai is the largest city in China and in the world as well. It has a population of 11 million, and is China's most important foreign trade port. Shanghai has the advanced industrial, scientific and technological base for future development and growth. Its major points of interest include the Shanghai Museum, Yu Yuen Garden, Jade Buddha Temple and the Children's Palace. The Shanghai antique and curio stores have the largest collection of antiques and jewelry for sale to foreigners and locals alike. The lingering influence of earlier Western colonial excursions is still visible, although now Shanghai is uniquely Chinese and international in flavor.

Just as with the Peking ducks, the lambs used by *Hong Cheong Hing* must be raised according to strict rules and regulations. None are to be more than three months old, and must weigh between 30 and 40 pounds with a moderate amount of marbling. The lamb is sliced very thin and cooked by dunking the meat into boiling broth. As each piece is cooked, the patron dunks the tender cooked meat into assorted dips and eats it with assorted vegetables.

Toward the end of the meal, additional vegetables and noodles are added to the broth to make a hearty soup. Other specialties at *Hong Cheong Hing* include Steamed Crab and Shanghai Style Steamed Fish.

*The Hong Cheong Hing Lamb Restaurant* was showcased on Chinese Television in 1979, and since then its reputation has grown. This is definitely a worthwhile stop the next time you are in Shanghai.

Another culinary highlight in Shanghai is *The Kung Duck Lum Vegetarian Restaurant,* 43 Wang Ho Road, (phone 531-313), established in 1922. Mr. Chou, the original owner, was a devout Buddhist, and was encouraged by friends and monks at a nearby temple to open a restaurant serving vegetarian dishes. Since the very first day, *Kung Duck Lum* has been successful, and today is the mecca of vegetarian cooking in Shanghai and perhaps in the world as well.

One of the fundamental principles of vegetarian cooking is the insistence on fresh, seasonal ingredients. Tofu which is used by the chefs at *Kung Duck Lum* is homemade daily, and because it is so fresh, it has an unusual taste and texture totally missing from commercially manufactured soybean products.

Tofu takes on a number of disguises, and appears in dishes like stir-fried shrimp, and sweet and sour yellow fish. The color, texture, fragrance and taste of these dishes compare favorably with dishes made with actual shrimp and fish. Tofu in its myriad forms – dried into sheets, fresh, fried and mashed – is magically transformed by these chefs into tasty meatless dishes that "fool" the eyes and tongues of foreign visitors and locals alike.

The restaurant lists more than 400 dishes on its menu, and in recent years many foreigners have become repeat visitors and have proclaimed *Kung Duck Lum's* vegetarian food to be the best of its kind in the world.

The vegetarian recipes in this book are healthful alternatives and may be combined with meat dishes to increase fiber and roughage in your diet. Also, practically speaking, cooking more seasonal vegetables on a regular basis will help to cut down on food costs for the average North American family. What could be better than learning to eat better for less? Try a number of these dishes, experiment with them, and I guarantee your family will become converts. There is much to be learned about non-meat cuisines, and starting with recipes from *Kung Duck Lum Vegetarian Restaurant* makes a wonderful beginning.

CHENGTU: Chengtu is the provincial capital of Szechwan Province, which is located 950 miles southwest of Beijing. It has a population of more than 4 million people. Chengtu is one of the ancient cultural cities in southwestern China. Two thousand years ago, at the end of the Chou dynasty, the King of Shu moved his capital to this place and named it Chengtu. Chengtu is not very hot in the summer, and seldom is there snow in the winter. The climate is mild and rainfall abundant. The soil is fertile and the natural produce is rich therefore the plains surrounding Chengtu have long been known as a land of great abundance.

Chengtu has a number of beautiful parks and places of historical interest, such as the House of Tu Fu (a famous poet), the Temple in Memory of Chu Ke Liang, the famous project of the Tuchiangyen Irrigation System, and the Exhibition Hall for Class Education. Chengtu also has, as a culinary resource, *The Sing Do Restaurant,* Sing Do Main Street, East #642, (phone 5338). Considered by many, myself included, as one of the most elegantly decorated restaurants in Szechwan Province, this restaurant can accommodate 1,300 persons at a time. It has a menu from which dishes may be selected to commemorate festive occasions as well as tasty economical home-style dinners.

The kitchen staff has a depth unequalled in the world today in preparing and teaching Szechwan cooking. Because of the location of Szechwan Province and its proximity to food resources, the restaurant is able to draw upon a wellspring of more than 8,000 dishes, and regularly prepares more than 120 dim sum tea snacks. The menu routinely highlights 60 traditional and popular dishes with chefs explaining how each dish is prepared. Dining at the *Sing Do Restaurant* can be a truly educational experience.

Regional favorites include Tea Smoked Duck and Pan Pan Chicken. This latter dish is also known as "Strange-Taste Chicken." Strange-Taste Chicken really just represents a Szechwan method of cooking.

*Kung Pao* is a method of cooking that was originated by Provincial Governor Ding nearly 100 years ago. Governor Ding was highly regarded for his administrative abilities as well as for his gourmet tastes, and when he directed his chefs to prepare food in a particular manner, and it was judged a great success, his friends honored him by naming the technique *Kung Pao* after Governor Ding's official title.

More recently Szechwan chefs have developed a number of so-called "show" dishes, otherwise known as decorated cold plates, where the food is arranged in beautiful and intricate patterns taking the shape of peacocks and other fanciful creatures.

HANGCHOW: Hangchow is the provincial capital of Chekiang Province, located along the southeastern coast of China on Hangchow Bay. Hangchow is an old city with a history of 2,500 years. This city is famous for its scenic beauty, especially the West Lake with its arching bridges, willows, plum blossoms and ponds. There are some other famous spots such as The Solidarity Hills, Pagoda of Six Harmonies, Ling Yin Temple, Tiger Spring and Jade Mountain. Hangchow silk is famous around the world. Other local products, such as glassware, scissors, wood and bamboo carvings are also popular. Hangchow also produces one of the best teas in China: Lung Chin (Dragon Wells) Tea. 

*The Hangchow Restaurant,* Hangchow City, 132 Yin On Road, (phone 234-77), is located near the beautiful West Lake in Hangchow. This restaurant has a kitchen staff of nearly 100. The restaurant itself is an imposing structure, three stories high. *The Hangchow Restaurant's* food has become so popular that more than 30 chefs who were trained at the Hangchow now reside in embassies and diplomatic mission around the world.

Visiting dignitaries and tired travelers have always found the Hangchow region relaxing and refreshing. Perhaps this is due in no small part to the simplicity in the preparation of the region's fresh fish; a single reminder to those wrapped up in life's complexities that some of the best things in life are also the simplest.

CHANGSHA: Changsha, the provincial capital of Hunan Province, is located in the south central part of China. The city has been inhabited for more than 3,000 years. Changsha is known as the boyhood home of the late Chairman Mao Tse Tung. The First Normal School was the school that Mao attended as a boy, and later he taught at the same school. There are other attractions such as the Self Study University, Clear Water Pond, Orange Island, and the lovely Greening Pavillion. In the Hunan Provincial Museum, there is a display of valuable artifacts, including the 2,000-year-old, well-preserved body of a royal princess found in the Han Tomb at Mawangtui. Changsha is also famous for its exquisite porcelain figures, fine embroidery and, of course, Hunan Cuisine.

*The Fire Palace Restaurant,* 149 Bor Jee Stret, (phone 235-91), Changsha, was established in 1932 after Changsha experienced a devastating fire. Like the legendary phoenix, *The Fire Palace Restaurant* rose from the skeleton of the Fire God Temple, a temple that dated back to the mid-1600s.

*The Fire Palace Restaurant* is not as elaborate as some of the other restaurants that I have visited, nor is it known for its extravagant and expensive dishes and culinary creations. Rather, this restaurant concentrates on preserving the best traditional dishes regardless of their origin, and has been able to turn the humble tofu into 120 unique incarnations of the fiery Hunan style.

As a matter of fact, the tofu that is made for this restaurant has become so famous that it is often flown to Beijing to be used in preparing authentic Hunanese dishes for visiting dignitaries. The Hunanese also excel in their creative use of Chinese black mushrooms, bamboo shoots and black beans to create tasty and unique dishes. *The Fire Palace Restaurant* has five dining rooms, each specializing in a particular kind of food.

★ ★ ★ ★

The reason for writing this chapter is to give you, the reader, a better idea of the background and a feeling for the foods that you may wish to prepare. These places are very special to me, and hold treasures beyond price. It is my fondest hope that many of you who read this book will be able to travel to China and experience for yourself many of the culinary pleasures that I have described in this brief armchair cook's tour. The next chapter is filled with practical suggestions, cooking tips and innovative ideas.

*Appetizers*

蝦片

# *Deep Fried Colorful Shrimp Chips*

This is great for entertaining. All you need to do is deep-fry the chips from the box. It is very colorful and takes only seconds to cook. If your company says that you must have spent a whole week in the kitchen, just keep smiling.

*1 8-ounce box shrimp-flavored chips (assorted colors)*
*3-4 cups vegetable oil*

Heat oil in a wok to approximately 400-450°. Deep fry a small handful of shrimp chips at a time. Use a wire basket to stir while deep frying. As soon as the chips puff up and stop expanding, in 5-10 seconds, they are done. Remove from oil and drain on paper towel. Serve hot or cold.

Serves: 10-12
Cooking time: 5 minutes

# 炸大蝦

## *Deep Fried Shrimp*

The Cantonese use this dish as an entree or as an hors d'oeuvre dish. For partying this is terrific because one can prepare the shrimp ahead of time, enabling the host or hostess time to get dressed. In two more minutes of deep-frying, you have a beautiful golden brown seafood dish for your company.

*½ pound shrimp (medium size)*
*Salt and pepper to taste*

*Batter:*
*1 egg, lightly whipped*
*½ cup cornstarch*
*2 teaspoons vegetable oil*
*1 tablespoon water*

*4-6 cups of vegetable oil*

*Pinch of salt*

Shell, butterfly and devein shrimp. Rinse and drain. Pat dry with towel. Add salt and pepper. (If used for appetizer, keep the shell on the tail.)

In a large bowl, combine the ingredients to form a batter. Dip shrimp in batter and coat well.

Heat oil in wok to 375°. Drop shrimp in the oil one at a time and deep fry 1½ minutes or until golden brown and floating.

Drain the shrimp on an absorbent towel. Immediately sprinkle with a pinch of salt. Serve hot or at room temperature.

Serves: 4-6
Cooking time: 20 minutes

蝦多士

# *Shrimp Toast*

This Cantonese hors d'oeuvre feature is especially appealing to the eye. Having the shrimp riding on a piece of golden brown toast creates an unusual textural effect when your company comes to the cocktail table.

*3 ounces ground pork*
*½ dozen water chestnuts, finely chopped*
*½ cup green onion, chopped*
*1 egg, whipped*

*Seasoning:*
*1 teaspoon vegetable oil*
*2 teaspoons oyster sauce*
*½ teaspoon sugar*
*2 teaspoons wine*
*1½ teaspoons corn starch*

*1 dozen shrimp (20-25 per pound size)*

*1½ teaspoons corn starch*
*1 egg white, lightly whipped*
*Salt and pepper to taste*

*6 slices of white bread, cut in half*

*3-4 cups vegetable oil*

*Pinch of salt*

In a large bowl, mix the egg, chestnuts, onions, pork and seasoning.

Shell and butterfly shrimp. Wash, drain and pat dry with paper towel.

In a bowl, combine shrimp, corn starch, egg white, salt and pepper. Mix well.

Spread the pork mixture evenly on each of the bread pieces, place 1 shrimp on top of the bread, lightly press down to stick. (Placing the back of the shrimp upward)

Heat oil to 300°, placing 3 or 4 pieces of bread mixture in the oil with the shrimp side down. Deep-fry for 1 minute. Turn to the other side and fry for another minute.

Take out and drain on absorbent towl. While it is hot, sprinkle with pinch of salt, serve hot or cold.

Makes 1 dozen toasts
Cooking time: 45 minutes

Note: May be made ready for deep frying 2 days ahead of time.

脆皮鮮蝦餃子



# *Deep Fried Shrimp Gau Gee*

This Cantonese deep-fried dish is like a deep-fried won ton. It is perfect to serve as "heavy hors d'oeuvres." Add a dish of chow mein and a few other items, and your guests can have a good happy hour, just enjoying the appetizers instead of a formal meal.

*2-3 ounces ground pork*
*½ dozen water chestnuts, finely chopped*
*½ cup green onion, chopped*

*Seasoning:*
*1 teaspoon vegetable oil*
*2 teaspoons oyster sauce*
*½ teaspoon sugar*
*1 teaspoon wine*
*1½ teaspoons cornstarch*

*1 dozen medium shrimp*

*1 egg white, lightly whipped*
*Salt and pepper to taste*

*12-16 pieces won ton skin (wrappers)*

*1 egg, lightly whipped*

*3-4 cups of vegetable oil*

*Pinch of salt*

In a large bowl, mix the water chestnuts, onion, pork and seasoning.

Shell and chop shrimp. Wash, drain and pat dry with paper towel.

Combine shrimp with the pork mixture. Well mix to form gau gee filling.

At the center of each wrapper, place 1-1½ tablespoons of filling. Seal edges of the skin with whipped egg; with a table knife or spoon, fold the skin in half and press down lightly to seal.

Heat the oil to 300-375°. Deep fry gau gee 1½ minute per side or until golden brown and floating. Drain on absorbent paper. When they are still hot, sprinkle with pinch of salt. Serve hot or cold.

Serves: 6-8
Cooking time: 20 minutes

# 油炸斑球

## *Golden Brown Sea Bass Fillet Appetizer*

This recipe is very good for serving as hors d'oeuvres during the cocktail hour. The sea bass meat is tender and firm, so it's easy for finger food.

*1 pound sea bass fillets (may substitute sole or snapper)*
*1 teaspoon vegetable oil*
*Salt and pepper to taste*

*Batter:*
*1 egg, lightly whipped*
*½ cup corn starch*
*1 tablespoon water*
*2 teaspoons oil*

*4-5 cups vegetable oil*

*Pinch of salt*
*1 cup catsup or oyster sauce*

Remove bone from fillet and slice it ½ inch thick by 1½ inch long by 1 inch wide. Add oil, salt and pepper and mix well. Combine the batter ingredients in a bowl. Coat the fillets with batter.

Heat oil in wok to 375°. Add coated fillet slices to wok, 1 (one) piece at a time. Stir and turn to keep fish separate. Cook 2-3 minutes.

Place fish on paper towel to drain. Sprinkle with pinch of salt while hot.

Place the catsup or oyster sauce in a small dish. Serve with the fillets as a dip.

Serves: 4-6
Cooking time: 20 minutes

# 四川棒棒雞

## *Szechwan Pan Pan Chicken*

There is more variety in cold foods in the Szechuan cuisine then in the Cantonese. Pan Pan Chicken is one of the examples, and is one of the very rare dishes that is somewhat close to the western taste, with the use of peanut butter. A delightful dish for your happy hour.

*1 fryer*

*Sauce:*
*2 tablespoons sherry*
*2½ tablespoons peanut butter*
*2½ teaspoons sesame oil*
*2 teaspoons sugar*
*2 teaspoons soy sauce*
*2 teaspoons Chinese red vinegar or cider vinegar*
*2 fresh or dried red chili pepper, seeded and thinly sliced*

Follow instructions for "Prepared Chicken" in chapter on poultry.

Debone and skin the prepared chicken. Cut chicken meat into strips approximately 1½ inches long and ¼ inch thick. One may use fully cooked chicken meat.

In a large bowl combine the peanut butter and sherry and mix well. Add the remaining ingredients. Add the chicken to the bowl and thoroughly mix. Place chicken on a serving plate and sprinkle chili pepper on top as garnish.

Serves: 12
Cooking time: 30 minutes

# 川式怪味雞

## *Szechwan Strange-Taste Chicken*

The people of Szechwan expect a certain spicy hot and peppery flavor to their cuisine. This chicken recipe has a well-blended flavor and thus in Szechwan it has a taste strange to their usual expectations. Because the title of this dish, "Strange-Taste Chicken" is often ignored by Westerners not willing to take a chance on such a dish. Thus many restaurants in America have changed the name to "Wonderful-Taste Chicken" and have won acceptance for it by their patrons.

*1 medium-size chicken fryer, fully cooked*

*3 cups green onion, cut into 1 inch long pieces*
*1 cup dry-roasted peanuts*

*Seasoning:*
*2 teaspoons red Chinese vinegar or cider vinegar*
*2 teaspoons chili paste with garlic or to taste, since this is very hot and salty*
*1 tablespoon sesame oil*
*2 teaspoons soy sauce*
*1 tablespoon light brown sugar*
*2 teaspoons straight sherry*
*Salt and pepper to taste*

*1 tomato*
*1 lemon*
*Few sprigs of parsley*

Debone the cooked chicken and cut into one-inch squares. For healthy eating, skin may be discarded.

Combine the green onion and ⅔ of the peanuts with the chicken in a large bowl.
Combine ingredients of the seasoning and mix well with chicken. Sprinkle the remaining peanuts on top.

Cut tomato in half, then cut into thin slices. Place the tomato around the rim of the platter and place the lemon on top of the tomato. Garnish with parsley.

Serve cold.

Serves: 4-6
Cooking time: 30 minutes

# 夏威夷式怪味雞

# *Wonderful Taste Chicken: Hawaiian Style*

*1 Prepared Chicken or pre-cooked or baked chicken from supermarket*

*Marinade:*
*1 tablespoon apple cider*
*2 teaspoons ground chili or hot sauce*
*1 tablespoon light brown sugar*
*1 tablespoons sherry*
*2 tablespoons soy sauce*
*½ tablespoon sesame oil*
*1 tablespoon oyster sauce*
*Salt to taste*

*½ round onion, cut into 1½ inch strips*

*2 cups deep fried won ton skin cut in ½-inch wide*
*2 inch long pieces or 2 cups deep fried Mai Fun (long rice)*

*1 tablespoon toasted sesame seeds*
*Pinch cilantro, cut in 1-inch pieces*

Debone Prepared Chicken and cut meat into 1-inch squares.

Mix marinade with chicken and onions. Serve immediately.

Serves: 8-10
Preparation time: 15 minutes

Right before serving toss in won ton skin or mai fun. Sprinkle with sesame seeds and top with cilantro or American parsley.

# 上海醉雞

## *Shanghai Drunken Chicken*

This involves a unique cooking method in the Shanghainese cuisine. Soaking the cooked chicken in wines makes a very different dish from the usual dishes prepared by stir-frying or deep frying. It is good to serve during the cocktail hour - but just watch yourself. The chicken can be a drunken chicken, and I don't want any drunken person.

*1 fryer in cold ginger-onion sauce*

*Sauce:*
*1 teaspoon salt*
*1 tablespoon peeled and chopped ginger root or garlic*
*3 cups sake or wine of your own choice*
*1 can or 2 cups chicken broth*

*Salt and pepper to taste*

Prepare chicken according to "Prepared Chicken" recipe.

Cut chicken in quarters and pat dry.

Mix ingredients in a pan, then add in the chicken. Cover and refrigerate for 24 hours. Turn chicken one or two times to make sure the chicken is well soaked in the wine sauce.

Cut the chicken into pieces approximately 1 inch wide and 2 inches long. Place on a serving plate, and sprinkle 2 tablespoons wine sauce on top before serving. Garnish with sprigs of cilantro (Chinese parsley) or regular parsley.

Serves: 12
Cooking time: 40 minutes

# 四川紅油雞塊

## *Szechwan Red-Oil Chicken*

Red oil is one of the cooking methods in the Szechwan cuisine, just like the stir-fry or steaming among the Cantonese dishes. This dish is easy to make because it is simple in nature, and it is a great dish to do because it can be prepared ahead. It is a delightful cold dish.

*1 fryer, 3-3½ pounds*

*Sauce:*
*1 tablespoon red Chinese vinegar or cider vinegar*
*1 tablespoon soy sauce*
*2 teaspoons sugar*
*2 teaspoons sesame seeds*
*2 teaspoons peeled ginger root, chopped*
*⅓ cup chopped green onion*
*Chili oil or chili paste to taste*

*¼ cup roasted peanuts, freshly crushed*

Prepare the chicken according to instructions for "Prepared Chicken."

Debone the chicken and skin the prepared chicken and cut meat into 1-inch by 1½-inch pieces.

Mix the sauce ingredients well and combine with the chicken meat. Mix well. Pour the contents into a serving plate. Sprinkle crushed peanuts as a garnish on top. Serve cold.

Serves: 4-6
Cooking time: 1 hour

# Golden Brown Vegetarian Spring Rolls

Spring rolls have been a great favorite of many westerners. We insert this recipe in our book to please the people who enjoy spring rolls, yet don't eat meat. By preparing the spring roll by the following method, you will enjoy this spring roll as much as those who enjoy the spring roll with meat.

*1 package spring roll wrappers*
*6 dried black mushrooms (may be substituted with 1 can stems & pieces), drained*
*1 cup chives*
*2 cups celery, thinly julienned 1-inch long*
*1 large carrot, grated*
*2 cups finely shredded cabbage*
*1 cup water chestnuts, finely chopped*

*Seasoning:*
*1½ tablespoons soy sauce*
*2 tablespoons oyster sauce*
*2 teaspoons sesame oil*
*2 teaspoons sugar*
*Salt and pepper to taste*

*2 tablespoons chicken broth or water*

*Thickening base:*
*2½ tablespoons cornstarch*
*3½ tablespoons water*

*Seal:*
*1 egg, lightly beaten*

*4-6 cups vegetable oil*

*Note: To make other types of Spring Rolls, add 1 cup of finely shredded, cooked chicken meat or 1 cup of fully cooked char siu or ham, shredded.*

Soak dried mushrooms in water for 30 minutes. Cut and discard stems. Squeeze out the water. Cut into thin strips.

Cut chives into 1-inch long pieces.

Stir-fry chives and celery until fragrant. Add the remaining vegetables and stir-fry for 1 minute. Put in all the seasonings and stir-fry for 30 seconds. Add 2 tablespoons chicken broth or water. When sauce comes to a boil, add in thickening base. Let cool and put in freezer for 30 minutes.

Spread each wrapper, and put about 2 tablespoons of mixture in the wrapper. Fold it as if folding an envelope. At the tip, use the egg as a seal, then roll to fold. Rolls may be prepared two days ahead and put in refrigerator. Cover with a damp towel.

Heat oil to 350°. Place 4-5 rolls at one time in the oil, deep-fry until they float and turn golden brown. Take out and drain on absorbent paper immediately. Sprinkle lightly with salt, if desired.

*Wrappers may be purchased in Chinatown or gourmet shops.*

Serve as an appetizer. May serve along with 1 cup of sweet and sour sauce.

Yield: 1½ to 2 dozen rolls
Cooking time: 1½ hours

## *Golden Brown Oyster Rolls*

*4-5 old fashioned oyster rolls*
*1 egg, lightly whipped*
*1½ cups cornstarch*

*4-6 cups vegetable oil*

*Parsley*

Dip each oyster roll into the egg and coat with cornstarch. Refrigerate for an hour, preferably overnight.

Heat oil to approximately 350 degrees. Deep fry 2 of the oyster rolls at a time for about 3-5 minutes or until golden brown.

Serve in a platter or bowl. Top with a pinch of parsley. Serve as heavy pupus (appetizers, hors d'oeuvres) or serve as an entree. It is better to serve this either before or after a dish that has a sauce or gravy.

Makes approximately 20 rolls.

# 舊式蠔豉卷

## *Old-Fashioned Oyster Rolls*

Oyster rolls may be served as an hors d'oeuvre or as an entree. Most of the preparation can be completed one to two days in advance; deep frying and sauce-making are done at the last moment.

You can buy the dried oysters and Chinese mushrooms in Chinatown. The caul fat is fat taken from pork and shaped like a net. Some people call it a net fat. It is already cleaned and you can purchase it from the pork stands in Chinatown. Fish cake is made from fish meat combined with cornstarch and water, and whipped by hand to form a paste. This can also be purchased in Chinatown.

*1/4 pound dried oysters*

*1 square inch ginger root, optional*
*6 green onions*
*3-4 cups water*

*1 8-ounce can or 1 1/2 cups water chestnuts*
*1 roll salted preserved turnip greens (tai tau tsoi)*
*1/4 cup roasted peanuts*
*1 egg*
*1/2 dozen dried Chinese mushrooms*
*1/4 cup ground pork*
*1/2 pound fish cake*

*Marinade:*
*1 1/2 tablespoons cornstarch*
*1 tablespoon straight sherry*
*2 teaspoons soy sauce*
*2 tablespoons oyster sauce*
*1 teaspoon sesame oil*
*2 teaspoons sugar*
*Salt and pepper to taste*

*1/2 pound caul fat (mong yau)*

Soak oysters in cold water for 1/2 hour or until softened, then hand pick fractured oysters shells, if any, from each oyster.

Crush the ginger and onions and add to oysters. Gently boil for about 1/2 hour or until tender. Discard vegetables and drain. Chop both oysters and chestnuts coarsely. Rinse turnip greens and chop finely. Crush peanuts. Lightly whip egg. Soak mushrooms in 2 cups of water for 20 minutes. Squeeze out water. Cut and discard stems and dice. Combine all of the ingredients, including pork and fish cake, in a large bowl.

Add all of the marinade in the bowl and mix well with the ingredients.

Spread caul fat on a cutting board and place marinated ingredients at the edge of it. Roll it once and tuck the end, rolling it twice to form a roll approximately 7-8 inches long and about 1½ inches in diameter.

In a steamer, bring water to a boil. Brush the steaming tray with a touch of vegetable oil and place the rolls on it. Cover and steam 15-20 minutes. Take out when cooled. Cut each roll into 5-6 equal segments. Cover and steam.

Yield: 4-5 rolls

# *Soft, Steamed Oyster Rolls In Oyster Sauce*

*Sauce:*
*2 teaspoons vegetable oil*

*2 teaspoons chopped garlic*

*1 tablespoon straight sherry or brandy*
*1 cup chicken broth*
*2 teaspoons soy sauce*
*1 teaspoon light brown sugar*
*1 teaspoon sesame oil*
*Salt and pepper to taste*

*Thickening base:*
*1 tablespoon cornstarch*
*2 tablespoons water*

*1 egg yolk, whipped*

*1 teaspoon vegetable oil optional*
*¼ cup peanuts, crushed*
*pinch of parsley*

Steam oyster rolls segments in a steamer or in a microwave oven. Arrange them in bowl.

Heat wok or a saucepan over medium high heat for 30 seconds. Spread vegetable oil at the bottom of wok. Stir-fry chopped garlic for a few seconds until it becomes aromatic. Sprinkle sherry around the edge of wok and add the chicken broth.

Add remaining ingredients. Mix well and bring to a boil.

Combine cornstarch and water in a cup. When sauce is boiling hard, mix thickening base and slowly stir it in the wok to make a nice sauce. Bring the sauce back to a boil and stir in the egg yolk.

Add touch of oil for a shiny effect. Pour sausce evenly over the steamed oyster rolls, sprinkle with crushed peanuts and top with parsley.

Makes: 20 rolls

Serves: 6-8
Cooking time: 2 hours

The steaming method is suggested as a more healthy cooking method; however, the traditional way is to deep-fry the rolls for 3-5 minutes in 350° oil. Take out and drain on absorbent towel to remove the excess oil. Pour the sauce over rolls. Serve hot.

# 湯水類

*Soups*

白菜湯

# Bok Choy Soup

To the Chinese, the soup is more than just another food. It is believed to have certain healing powers and is often served to people who are ill to assist their recovery.

*3 cups water*
*1 can or 2 cups chicken broth*

*½ pound bok choy*

*1 tablespoon Chinese fungus*

*1 cup young corn, diced*

*½ teaspoon MSG (monosodium glutamate) optional*

*Salt and white pepper to taste*

*2 teaspoons brandy*

*You may substitute spinach, broccoli or choy sum for bok choy.*

Bring the liquid to a boil. Remove any fat that may be floating on top.

Wash, clean and separate stems from leaves of the bok choy. Cut stems at an angle, in 1-inch lengths. Add stems to liquid and boil 1 minute.

Soak fungus in warm water for 20 minutes. Use fingers to pick up the fungus and discard the water.

Add leaves, fungus and young corn to the soup. Gently cook for 3 more minutes.

Add MSG, salt and pepper and stir well. Ladle into a serving bowl.

Add brandy to the bowl, stir well and just before serving the soup, ladle into individual bowls.

Serves: 4-6
Cooking time: 15 minutes

# *Fresh Vegetable Soup*

Cantonese people enjoy using fresh vegetables to make a clear soup without a thickening base.

*4 cups or 2 cans chicken broth*
*1 cup water*

*Dried vegetables:*
*½ cup gum jum*
*(dried lily flower – Fleurs de lis Sechees)*

*Fresh vegetables:*
*4 ounces Chinese broccoli or American broccoli, sliced on an angle (may substitute ½ small head of cauliflower, cut in pieces)*
*1 carrot peeled and thinly sliced*

*Salt and pepper to taste*

Bring the broth and water to a boil in pot or wok. Remove any oil floating on the surface.

Soak gum jum in 2 cups of water for 20 minutes. Pick up gum jum with fingers and squeeze off water. Discard the water.

Place all fresh vegetables in the stock, gently cook for 2 minutes. Add gum jum and cook for another 2 minutes until fresh vegetables are tender. Add salt and pepper and serve.

Serves: 4-6
Cooking time: 20 minutes

# 杭州魚丸湯

## *Hangchow Fish Ball Soup*

Hangchow is one of the most scenic cities in China. There are many lakes, so that fish are readily available, and thus, it is not surprising that they have developed many fine fish recipes.

*½ pound fish cake (may be purchased in Chinese market)*

*2 teaspoons chopped garlic*
*2 teaspoons chopped ginger root*
*1 tablespoon wine*
*2 cups chicken broth*
*1 cup water*
*(or water may be substituted for broth)*

*Garnish:*
*6 pieces fully cooked ham, cut 1 inch by 1½ inch*

*Salt and pepper to taste*

Using a teaspoon, scoop out a teaspoon of fish cake to form a ball, and place in a bowl of cold water until all fish cake has been used.

Stir-fry garlic and ginger root until fragrant. Around the edge of wok, add wine, pour in the broth and just bring to a boil. Add the drained fish balls to the wok. Reduce to low heat and gently simmer for 3 minutes. Put the ingredients in a large bowl and garnish with ham slices. Serve hot.

Serves: 2-4
Cooking time: 20 minutes

# Fish and Seequar Soup

Simple to prepare, fish and seequar soup gives interesting color contrasts, as a typical Cantonese dish should. Seequar may have to be purchased in Chinese stores. Some refer to it as string melon. It can be eaten with the seeds inside and is a very tasty vegetable.

*½ pound fish fillet*

Cut fillet 1 inch by 1½ inch in size and ¼ inch thick.

*2 teaspoons cornstarch*
*2 teaspoons water*
*Salt and pepper to taste*

Combine fish slices, cornstarch, water, salt and pepper, mix well.

*½ pound seequar (Chinese string melon); other melon may be substituted*

Lightly peel seequar and cut in half, then into ¼-inch thick slices.

*1 cup carrots, thinly sliced*
*1 cup water chestnuts, thinly sliced*

*5 cups water*

Bring water to a boil in a pot. Add seequar, carrots and water chestnuts. Gently boil for 4 minutes uncovered, until seequar is green and tender. Add fish and cook 2 more minutes.

*½ teaspoon MSG (optional)*
*Salt and pepper to taste*

Mix in MSG, salt and pepper. Ladle into large bowl.

*2 teaspoons whiskey or brandy*

Pour brandy or whiskey in the serving bowl. Mix well before serving into individual bowls.

Serves: 4-6
Cooking time: 20 minutes

# 瓜菜肉片湯

## *Meat and Vegetable Soup*

*½ pound pork butt (or beef)*

*Salt and pepper to taste*
*2 teaspoons vegetable oil*
*1 teaspoon cornstarch*

*½ pound choy sum*

*5 cups water*
*½ square inch ginger root, crushed*

*1 cup bamboo shoots, thinly sliced*
*½ teaspoon M.S.G. (Monosodium glutamate) optional*
*Salt and pepper to taste*

*2 teaspoons sherry*

*Note: Bok choy or spinach may be substituted for choy sum.*

Cut thinly sliced meat into 1 inch by 2 inch rectangles.

Marinate meat with oil, cornstarch, salt and pepper for 10 minutes.

Wash the vegetables. Cut into 2½ inch segments, and separate stems from leaves.

Bring water to a boil, add ginger and meat, stir gently, cook for 3 minutes. Scrape off floating fat, if any. Add stems of choy sum, cook for 1 minute.

Add the leaves, bamboo shoots, M.S.G., salt and pepper, cook for 1 more minute until the leaves are tender, ladle into a serving bowl.

Add sherry to soup before serving in individual bowls.

Serves: 4-6
Cooking time: 20 minutes

# 粉絲青菜湯

## *Vegetable and Bean Thread Soup*

Bean thread is a popular food item among the Chinese people. It contains much protein and is inexpensive.

*2 ounces bean thread (long rice)*
*2 ounces la choy (perserved turnip)*
*1 small carrot*
*1 medium size Seequar (optional)*
*6 black dried mushrooms or 1 small can regular mushrooms*

*2 teaspoons chopped fresh ginger*
*2-3 teaspoons sherry*
*2 cans or 4 cups chicken broth*
*2 cups water*
*1 teaspoon sesame oil*

*Salt and pepper to taste*

Soak bean thread in warm tap water for 15 mintues or until soft. Discard water. Rinse and cut la choy and carrot in thin slices.

Lightly peel seequar cut in half, then diagonally in ¼ inch thick pieces. Use seeds and all. Soak dried mushrooms in warm tap water for 30 minutes. Discard stems. Squeeze out water. Cut into strips.

Stir-fry the ginger for 30 seconds in a few drops of oil. Add sherry and the rest of the ingredients. Simmer for 3 minutes and serve hot.

Serves: 4-6
Soaking Time: 30 minutes
Cooking Time: 10 minutes

# *Tofu and Spinach Soup*

Tofu cooking is now very popular. Recently there have been cookbooks written on tofu alone. The author recommends that you use more tofu in your diet, as it is very nutritional, low fat and low in calories. If prepared correctly, it can be a gourmet dish.

*1 bundle spinach*

*2 cans chicken broth or 4 cups home-made stock*
*1 cup water*

*12 ounces tofu (1 block, well drained)*

*2 teaspoons brandy, optional*
*Salt and pepper to taste*

Clean and wash spinach. Cut in segments of 1½ inches in length. In a saucepan, bring the broth and water to a boil. Add the stem part. Let it gently boil for 30 seconds.

Cut tofu into 1-inch cubes. Add tofu and the spinach leaves and let boil for 1 more minute until spinach is tender and crisp.

Put in a soup bowl. Add brandy and serve.

Serves: 6
Cooking time: 15 minutes

# 沙律類

*Salads*

# 手撕雞

# *Chinese Chicken Salad*

*2 cups cooked chicken meat*

*Marinade:*
*2-3 teaspoons sesame oil*
*½ teaspoon salt*
*Dash white pepper*
*3 teaspoons brandy*
*2 teaspoons peanut or vegetable oil*
*2 tablespoons oyster sauce*
*2 tablespoons Chinese red vinegar*
*1 tablespoon soy sauce*

*3 cups shredded head lettuce, butter lettuce and romaine lettuce, mixed*
*½ cup green onion*
*1 cup celery*
*1 cup cilantro*

*Dressing:*
*½ teaspoon sugar*
*½ teaspoon salt*
*½ cup Chinese red vinegar or Italian red wine vinegar*
*⅓ cup roasted and salted peanuts, crushed*
*1½ cups crushed won ton pi chips, optional*
*Dash white pepper*

Use chicken that has been deep-fried, roasted or boiled, but not barbecued. Shred the meat into 2-inch strips. Combine the chicken with marinade ingredients and mix well, then let it sit for at least ½ hour.

Shred all the lettuce. Cut the green onion into thin strips, about 1½ inches in length, and also cut the celery into thin pieces, julienne style. Cut the cilantro in 2-inch sprigs.

Gently mix the vegetables and dressing in a large salad bowl. Combine the chicken and the peanuts. Add won ton pi chips. Mix well and serve immediately.

Serves: 4-6
Cooking time: 45 minutes

# 叉燒沙律

## *Chinese Char Siu Salad*

One should become familiar with char siu. Then you can make salad with the char siu, a dish that is not only tasty, but has a lot of eye appeal because the char siu has a deep red color.

*2 cups cooked char siu**

*Vegetables:*
*3 cups total: head lettuce, butter lettuce and romaine lettuce, mixed and shredded*
*½ cup chive*
*1 cup bean sprout*
*½ cup cilantro*
*1 small can shredded bamboo shoots*
*½ cup peeled and grated carrots*

*Dressing:*
*¼ teaspoon salt*
*Dash white pepper*
*½ cup Chinese red vinegar*
*½ teaspoon sugar*

*⅓ cup roasted and salted peanuts, crushed*
*2 teaspoons toasted sesame seeds*
*1½ cups deep fried, crushed won ton pi chips optional*

**Cooked ham may be substituted for Char Siu.*

Cut char siu, julienne-style. Shred all lettuce. Cut chive into strips, about 1½ inches long. Cut cilantro into 2-inch sprigs. Gently mix vegetables and dressing in a large salad bowl.

Mix sesame seeds, peanuts and won ton chips in bowl. Put half of these with the char siu and use the remainder for garnish.

Serves: 4-6
Cooking time: 20 minutes

# 中式燒肉沙律

## *Chinese Roast Pork Salad*

Chinese roast pork, not to be confused with Char Siu, is another good ingredient for salad, as you can roast a big piece of pork and keep it in the freezer. When you need to use it, simply defrost, and you can make a salad in a very short time. Good for busy and working people.

*2 cups cooked roast pork*

*Vegetables:*
*3 cups total: head lettuce, butter lettuce and romaine lettuce*
*½ cup chives, cut in 1-inch segments*
*1 cup celery*
*½ cup cilantro or American parsley*
*½ round onion, thinly sliced*
*½ small red bell pepper, thinly sliced*

*Dressing:*
*½ teaspoon sugar*
*½ teaspoon salt*
*½ cup Chinese red vinegar or Italian red wine vinegar*

*⅓ cup roasted and salted peanuts, crushed*
*Dash white pepper*

*½ tablespoon oyster sauce*
*½ tablespooon soy sauce*

Cut the pork into 2-inch strips.

Shred all the lettuce. Cut the celery into thin pieces, julienne style. Cut the cilantro into 2-inch sprigs.

Gently mix the vegetables and dressing in a large salad bowl. Add the pork and half of the peanuts. Mix well, top with remaining peanuts, and serve immediately.

Serves: 4-6
Cooking time: 20 minutes

三絲沙律

# Sam See Salad

Sam means three, and see means strips in Chinese, so this dish is very versatile. You can use 3 different types of fully cooked meat or seafood, and can make a wonderful salad. The meat is up to your own choice. If abalone is too expensive, one may substitute with roast duck. So this recipe has a great adjustability for people who want to make it an expensive or an inexpensive dish.

*1 cup cooked chicken strips*
*½ cup abalone strips*
*½ cup ham strips*

*Marinade:*
*½ teaspoon sugar*
*½ teaspoon salt*
*3 teaspoons dry sherry*
*2 teaspoons oyster sauce*
*2 teaspoons soy sauce*
*1 teaspoon peanut oil*
*½ teaspoon sesame oil*
*2 tablespoons red Chinese vinegar*
*Hot pepper sauce to taste*

*Vegetables:*
*2 cups won bok strips or romaine lettuce*
*2 cups head lettuce strips*
*1 cup sliced celery*
*½ cup 1½-inch green onion strips*
*1 cup 1½-inch Chinese parsley*

*Seasoning:*
*⅓ cup red Chinese Vinegar*
*1 tablespoon oyster sauce*
*1 teaspoon soy sauce*
*½ teaspoon sesame oil*
*¼ teaspoon hot pepper sauce*
*½ teaspoon sugar*
*¼ teaspoon pepper*

*¼ cup salted peanuts, crushed*

Cut chicken, abalone, ham, won bok and lettuce into 1½ by ¼ inch strips.

Combine marinade ingredients. Mix in chicken, abalone and ham strips. Let stand for 30 minutes.

Put vegetables into a salad bowl. Combine seasoning and pour over vegetables, tossing lightly. Gently mix in chicken, ham and abalone and half of the peanuts. Sprinkle with remaining peanuts.

Serves: 4
Cooking time: 30 minutes

# 豆腐沙律

## *Tofu And Bean Sprout Salad*

With the emphasis on healthy eating recently, tofu has been placed in a role of much greater importance in cooking than ever before. Though salad is not a real Chinese dish, as Chinese rarely eat vegetables uncooked, combining the tofu and vegetables, such as in this recipe, will make a very refreshing dish.

*12 ounces tofu (1 block, well drained)*

*2-4 ounces fully cooked ham, optional*
*6-8 ounces fresh bean sprouts or alfalfa sprouts or 1 can bean sprouts, drained*
*1 cup celery, julienned*

*Seasoning:*
*1 tablespoon soy sauce*
*1 teaspoon sugar*
*1 teaspoon cider vinegar*
*Dash white pepper*

*Sauce:*
*1 teaspoon sesame oil*
*2 tablespoons straight sherry*
*2 tablespoons soy sauce*

Cut tofu lengthwise into 4 pieces. Scoop 1 tablespoon tofu out from center of each. Cut in thin strips.

In a small bowl, combine ham, sprouts, celery and tofu strips. Mix in seasoning, and then fill the hole in each of the four pieces of tofu. Place each tofu onto one individual serving plate.

Combine sesame oil, sherry and soy sauce in a small bowl. Serve as a salad dressing.

Serves: 4-6
Cooking time: 30 minutes

*For Vegetarians*

# *Thoughts On Vegetarian Food*

Vegetarian dishes flourished early in China. At that time, it was mostly due to the Buddhist influence. The followers of Buddhism, in honoring the Buddha's merciful philosophy, did not slaughter. Later, some people enjoyed vegetarian food for no religious reasons, but simply because it is good food. Nowadays, some people choose vegetarian food for health reasons, to avoid animal fat and cholesterol, and to look slim and trim. This section is written with this thought in mind.

The word vegetarian has various interpretations. Some people, for religious or moral reasons, would never use chicken broth to cook a vegetable dish and call it vegetarian. In such a case, one should simply substitute with water. Due to some religious beliefs, even garlic and onions are not included in some vegetarian meals. In such a case, simply omit them, should our recipes suggest them. We feel, each to his own.

In this book, we do not cater to any particular religious or moral philosophies. Our interest is in cooking non-meat dishes with a gourmet touch, as some vegetarian dishes can be bland. The recipes in this section are concerned with not using red meat, but cooking instead with vegetables and bean products and adding chicken broth. We suggest that in following these recipes, the reader use their own discretion as to whether to include certain ingredients.

Bean products such as tofu are getting easier to obtain and fresh vegetables are very good for one's health. Try our recipes. You will find they are tasty and good for you.

禪堂青芥

# *Tofu and Broccoli*

*2 teaspoons vegetable oil*
*2 teaspoons garlic, chopped*

*1 pound Chinese broccoli or American broccoli*
*2 teaspoons white wine*
*1 cup chicken broth*
*1 block tofu, cut in 8 equal segments*

*1-1½ cups shredded bamboo shoots*
*1 small grated carrot*

*Seasoning:*
*2 teaspoons Hoisin Sauce*
*2 teaspoons bean sauce*
*1 teaspoon sesame sauce*

*Seasoning:*
*2 teaspoons Hoisin Sauce*
*2 teaspoons bean sauce*
*1 teaspoon sesame oil*
*1 tablespoon soy sauce*
*Salt and pepper to taste*

*Thickening base:*
*1 tablespoon cornstarch*
*2 tablespoons water*

Place the wok over medium-high heat for 30 seconds. Spread oil in the wok and wait for 30 seconds more. Quickly stir-fry garlic.

Cut broccoli into spears approximately 2 inches long. Add broccoli to the wok, stir-fry 1 minute. Pour wine at the edge of wok and follow with chicken broth, stir-fry for 2 more minutes.

Cut tofu into 8 equal segments. Add tofu and bamboo shoots and mix gently.

Add seasoning to wok. Gently mix and cook for 2 more minutes. Add grated carrot. Gently mix. Make a well in the center of wok.

Combine water and cornstarch in a bowl. Stir in the wok to make a sauce. When it comes back to a boil, mix the contents well and serve.

Serve: 4-6
Cooking time: 15 minutes

腰菓荳腐

# *Tofu with Cashew Nuts*

This dish is fashioned after the popular Cantonese dish called Chicken Cashew. For people who enjoy vegetarian dishes, this is certainly a good dish to try.

*12 ounces tofu ( 1 block, well drained)*

*2 teaspoons vegetable oil*
*12 ounces bean sprouts*
*½ cup chopped green onion*

*Seasoning:*
*1 teaspoon sugar*
*1 tablespoon soy sauce*

*2 eggs, lightly whipped with a touch of salt and white pepper*

*¼ cup cashew nuts*
*2 teaspoons toasted sesame seeds*
*Salt and pepper to taste*

Cut tofu lengthwise in half, then cut crosswise in half, and slice into ½-inch pieces.

Heat wok, add 2 teaspoons oil, heat 30 seconds, spreading oil over bottom of wok with a spatula. Stir-fry tofu until both sides are lightly brown. Put on a plate. Then stir-fry the bean sprouts and green onions in the wok for 1 minute. Return the tofu to the wok, mix in seasoning. Pour in beaten eggs. Cook until eggs are set.

Place on serving plate, sprinkle evenly with cashew nuts and sesame seed. Serve hot.

Serves: 4
Cooking time: 15 minutes

# Sauteed Broccoli in Mock Crab Meat Sauce

You will find the word "mock" in many vegetarian dishes. The mock chicken, the mock abalone, and the mock char siu come from different ways of treating the gluton balls, a skillful combination of wheat flour, salt, safflower, a soybean extract, sugar, water and a few other tasty ingredients. This is a good dish for people who enjoy seafood and meat, yet follow the vegetarian diet.

*1 block or 12 ounces tofu (soft)*

*1 pound broccoli*
*4-6 cups water*
*1 tablespoon sugar*

*1 teaspoon fresh ginger*
*2 cloves garlic*

*2 teaspoons vegetable oil*
*1 tablespoon sherry*

*½ cup chicken broth*

*Seasoning:*
*½ teaspoon salt*
*1 teaspoon sugar*
*1 teaspoon cider vinegar*
*1 teaspoon sesame oil*
*1 tablespoon oyster sauce*
*1 egg white, lightly beaten*

*Thickening base:*
*2 teaspoons corn starch*
*2 tablespoons water*

*1 medium carrot, grated*

Drain tofu, then dice.

Peel broccoli. Cut stems into small pieces on a diagonal slant. Break tops into florets. Parboil for 1 minute with the sugar.

Peel and chop ginger and drain.

Add oil to wok, spread it around the bottom and let it heat for 1 minute. Stir-fry ginger and garlic until fragrant. Add broccoli and stir-fry for 2 minutes. Then add sherry. Remove contents and place on a plate.

Add the chicken broth and bean curd to the wok and bring to a boil. Add seasoning and egg white and return to a boil. Add thickening base, stirring constantly until it again returns to a boil. Add grated carrot and cook until heated through. Put mixture onto the broccoli.

Garnish with grated carrot.

Serves: 4-6
Cooking time: 15 minutes

# 菜心伴齋鮑魚

## *Mock Abalone with Choy Sum*

This dish is made with vegetables, but it is made to look as if it were seafood. In some fancy Chinese restaurants, or some great temples, you may order a banquet of 21 courses made out of vegetable ingredients, but presented in the shape of a duck, chicken, or shrimp. And that's why this dish is called "mock" abalone. It looks like, and somewhat tastes like, abalone, although it's made out of vegetable ingredients.

*5-6 cups water*
*1 tablespoon sugar*
*1 tablespoon oil*
*1 bundle or 1 pound choy sum*

*Salt and pepper to taste*
*1 teaspoon sesame oil or*
*2 teaspoons vegetable oil*

*1 10-ounce can mock abalone (chai pow yu)*
*Pinch of parsley*

Bring water to a boil in a wok. Add sugar and oil. Wash choy sum and place the whole bundle in water. Boil for 3 minutes. Remove choy sum and drain. Cut into 2-inch segments and arrange around the edge of serving platter. Sprinkle salt and pepper and oil on top of choy sum.

Place mock abalone in center of platter. Garnish with parsley. Serve either hot or cold.

Serves: 4-6
Cooking time: 15 minutes

# 蠔油假鮑魚

## *Mock Abalone in Oyster Sauce*

Some people who don't eat meat like the feeling that they are eating meat, and so the "mock" recipe was created. Actually, the abalone is made out of gluton balls, which are in turn made skillfully with flour water, salt, seasonings, etc. And from that you cut the shape of abalone. This is a popular dish among the vegetarian cuisine.

*½ medium-size head lettuce*
*1 teaspoon chopped ginger*
*1 can (8-ounce) abalone mushrooms**
*1 pound fully cooked gluton balls*
*1 small can bamboo shoots*
*1 dozen Chinese pea pods*

*1 teaspoon sherry*
*⅔ cup chicken broth or water*

*Seasoning:*
*2 tablespoons oyster sauce*
*1 tablespoon soy sauce*
*1 teaspoon sesame oil*
*2 teaspoons sugar*

*Thickening base:*
*1 tablespoon cornstarch*
*1½ tablespoons water*

*¼ cup chopped green onion*

*Salt and pepper to taste*

**May substitute with straw mushrooms.*

Cut lettuce into 4 wedges, drain mushrooms. Cut gluton balls in slices, and slice bamboo shoots thin.

To prepare lettuce use 6 cups of hot boiling water. Loosen lettuce leaves and par boil for 30 seconds. Take out and drain.

Heat the wok. Stir-fry ginger and garlic in a few drops of oil until fragrant. Add the abalone mushrooms or straw mushrooms, and stir-fry for 2 minutes. Add the gluton balls slices, the bamboo shoots, and then sprinkle the sherry around edge of wok. Next add the chicken broth. Combine the rest of the seasonings and cook gently for 3 minutes. Stir in the peapods and bring the sauce to a boil. Stir in the thickening base.

Place lettuce on serving plate. Scoop the contents of the wok on top of the lettuce. Sprinkle green onion on top as garnish (optional).

Serves: 4-6
Cooking time: 15 minutes

# Mock Sweet and Sour Pork

This is such a clever dish that the "mock" pork looks, and even somewhat tastes, like real pork – a delight for vegetarians, who enjoy sweet and sour dishes.

*6 ounces walnuts*

*Batter:*
*2 teaspoons baking powder*
*2/3 cup cornstarch*
*2/3 cup flour*
*1/2 cup water*

*4-6 cups vegetable oil for deep frying*

*Sweet and sour sauce:*
*1/2 cup cider vinegar*
*1/2 cup water*
*1/2 cup light golden brown sugar*
*1/4 cup catsup*

*Thickening base:*
*1 tablespoon cornstarch*
*2 tablespoons water*

*1 can pineapple chunks (6-8 ounces) drained*
*1/2 small round onion, cut in bite-size pieces*
*2 teaspoons toasted sesame seeds*

In a bowl, mix the batter ingredients well. Toss walnuts in batter for a good coating.

Heat oil to 375°. Deep-fry coated walnuts in oil until golden brown. Drain. When cool, deep-fry quickly for second time for extra crispy effect. Take out and drain.

In a small saucepan, mix all the sauce ingredients and bring to a gentle boil. Mix thickening base well in a small bowl, and stir into ingredients in sauce pan.

Stir-fry onion until fragrant. Add pineapple chunks. Gently mix in fried walnuts. Pour in thickened sweet and sour sauce. Quickly toss together and serve immediately. Sprinkle sesame seeds on top.

Serves: 4-6
Cooking time: 15 minutes

# Low Hon Jai

Jai means a vegetarian dish. Low Hon is the name of a Buddha. In China, when you walk in a temple, you will see two large Buddha images guarding the temple. One looks very fierce and mean – his name is Gum Kong. The other one looks very kind and serene – his name is Low Hon. It is said that Low Hon enjoys this vegetarian dish the most, and that is why it is named Low Hon Jai.

*1 can bamboo shoots (8-12 ounces)*
*1 dozen black mushrooms*
*1 can straw mushrooms (8-10 ounces)*
*1 can button mushrooms (8-10 ounces)*
*1 ounce fungus*
*1 dozen gluton balls*
*1 tablespoon straight sherry*
*2/3 cup chicken broth or water*
*1 dozen fresh broccoli spears or asparagus*
*1 can Ginko nuts*
*12-18 ounces bean sprouts, fresh or canned*
*2 teaspoons vegetable oil*

*Seasoning:*
*1 teaspoon sugar*
*1 tablespoon oyster sauce*
*1 tablespoon red bean curd mashed*
*1 tablespoon bean sauce (brown)*
*2 teaspoons sesame oil*

*Thickening base:*
*2 teaspoons cornstarch*
*1½ tablespoons water*

*Salt and pepper to taste*

Rinse and thinly slice bamboo shoots approximately 1 inch by 1½ inch by 1/5 inch thick. Soak black mushrooms in warm tap water for 30 minutes. Cut and discard stems. Tightly squeeze and discard water. Rinse and drain straw and button mushrooms. Soak fungus in tap water for 15 minutes or until soft. Pick up fungus with your fingers. Discard water.

Rinse and drain ginko nuts and bean sprouts.

Mix thickening base well in a small bowl.

Heat the wok. Combine bamboo shoots, mushrooms, fungus, and gluton balls and stir-fry for 2 minutes. Sprinkle in sherry around edge of wok, follow with chicken broth or water. Add in ginko nuts and broccoli. Stir-fry for 2 minutes until crisp and tender, yet retaining the green look. Add seasoning and mix well. Put in bean sprouts quickly and stir-fry for 30 seconds. Make a well in the center of the wok and wait until sauce comes back to a boil. Stir in thickening base. Then mix well with the ingredients. Serve hot.

Serves: 4-6
Cooking time: 15 minutes

In Hawaii beautiful orchids are used to decorate food. You can also tell a girl's marital status by where she places a flower in her hair.

If she wears it on the left, she is married; if she wears it on her right, she is looking. If she wears it in the middle, she is married AND looking!

中式齋菜

# Jai, Chinese Vegetarian Food

Jai in the Chinese sense means that kind of vegetable dish enjoyed mostly by monks in the missions. Therefore, it is simply referred to as "Monks Food." It is also a great favorite Cantonese dish cooked during Chinese New Year's Eve and Chinese New Year's Day to show the kindness of the people – they don't want to have any slaughtering at the end of the old year and the beginning of the new year.

*2 teaspoons vegetable oil*
*2 teaspoons ginger root, chopped*
*1 tablespoon ground bean sauce*

*2 cups won bok (Chinese cabbage)*
*1 tablespoon water*

*2 teaspoons vegetable oil*
*1 medium size carrot, peeled and thinly sliced*
*1 cup deep fried bean curds*

*1 cup raw white peanuts*
*1 can or 2 cups straw mushrooms*
*1 block wet tofu, cut in large pieces*
*1 tablespoon Chinese fungus*

*1 small bundle Chinese long rice*

*1 cup water*

*Seasoning:*
*1 tablespoon sugar*
*2 teaspoons soy sauce*
*Salt and pepper to taste*

Place wok over medium-high heat for 30 seconds. Spread oil in bottom of wok and wait for another 30 seconds. Quickly stir-fry ginger and ground bean sauce.

Cut cabbage into 1-inch by 1½-inch pieces. Add cabbage to wok. Stir-fry for 1 minute. Add water and stir-fry for another minute. Remove cabbage and clean wok.

Soak bean curds in warm water until soft. Cut into 1-inch segments. Boil peanuts until tender. Soak fungus in warm water for 20 minutes until soft. Use fingers to pick out fungus. Discard water. Soak long rice in warm water for 20 minutes or until soft. Drain.

Heat up the clean wok, and spread in the oil. Then add carrots, bean curds, peanuts, straw mushrooms and water. Stir-fry for 2 minutes. Add Chinese cabbage, tofu, Chinese fungus and long rice. Stir well. Add seasoning to wok. Cook for another 3 minutes.

Serves: 6-8
Cooking time: 30 minutes

# 新式鼎湖上素

## *Monk's Food*

In the old days, this was a Chinese vegetarian dish mostly used for Chinese New Year's Eve as an offering to the Buddha.

*1 dozen cherry tomatoes, halved*
*1 4-ounce can button mushrooms, drained (Stems and pieces can also be used)*
*1 10-ounce package frozen cut green beans, thawed*
*1 8-ounce can baby corn, drained (optional)*

*5 teaspoons vegetable oil*

*Seasonings:*
*2 tablespoons soy sauce*
*2 tablespoons oyster sauce*
*1 teaspoon sugar*
*Salt to taste*
*Dash pepper*

*½ cup chicken broth*

*Thickening base:*
*2 teaspoons cornstarch*
*4 teaspoons water*

Heat wok over medium-high heat for 1 minute. Spread 1 tablespoon oil in a large area on the bottom of the wok. Add all the vegetables and seasonings. Stir fry all until hot, then add chicken broth. Make a well in the center and when sauce comes to a boil, add thickening base. Add 2 teaspoons oil for shiny effect. Serve on a preheated platter.

Serves: 4
Cooking time: 15 minutes

Note: This is a simplified version of Monk's food with the emphasis on easy preparation rather on a strictly vegetarian regimen. This explains why we have used oyster sauce and chicken broth throughout the Vegetarian section. Also, this recipe will not look like the photo of Monk's Food, because we have used different foods, however, you can substitute those foods and make it look like the photograph.

# 核桃素菜

## *Crispy Walnuts with Diced Mushrooms*

This vegetarian dish is one of the typical Cantonese dishes. By combining ingredients with the same form, such as the way the mushroom is diced, it looks pretty much in the same shape as the walnuts, so it has the taste as well as eye appeal in presentation.

*3-4 ounces walnuts*

*1 cup celery, diced*
*2 teaspoons vegetable oil*

*1 can (6-8 ounces) straw mushrooms*
*1 can (6-8 ounces) button mushrooms*
*1 can (6-8 ounces) ginkgo nuts*
*2 pieces spiced bean curd (diced)*
*1 package (8 ounces) frozen peas and carrots*

*Seasoning:*
*1 tablespoon sherry*
*¼ cup chicken broth*
*1 tablespoon soy sauce*
*1 tablespoon oyster sauce, optional*

*½ cup white part of green onion, diced*

*Thickening base:*
*2 teaspoons cornstarch*
*1 tablespoon water*

*Parsley for garnish*

*Salt and pepper to taste*

Deep fry walnuts in 2 cups of vegetable oil for 15 seconds at 300°. Take out, drain and let cool. Set aside for garnish.

Stir-fry celery in oil until fragrant.

Rinse and drain the mushrooms and ginkgo nuts. Dice the mushrooms about the same size as walnuts. Combine all the vegetables, ginkgo nuts and bean curd and stir-fry 3 minutes.

Add sherry to the wok, followed by the chicken broth. Then add soy sauce and oyster sauce if used. Stir-fry 1 minute, until the mixture comes to a boil.

Combine cornstarch and water.

Add onions, along with the thickening base and mix well. Return to a boil.

Place on a serving platter, garnish with walnuts sprinkled over the top and a few sprigs of cilantro or American parsley.

Serves: 6
Cooking time: 15 minutes

# 雜菜伴粉絲

## *Preserved Vegetables with Rice Vermicelli*

In this dish the long rice, after it is deep fried, becomes crispy and has the ability to absorb taste from the preserved vegetables. Cantonese people skillfully combine the ingredients together so that they enhance each other.

*4 ounces la choy (preserved turnip)*
*4 ounces pickled ginger*
*2 dried red chili peppers*
*2 pieces spicy bean curd, diced*
*1 can (6-8 ounces) mushroom stems and pieces, drained*
*1 package (8 ounces) frozen peas and carrots*

*8 ounces vermicelli*
*2 teaspoons vegetable oil*
*2 teaspoons chopped garlic*

*1 tablespoon sherry*
*½ cup chicken broth or water*

*Seasoning:*
*1½ tablespoons oyster sauce*
*1½ tablespoons soy sauce*
*2 teaspoons sugar*
*1 tablespoon sesame oil*

*Thickening base:*
*2 teaspoons corn starch*
*1 tablespoon water*

*Salt to taste*

*Garnish:*
*⅓ cup dry roasted peanuts*
*⅓ cup chopped green onion*

Rinse la choy, drain and dice. Drain and dice pickled ginger. Discard seeds and coarsely chop red pepper.

Heat oil to 400°. Put small portion of vermicelli in at a time, deep fry until it stops expanding (approximately 5-10 seconds). Take out, drain. This can be done ahead. Strain oil and save for later use.

Mix thickening base well in a small bowl.

Stir-fry with 2 teaspoons of oil the garlic, preserved turnip, pickled ginger, spicy bean curd, mushrooms and chili peppers for about 2 minutes. Add carrots and peas. Pour sherry around edge of wok and follow with ½ cup chicken broth or water. Cook another minute. Add the seasoning to the wok. Stir-fry for 2 more minutes. When the sauce comes to a boil, stir in the thickening base, and return to a boil. Pour on a platter, top with chopped green onions and peanuts, then vermicelli.

Serves: 6-8
Cooking time: 20 minutes

# Vegetarian Fried Rice

Fried rice, like sweet-sour pork and crispy spring rolls, is a great favorite among Western people. To those who enjoy fried rice, yet don't want to eat meat, this recipe is the answer. It tastes as good as any other fried rice, and it has no meat. A good dish for home.

This is the basic fried rice recipe. You may add 1 cup of fully cooked shrimp or char siu. If both shrimp and char siu are added it is called Young Chow Fried Rice.

*4 cups cooked rice, cooled*
*2 eggs, lightly beaten and scrambled*
*2 pieces of dried bean curd, diced*
*1/3 cup frozen peas and carrots, thawed*
*2 teaspoons vegetable oil*

*Seasoning:*
*2 teaspoons oyster sauce, optional*
*2 teaspoons soy sauce*
*1 teaspoon sesame oil*
*2 teaspoons sherry*

*1 small ripe tomato, diced*
*1 small can mushrooms, stems and pieces, drained*

*Salt and pepper to taste*

Add 2 teaspoons oil to wok and let it get hot. Stir-fry the cooked rice for 2 minutes or until it is hot. Combine 2 scrambled eggs, peas, carrots and the diced bean curd. Add seasoning. Stir-fry for 2 minutes, then add tomato and mushrooms. Stir-fry for 2 minutes. Serve.

Serves: 4-6
Cooking time: 15 minutes

*Top:* Decorative vegetable cutting is an ancient art now growing in popularity. *Center:* A cold plate with decorated vegetables to start a formal dinner. *Below:* Crab Meat with Noodles.

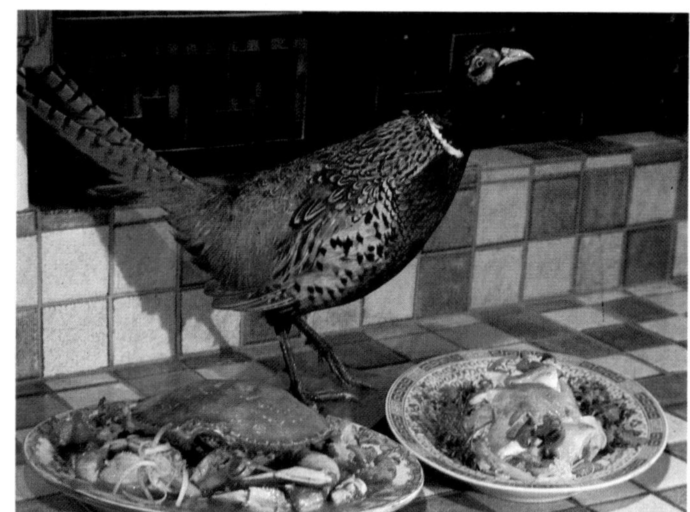

*Right:* Crab in Ginger-Onion Sauce and Golden Brown Deep-Fried Chicken. *Center:* Sweet and Sour Pork. *Below:* Pork with Walnuts originated in Canton and is an all-American favorite; and a specialty of the Aloha State, Pork Fillet with Chinese Vegetables.

*Above:* Chinese Chicken Salad. *Center:* Tofu Soup garnished with shrimp. *Below:* Three dishes for healthy eating: Egg Flower Soup, Fresh Vegetable Soup, and Steamed Fish.

*Top:* Titus Chan poaching a fresh fish. *Center:* Kung Pao Chicken is a spicy, hot, boneless chicken created by the Chinese gourmet and scholar Kung Pao Ding. The other dish is the new favorite of the Northern cuisine, Mongolian Beef. *Below:* Smoked Tea Duck, with many varieties of tea accompanying it is a favorite delicacy of Szechwan.

*Above:* Monk's Food is a Chinese vegetarian dish used for the Chinese New Year's Eve as an offering to the Buddha. *Below:* Peking Duck originated in Peking but has been adapted to the Cantonese cuisine.

*Above:* Kung Pao Fish, a spicy, hot Szechwan specialty, and a Western chef's rendition of Gray Snapper Fillet with Ginger. *Right:* In the bowl are Stir-Fried Straw Mushrooms with Tofu and in the other are Black Mushrooms with Chinese Pea Pods accompanied by a decorative cucumber carving. *Below:* Three fish dinners which are steamed to satisfy those concerned with health and fitness.

*Above:* Lobster in Black Bean Sauce presented with vegetable and fruit decorations.
*Below:* Sweet and Sour Lichee Shrimp accompanied by a carved apple "swan."

*Above:* Titus Chan prepares to serve a banquet. *Below:* The Mongolian Firepot is a fun way of table-top cooking for a cold winter's evening.

*Recipes from Famous Honolulu Restaurants*

# *Recipes from Famous Honolulu Restaurants*

Here are some recipes by great chefs of outstanding restaurants in Hawaii who have participated in our television shows.

## *Tempura*

### *(Shogun Restaurant – Pacific Beach Hotel)*

Restaurants in the Pacific Beach Hotel have provided a unique setting for the kamaainas and the malihinis in Hawaii to enjoy. Their aquarium is three stories high and is said to be the largest indoor aquarium in the world.

*The Shogun Restaurant* offers authentic and beautifully decorated Japanese cooking along with a sushi bar, which are now getting popular in America. The *Neptune Restaurant* offers fantastic seafood. *The Oceanarium Restaurant* on the bottom level offers buffets featuring ethnic foods. And we asked an outstanding Japanese chef from *Shogun* to share his secret tempura recipe for our readers.

We have video-taped beautiful dishes from *The Neptune Restaurant* for our viewers. We feel that you will enjoy this tempura dish directly from this popular *Shogun Restaurant.*

*½ pound medium size shrimp*

*Batter:*
*1 cup cold water*
*1 cup flour*
*1 egg*

*1 cup flour for dredging*

*Eggplant, cut in strips**
*String beans*
*Shiso Leaf*

*Somen*

Clean and devein shrimp, cutting them down the back to make them straight. Leave the tails intact.

Make batter by mixing ingredients thoroughly. It should be somewhat thinner than pancake batter.

Dredge shrimp in flour, then dip in batter, then place in hot oil (375°) and fry until golden brown. Sprinkle a little batter over the shrimp to make it extra flakey.

Break somen in half. Holding several strands together, dip one end in the batter and then toss the small bunch into the hot oil until it turns crisp.

Serves: 4-6
Cooking time: 45 minutes

*These are the vegetables used at Shogun. You may use any vegetable of your choice. Mushrooms, onions, green peppers, and zucchini are all excellent to make vegetable tempura. No amounts are given because it is a matter of personal choice.

# 西式羌葱魚塊

## *Opakapaka with Ginger Sauce*

### *Protea Restaurant*
### *Outrigger Prince Kuhio Hotel*

The luxurious Outrigger Prince Kuhio Hotel in Waikiki on the island of Oahu impressed me when I first walked in the hotel lobby and saw beautiful hors d'oeuvres that had been eloquently prepared and were being offered to whoever happened to be in the lobby.

The hotel's unique Sunday buffet offered on Oahu features all the champagne you can drink. I have enjoyed many dinners at the *Protea Restaurant,* which features a rather romantic South Pacific setting. Beautiful fresh protea flowers are flown in from the island of Maui to the *Protea Restaurant,* as a unique decoration.

We have asked that the management provide a few recipes in our book, so we can unveil their secret of success to our readers, and we have taped several shows in the restaurant and in the hotel.

*2 opakapaka fillets, about 6 ounces each*
*1/4 pound butter, clarified (You may not need all of it.)*
*Salt and pepper to taste*
*Flour*

*2 teaspoons shallots*
*1 1/2 teaspoons fresh ginger, peeled and chopped*
*2 bay leaves*
*1 teaspoon peppercorns*

*1 cup dry white wine*
*2 teaspoons butter*

*Parsley for garnish*

Place frying pan on medium heat. Add a little clarified butter. Salt and pepper fish, dredge with flour, rubbing it in, but shaking off the excess. Place fish in pan. Cook 4-6 minutes. Turn and cook other side in the same manner.

In another pan on medium heat, add a little clarified butter and shallots and saute until translucent. Add ginger root, bay leaves and peppercorns and quickly saute.

Add wine and bring to a boil. Boil until amount has been reduced to half. Turn off heat. When boiling stops, add one spoon of butter at a time, whipping each into the pan.

Strain sauce. Ladle over fish on serving plates. Garnish with parsley.

Serves: 2
Cooking time: 15 minutes

# 甜酸荔枝蝦

## *Sweet and Sour Lichee Shrimp*

### *John Dominis Restaurant*

*John Dominis Restaurant* is one of the most popular and prosperous seafood and steak restaurants on the island of Oahu. It is located on the ocean, looking toward majestic Diamond Head and the beach at Waikiki.

We were very fortunate in prying the secrets of this marvelously successful shrimp dish for you from *John Dominis Restaurant.*

*½ pound shrimp, shelled and deveined*
*Vegetable oil*

*John Dominis batter:*
*1 cup cornstarch*
*1 cup ice water*
*1 cup flour*
*1 egg yolk, lightly beaten*
*¼ teaspoon salt*
*1 tablespoon sherry*

*2-3 ounces lichee, fresh or canned, peeled and pitted*
*1-2 ounces bell peppers, cut in strips*
*2-3 ounces loquats*

*Sauce:*
*¼ cup cider vinegar*
*¼ cup sugar*
*¼ cup water*
*¼ cup catsup*
*½ fresh lemon*
*Drop of red food coloring*

*Thickening base:*
*1 teaspoon cornstarch*
*2 teaspoons water*

Mix the ingredients for the John Dominis batter. Pat the shrimp dry with a paper towel. Dip in batter and deep-fry quickly in hot oil (375°) until lightly browned. Do not overcook.

In another sauce pan, saute the bell pepper for 30 seconds on high heat with a little oil. Add loquats and lichee.

Mix the cornstarch and water together in a small bowl.

Combine all other sauce ingredients in a sauce pan or wok and bring to a boil. Add cornstarch and stir into the sauce, until it returns to a boil.

Add shrimp, lichee, pepper and loquats and heat through. Serve immediately.

Serves: 4-6
Cooking Time: 40 minutes

乾燒蝦

# *Spicy Prawns*

## *John Dominis Restaurant*

*1 pound giant prawns, cleaned & butterflied (about 8 pieces)*
*2 tablespoons peanut oil*
*1 teaspoon sesame oil*

*2 tablespoons green onions, chopped*
*1 teaspoon peppercorns*
*2 small red chili peppers*

*2 tablespoons oyster sauce*
*½ cup chicken broth*

*Thickening base:*
*1 teaspoon cornstarch*
*2 teaspoons water*

In a hot wok, quickly saute the giant prawns in 1 tablespoon peanut oil and the sesame oil. Add ¼ of the green onions and toss. Remove to a warm platter and set aside.

In a hot wok, add remaining oil, green onions, peppercorns and the red chili peppers, and quickly stir-fry.

When the onions have wilted, add oyster sauce and chicken broth.

Mix cornstarch and water and add to the above, stirring constantly until thickened. Return prawns to the mixture and heat just long enough to thoroughly heat the prawns. Do not overcook, or the prawns will be rubbery and lack flavor.

Serves: 4-6
Cooking time: 20 minutes

豉汁龍蝦

# *Lobster in Black Bean Sauce*

## *John Dominis Restaurant*

*1 whole lobster (about 2 pounds)*

*1 tablespoon black beans, mashed**
*1 teaspoon vegetable oil*
*1 teaspoon garlic*
*¼ teaspoon brown sugar*
*1 tablespoon oyster sauce*

*½ cup chicken broth*

*Thickening base:*
*1 teaspoon cornstarch*
*2 teaspoons water*

Boil lobster 3 minutes in its shell. Remove shell and cut in bite-size pieces.

In a hot wok, combine the black beans, oil, sugar and garlic. Stir-fry until flavors are enhanced (about 45 seconds.)

Add chicken broth and bring to a boil. Add oyster sauce, then stir in the thickening base.

When the black bean sauce is thick, quickly add in the lobster and toss until it is well coated. Turn out onto a heated platter and serve immediately.

Note: Be sure to add the lobster at the last minute and just heat through. If you cook the lobster too long, it will be tough and stringy.

**John Dominis Restaurant* makes black bean sauce by the gallon because they use it in so many recipes. Their formula is 1 pound of brown sugar for each 5 pounds of black beans and ½ cup of sesame oil.

冬菇鮑魚

# *Abalone with Black Mushrooms*

*John Dominis Restaurant*

*1 teaspoon sesame oil*
*2 tablespoons peanut oil*

*6-8 ounces abalone, canned or fresh*
*4 ounces black mushrooms**

*1 tablespoon oyster sauce*
*2 ounces snow peas*
*2 ounces bamboo shoots*
*½ tablespoon soy sauce*
*½ cup chicken broth*

*1 teaspoon corn starch*
*2 teaspoons water*

In a hot wok, add sesame and peanut oil.

When oil begins to smoke, add abalone which has been sliced thinly across the grain, and the black mushrooms, also sliced thinly. Stir-fry until both ingredients are heated through.

Add oyster sauce, snow peas, bamboo shoots and soy sauce. When all the ingredients are evenly coated, add chicken broth.

Combine corn starch with the water, and stir into the above ingredients. Turn onto a heated platter and serve immediately.

*John Dominis's Restaurant uses a tremendous amount of Chinese Black Mushrooms. They prepare them in a large batch, simmering for about half an hour, with a little seasoning. If you don't simmer them for half an hour, be sure to soak them in warm water until they are soft. Squeeze the water out of the mushrooms, cut off and discard the stems.

# *Crab Soup Supreme*
## *John Dominis Restaurant*

*1 whole roasting chicken (about 3 pounds)*
*2 quarts water*
*½ square inch fresh ginger, crushed*

*2-3 ounces bamboo shoots*
*2-3 ounces Chinese black mushrooms**
*4 ounces long rice, soaked until soft*

*2 ounces pea pods*
*2 ounces baby corn*
*4 ounces crabmeat*

*1 whole crab, quickly boiled (2 minutes) cleaned and cracked in half*
*1 teaspoon sesame oil*
*Green onions and parsley for garnish*

In a large stockpot, simmer chicken with ginger for 1 hour. Remove from pot, cool and shred chicken and set aside. Remove ginger from broth.

Reheat broth and add bamboo shoots, mushrooms and long rice. Simmer about 5 minutes.

Add baby corn, pea pods and crabmeat and simmer another 3 minutes. Add shredded chicken and cook 1 more minute.

Ladle hot soup into a soup tureen. Place whole crab on top and drizzle a little sesame oil onto the crab. Garnish with green onions and parsley, if desired.

Serves: 8-10
Cooking time: 1½ hours

*See recipe for Abalone with Black Mushrooms. *John Dominis* has their own special way of treating Chinese Black Mushrooms. If you don't simmer them for half an hour, be sure you soak them in warm water for 20 minutes, until soft.

# 宮保雞丁

## *Kung Pao Chicken*
### *John Dominis Restaurant*

*3-4 teaspoons peanut oil*
*1 teaspoon garlic*
*8 ounces uncooked chicken, deboned and cut in cubes*

*1 ounce bell pepper, cubed*
*2 ounces bamboo shoots, cubed*
*2 ounces peanuts*
*2 ounces water chestnuts*

*1½ teaspoons oyster sauce*
*1 tablespoon soy sauce*
*¼ cup chicken broth*

*1 teaspoon cornstarch*
*2 teaspoons water*

Heat a wok and, using ½ of the peanut oil, quickly saute the garlic and chicken for 2 minutes.

Add bell pepper, bamboo, peanuts and water chestnuts and stir-fry another 2 minutes. Remove from the wok and set aside on a heated platter.

Reheat wok, add the remaining oil, the oyster and soy sauces, and the chicken broth. Bring to a boil.

Mix together cornstarch and water and blend into the above sauce, stirring until thickened.

Return chicken and other ingredients to the wok and toss a few times until heated through. Turn onto a platter and serve immediately.

Serves: 2-4
Cooking time: 20 minutes

# 海鮮類

*Seafood*

海鮮舫浸魚

# *Poached Fish Cantonese Style*

Cantonese are very good with their seafood, because the city is located at the mouth of the Pearl River. Beautiful seafood dishes are presented at the beautiful, highly decorated, large floating restaurants, and also by small sampans. Prices are expensive, but the food is excellent. Poached fish dishes are one of the best ways to keep a person slim and trim. This method of cooking fish is not only good for the person who has healthy eating in mind, but features simplicity, and takes so very little time and attention.

Fresh or live fish are considered expensive. Therefore, when presenting this dish, the Chinese usually decorate it with a few leaves of lettuce or a few pieces of flowers cut from vegetables, so as to make the food look plentiful and expensive.

*A pot of water, enough to cover fish*
*6 pieces green onions, crushed*
*8 sprigs parsley, crushed*
*1 square inch ginger, crushed*

*1½ pounds fresh fish (any kind)*

*1 cup fish broth from wok*
*3 tablespoons soy sauce*
*2 teaspoons sherry*
*2 teaspoons sesame oil*
*1 teaspoon vegetable oil*

*Parsley for garnish*

*Salt and pepper to taste*

Bring water to a boil. Toss in green onions, parsley and ginger. Stir.

Score sides of fish 2 inches apart on the heavy meat side and place in water. Poach for 5 minutes and turn over. Simmer for 15-18 minutes total uncovered.

Using water from pot, heat platter and place fish on platter.

Pour the soy sauce, sherry, pepper and fish broth over the fish.

Garnish with parsley and serve.

Serves: 4-6
Cooking time: 30 minutes

# 港式畫舫浸魚

## *Poached Fish Hong Kong Fancy Floating Restaurant Style*

Those who have been patronizing the most beautiful, most orientally decorated, floating Chinese restaurants in Hong Kong, will certainly remember this simple, yet elaborately prepared poached fish. It is a dieter's delight for a gourmet dish. Now we unveil the excitement of the floating restaurants. The secret is the perfect "doneness" and the making of the sauce. Try it and happy cooking!

*1½-pound fresh or chilled fish (salmon, red snapper or mullet)*

*Cooking liquid:*
*9-10 cups hot water*
*2 square inches fresh ginger, or 1 tablespoon ginger powder*
*2 sprigs cilantro*
*3 stalks green onion*

*½ round onion quartered if ginger is not used*

*Sauce to pour over fish:*
*½ cup soy sauce*
*2 teaspoons sesame oil*
*2 tablespoons sherry*
*Dash of white pepper*
*1 cup chicken stock, heated*
*3 green onions, crushed, then sliced diagonally into 1½-2-inch thin strips*

*¼ cup vegetable oil*

*Parsley for garnish*

Clean fish, leaving head and tail on. Score body of fish with knife, making a row of diagonal cuts about 2 inches apart and ½ inch deep from head to tail. Repeat on other side.

Pour water into a wok. Coarsely chop ginger, cilantro and green onions. Add to water and boil for 10 minutes.

Place fish in water, making sure it is completely covered with at least ½ inch of water. When water returns to a boil, lower heat so it continues to cook at a gentle boil. Cook uncovered 14 to 20 minutes. With a fork, prick meaty part of fish. It is done if it flakes off easily. Transfer promptly to a large, heated platter. Discard stock.

While fish is cooking, heat oil in pan to 350°. Pour soy sauce, sesame oil and sherry over fish on the platter. Add chicken stock over fish. Then sprinkle green onions over fish from head to tail.

Carefully pour oil over top of fish. (Caution: When adding hot oil to the liquid, it will create a splattering effect.)

Garnish with sprigs of parsley that have been soaked in ice water for 5 minutes.

For a special effect underline the large heated platter holding the fish, with a silver platter.

Serves: 2-4
Cooking time: 30 minutes

Sea food is somewhat on the expensive side. It's good to use parsley or some lettuce leaves to decorate steamed fish to make the platter look big and plentiful. The Chinese are good at stretching, and making things look good.

At home in my tiny, one bedroom apartment, I let the telephone ring 8 times before I pick it up. People say "Wow! This guy must live in a big house!"

# 畫舫蒸魚

## *Steamed Fish Cantonese*

*1½-2 pound fresh fish (sole, snapper, mullet, sea bass, rock cod)*

*1 square inch fresh ginger, crushed*
*1 tablespoon wine*

*8-10 cups water*

*Sauce:*
*2 teaspoons vegetable oil*
*2 tablespoons soy sauce*
*1 teaspoon sesame oil*
*1 teaspoon sugar*

*Salt and pepper to taste*

Clean, wash and drain the fish and cut it into 2 sections, leaving head and tail intact.

Place the ginger in your palm, pour the wine over ginger, tightly squeeze and let the liquid drop on the fish.

Place water from tap in the bottom of a steamer. Cover and bring to a rapid boil over high heat. Place the steaming tray on top of the pot, then put the platter that contains the fish inside the tray. Tightly cover and steam over high heat for 12-14 minutes.

Two to 3 minutes before it's done, test by sticking a fork into the meaty part of the fish. If it is easy in and out and flakes easily, then the fish is done. Remove immediately.

Combine vegetable oil, soy sauce, sugar and sesame oil, to make sauce. Pour sauce over fish and serve hot.

If the steamer has been used for some time and the steam escapes, cover it with a damp towel. Do not remove cover unless you are checking the doneness.

To serve, use a large tablespoon and fork to scoop the fish into individual plates. Spoon some of the sauce over the fish.

Serves: 2-4
Cooking time: 20 minutes

# 上海蠔油蒸魚

## *Shanghai Steamed Fish with Oyster Sauce*

Shanghai is a seaport and a center for trading and business activity. It is comparable to Chicago in America. Due to the fact that many big businesses are there, wealthy merchants demand gourmet food. Therefore, Shanghai cuisine, to a certain extent, caters to the elite.

*1-1½ pound fresh whole fish (snapper, mullet, or any other fresh fish)*

*4 black Chinese mushrooms*

*1 oz. lean pork, cut in strips*

*1 tablespoon fresh ginger root, peeled and shredded*

*Seasoning:*
*2 tablespoons soy sauce*
*2 tablespoons wine*
*3 tablespoons oyster sauce*
*2 teaspoons sugar*
*Dash pepper*

*8 cups water*

*Garnish:*
*¼ cup chopped green onion*

*Salt and pepper to taste*

Thoroughly scale and gut the fish, leaving tail and head on. Lay the fish on a chopping board and with a knife, score the body of the fish, making one row of diagonal cuts about 2 inches apart and ½ inch deep from head to tail. Repeat on the other side.

Soak mushrooms in water until soft. Squeeze out the water and discard, and cut mushrooms in fine shreds.

In a bowl, combine the mushrooms, ginger root, pork and seasoning. Mix well.

Put the 8 cups of water into a large pot and bring to a boil. When the water is boiling, poach the fish for 4 minutes, (2 minutes for each side) to get rid of the fishy smell.

Place the fish on a steaming plate and pour the seasoning, mushrooms, ginger root and pork evenly on top of the fish. Wait until water is boiling. Place the plate of fish on top of the rack. Cover and steam fish for 10-13 minutes. Do not uncover during steaming period. Garnish with green onion.

Serves: 4
Cooking time: 25 minutes

# 紅燒焗魚

## *Baked Fish in Red Cooked Sauce*

*1½-2 pound fish*

*Marinade:*
*¼ cup peanut oil*
*1 tablespoon sesame oil*
*3-4 tablespoons wine (sherry or brandy)*
*½ cup soy sauce*
*Dash of pepper*

*1 square inch ginger*
*1 bundle green onions*
*2-3 cloves garlic*

*Sauce:*
*1 tablespoon dried tangerine peel*
*1 ounce dried lily flower (gum jum)*
*1 cup dried mushrooms*

*1-medium-sized round onion*
*4-8 ounces fresh pork*
*1 can chicken broth*

*1 tablespoon oil*
*½ square inch ginger, chopped*
*2-3 cloves garlic, chopped*
*3 tablespoons mui kwe lu or white wine*

*Seasoning:*
*2 tablespoons oyster sauce*
*1 tablespoon soy sauce or mushroom soy*
*Dash white pepper*
*Salt to taste*

*Thickening base:*
*2 tablespoons of cornstarch*
*4 tablespoons of water*

*Sprigs of parsley*

Score fish once on each side. Mix the marinade in a bowl. Crush ginger, green onions and garlic and use the vegetables as a brush with which to rub the marinade on the fish, both inside and out. Let it set for 30 minutes and discard vegetables. Bake the fish in a 350°-375° oven for 45 minutes to an hour. Use wax paper to cover the fish for the first 20 minutes and then discard paper.

Soak the dried tangerine skin one hour and then slice thinly. Soak the dried lily flower and dried mushrooms ½ hour and then squeeze out the water and slice the mushrooms in thin strips. Cut the onion and pork into thin strips.

To make the sauce you must first heat the wok to medium heat, and spread the oil in the bottom. Stir-fry the pork for two minutes. Add the onions, garlic and ginger and stir-fry 1 more minute. Then add the wine and follow with the chicken broth. Bring to a boil. Add tangerine, gum jum and mushrooms. Stir for 30 seconds. Add seasoning to the sauce. When boiling, stir in thickening base. Bring back to a boil again and then pour evenly over the fish. Serve with a fork and a large spoon. You may decorate it with sprigs of parsley.

Serves: 8-10
Cooking time: 1 hour, 30 minutes

# Kung Pao Fish

Kung Pao is the name of a statesman in China a few hundred years ago. He invented dishes that feature that spicy hot taste. So every time you see the words "Kung Pao," whether applied to chicken, shrimp or whatever, then you know it is spicy hot.

*1 pound red snapper*

*Salt and pepper to taste*
*2 teaspoons vegetable oil*

*2 egg whites, whipped*
*½ cup cornstarch*

*3-4 cups vegetable oil*

*2 teaspoons chopped ginger*
*½ cup chopped green onion*

*1 cup chicken broth*
*2 teaspoons sugar*
*2 teaspoons vinegar*
*Touch of red pepper sauce*

*Thickening base:*
*1 tablespoon cornstarch*
*2 tablespoons water*

Slice the fish ⅓ inch thick by 1 inch wide and 2½ inches long.

Marinate fish in oil and salt and pepper for 5 minutes.

Whip egg whites and cornstarch together to make a batter. Coat fish thoroughly.

Heat oil in wok to 300-325°. Add fish, one piece at a time. Deep-fry for 1-2 minutes. Drain on absorbent paper and place in a serving platter. Pour oil out of wok, leaving a little of the residue.

Turn up wok to medium-high. Add ginger and onion and stir. Add rest of ingredients and cook another minute. When sauce has returned to a boil, add thickening base which has been thoroughly mixed, and stir constantly until thickened.

Ladle sauce over fish and serve immediately.

Serves: 2-4
Cooking time: 20 minutes

甜酸魚球

# *Cubed Sweet and Sour Fish*

Here is a very tasty way to prepare fish in a different manner than usual. The sauce adds a sweet yet piquant taste.

*1½ pound fish fillet*

*Marinade:*
*1 teaspoon cornstarch*
*1 teaspoon soy sauce*
*1 teaspoon vegetable oil*
*2 teaspoons dry sherry*
*Dash of pepper*

*Sauce:*
*⅓ cup light brown sugar*
*⅓ cup cider vinegar*
*⅓ cup water*
*¼ cup catsup*
*Hot sauce to taste*
*⅛ teaspoon orange coloring*

*Thickening base:*
*1½ teaspoons cornstarch*
*1 tablespoon cold water*

*Batter:*
*1 egg*
*4 teaspoons cold water*
*½ teaspoon oil*
*½ cup cornstarch*

*4 cups vegetable oil heated to 375°*

*1 round onion cut in bite-size pieces*
*1 tomato cut in wedges*

Choose fish that does not flake easily when cooking. Mix the marinade ingredients. Cut the fish into 1-inch cubes and put into the marinade.

In a separate bowl, mix the water and cornstarch until you have a smooth paste. In a large saucepan, bring to a boil the well-mixed sugar, vinegar, water, catsup and coloring. Once it boils, gradually add the cornstarch mixture, being careful to continue stirring to prevent lumps from forming. You will have a thin sauce which is a lovely pink color.

In a separate bowl, make the batter. Beat the egg lightly until blended, then add the oil, water and cornstarch to make a batter. Dip the fish cubes into the batter, making sure to coat each piece well. Deep-fry one batch at a time, for approximately 6-7 minutes. The fish will float to the top when done and the batter will cook to a golden brown. Drain excess oil.

As the final step, combine the fish, sauce and vegetables until heated and serve at once. The trick in preparing this dish is to serve it as soon as it is completed. If you try to hold the fish in the sauce it will become soggy and unappealing.

Serves: 4-6
Cooking time: 45 minutes

## *Baked Fish with Pineapple in Sweet and Sour Sauce*

*2½ pound fish cleaned with head and tail*
*1 teaspoon salt*
*½ teaspoon white pepper*
*½ tablespoon vegetable oil*

*Sweet and sour sauce:*
*1 cup light brown sugar*
*1 cup apple cider vinegar*
*1 cup water*
*½ cup catsup*
*½ square inch ginger, crushed*
*Hot pepper sauce to taste*
*¼ teaspoon orange coloring*

*Thickening base:*
*2 tablespoons cornstarch*
*3½ tablespoons water*

*½ pound pineapple, fresh or canned cut in bite-size pieces*
*1 large tomato cut in bite-size pieces*

*2 teaspoons sesame seeds*

Slit fish's back about ½ inch in both sides. Put fish in an oiled shallow baking pan and sprinkle with salt and pepper.

Drizzle oil over fish. Cover with waxed paper. Bake at 400° for ½ hour, then remove paper and bake at 350° until done. Remove fish to a large platter.

Combine sauce ingredients. Bring to a boil slowly. Then add thickening base, mix well and bring back to a boil. Add pineapple and tomatoes to the sauce until the tomatoes barely start to cook. Bring to a boil and pour sauce on fish just before serving. Top the dish with toasted sesame seeds.

Serves: 4-6
Cooking time: 1 hour, 15 minutes

# 蟹肉海鮮煲

## *Seafood Casserole Hong Kong Style*

*6 large shrimp*
*4-6 ounces crab meat*
*½ pound fish fillet*

*Marinade:*
*1 teaspoon sugar*
*1-2 teaspoons sesame oil*
*2 teaspoons straight sherry or brandy*
*2 teaspoons cornstarch*
*Salt and pepper to taste*

*2 teaspoons vegetable oil*
*½ pound lotus root (fresh or canned) (Taro, potato or daikon may be substituted)*
*1 small carrot, peeled and thinly sliced*
*½ cup white part of green onion, diced*

*1 tablespoon dried fungus*

*Seasoning:*
*2 teaspoons hot bean sauce*
*1 cup chicken broth or water*
*2 teaspoons soy sauce*
*2 teaspoons oyster sauce*
*1 teaspoon sugar*
*Salt and pepper to taste*

*2 green onions cut in one-inch segments*

Shell, butterfly, wash and drain shrimp.
Slice fish into cubes approximately ¼-inch thick, 1½ inches square.

Marinate seafood. Set aside for 5-10 minutes.

Cut lotus root into thin slices. Place the wok over medium high heat. Spread oil in wok. Stir-fry lotus root and carrot for 5 minutes. Add the onion and stir-fry for 1 more minute.

Soak fungus in 2 cups of water until soft. Pick out with fingers and coarsely dice. Discard water. Add to wok and stir-fry.

Add hot bean sauce. Stir-fry until well mixed. Add chicken broth, soy sauce, oyster sauce and sugar. Gently mix. Empty the contents into a casserole dish.

Spread seafood on top of the vegetables. Cover. Over medium-high heat, cook for 15 minutes or until the vegetables are tender. Garnish with green onions.

Serves: 4-6
Cooking time: 30 minutes

# 四川干燒蝦

## *Dry-Braised Shrimp Szechwan Style*

Dry braising is a popular method of Szechwan cuisine. Once the sauce is dried up, it gives the ingredients being cooked a stronger taste because all the sauce has been slowly cooked away and absorbed by the object. This is one characteristic that Cantonese cooking doesn't have.

*1 pound medium size shrimp*

*Marinade:*
*1 egg white, lightly whipped*
*1½ tablespoons cornstarch*
*1½ tablespoons oil*
*Salt and pepper to taste*

*4 cups vegetable oil*

*2 teaspoons hot bean sauce*
*½ cup leeks, chopped*
*2 teaspoons chopped garlic*
*1 teaspoon chili paste or to taste*
*2 tablespoons sherry*

*Seasoning:*
*1 tablespoon soy sauce*
*2 teaspoons sugar*
*½ teaspoon salt*
*2 teaspoons sesame oil*
*½ cup catsup*
*½ cup chicken broth*

Shell and devein shrimp, keeping the tails on. Rinse and dry.

In a bowl, mix shrimp and marinade together. Let stand for 15 minutes.

Heat oil to 375°. Put in marinated shrimp. Stir it loose with a spatula until shrimp just turns pink, (not more than 1 minute). Drain. When oil is cool, clean and refrigerate for another use.

Stir-fry bean sauce with a drop of oil for 30 seconds. Add leeks and garlic. Stir-fry for another 30 seconds using a spatula to stir up the ingredients to avoid burning. Combine the drained shrimp in the wok, add chili paste. Add sherry. Cook for 1 minute or until shrimp is tenderly done.

Add seasoning to wok, toss well and then raise to high heat until sauce is somewhat dry. Serve hot.

Serves: 4-6
Cooking time: 20 minutes

上海鮮蝦青荳

# *Shanghai Prawns with Green Peas*

This dish in Shanghai cuisine is as popular as Sweet and Sour Pork is in Cantonese cuisine. It features simplicity, turns out well for home use and for entertaining. If you travel to Shanghai, this is a dish you should definitely order in a restaurant.

*1 pound prawns, 15 to 20 pieces*

*Marinade:*
*1 egg white, lightly whipped*
*1½ tablespoons cornstarch*
*1½ tablespoons oil*
*Salt and pepper to taste*

*4 cups vegetable oil*

*2 teaspoons fresh ginger peeled and chopped*
*2 teaspoons chopped garlic*
*½ small round onion, chopped*
*1 small can button mushrooms, drained*
*1 cup frozen green peas, thawed*

*Seasoning:*
*2 tablespoons sherry*
*2 tablespoons chicken broth or water*
*1 tablespoon soy sauce*
*1 teaspoon vinegar*
*1 teaspoon sugar*
*½ teaspoon salt*
*2 teaspoons sesame oil*

Shell and devein prawns. Cut each into 2 to 3 segments. Rinse and pat dry.

In a bowl, mix prawns and marinade together. Let stand for 15 minutes.

Heat oil to 375°. Put in marinated prawns. Stir with a spatula until pink and tenderly done – not more than 1 minute. Remove from wok.

Stir-fry onion for 30 seconds. Add ginger, garlic, mushrooms and peas. Stir-fry for another 30 seconds and add the drained prawns to the wok.

Add seasoning to the wok, and stir for 30 seconds to 1 minute. Serve hot.

Serves: 4-6
Cooking time: 20 minutes

# 湖南炒鮮蝦

## *Hunan Shrimp*

This is one of the most popular ways that Hunan people cook shrimp. The shrimp is tender and succulent with a touch of spicy hotness. It has the characteristic of Northern cuisine in terms of the spicy hotness, yet it embraces beautiful color contrast – a characteristic of Cantonese cooking.

*1 pound medium-size shrimp*

*Marinade:*
*1 egg white, lightly whipped*
*1½ tablespoons cornstarch*
*1½ tablespoons oil*
*Salt and pepper to taste*

*4 cups vegetable oil*

*½ cup leeks, coarsely chopped*
*2 teaspoons ginger root, peeled and chopped*
*2 teaspoons chopped garlic*
*1 cup water chestnuts, sliced*

*Seasoning:*
*2 teaspoons sugar*
*½ teaspoon salt*
*1 tablespoon soy sauce*
*1 teaspoon sesame oil*
*1 tablespoon sherry*
*2 teaspoons red Chinese vinegar or cider vinegar*
*Dash hot sauce*

*½ cup peanuts*
*½ cup green onion, cut in ½-inch pieces*
*1 or 2 small fresh or dried chili peppers, seeded and chopped*

Shell and devein shrimp. Rinse and pat dry.

In a bowl, mix shrimp and marinade together. Let stand for 15 minutes.

Heat oil to 300°. Add marinated shrimp. Stir it loose with a spatula until the shrimp just turns pink (not more than 1 minute), drain. When oil is cool, clean and refrigerate for another use.

Stir-fry leeks for 30 seconds. Add ginger, garlic and water chestnuts. Stir for another 30 seconds, using a spatula to stir the ingredients to avoid burning. Add the drained shrimp to the wok. Add seasoning to wok. Toss well for 30 seconds.

Add peanuts, green onion and chili pepper to the wok and mix well. Serve hot.

Serves: 4-6
Cooking time: 20 minutes

# Shrimp with Pineapple

Once you learn how to deep-fry a shrimp, adding a handful of fresh pineapple chunks, to the shrimp or fish in the popular sweet-sour sauce, makes a dish your family and your company will long remember. This is one of the popular Cantonese entrees.

*15 medium-size shrimps*

*Marinade:*
*½ teaspoon sugar*
*2 teaspoons sherry*
*1 teaspoon oil*
*Salt and pepper to taste*

*Batter:*
*2 eggs*
*2 tablespoons cold water*
*2 teaspoons oil*
*1 cup cornstarch*

*4-6 cups vegetable oil*

*Sweet and Sour Sauce:*
*⅓ cup water*
*⅓ cup apple cider vinegar*
*⅓ cup light brown sugar*
*¼ cup catsup*

*Thickening base:*
*2 teaspoons cornstarch*
*3 teaspoons water*

*1 cup pineapple chunks*

Shell, devein, rinse and drain shrimp with paper towels.

Mix the marinade ingredients in a bowl. Add shrimp and let marinate for at least ½ an hour.

Beat the eggs lightly with a fork, then combine with the water, oil and cornstarch to make a batter. Add a little more water if a thinner batter is desired.

Turn the shrimp into the bowl of batter. Using your hands, mix it well so that each piece of shrimp is well-coated. Pour oil into a wok set over medium high heat. When the oil reaches 375°, add shrimp one piece at a time, until it is all in. Deep-fry for 2 minutes or until the shrimp is floating freely and has a rich brown color. Remove them from the oil and drain on absorbent paper.

Put the sweet and sour sauce in a wok, and bring to a boil.

Mix corn starch and water in a small bowl. Slowly stir the thickening base into the boiling sauce. Wait until it comes back to a boil. Quickly toss the shrimp and pineapple in the sauce. Stir, serve hot.

To prepare ahead, shrimp may be deep-fried 1 minute, taken out and allowed to cool. Just before serving, deep-fry shrimp 1 minute.

Don't combine the shrimp with sauce until just before serving.

Serves: 4-6
Cooking time: 30 minutes

# *Soochow Fried Prawns*

Soochow is a place in China with many waterways, and the seafood is very fresh. Soochow is also known for its embroidering.

*1 pound prawns, 15 to 20 pieces*

*Marinade:*
*1 egg white, lightly whipped*
*1½ tablespoon cornstarch*
*1½ tablespoons oil*
*Salt and pepper to taste*

*4 cups vegetable oil*

*½ cup white part of green onion, chopped*
*1 square-inch fresh ginger root, peeled and sliced*
*2 teaspoons chopped garlic*

*Seasoning:*
*2 tablespoons sherry*
*2 tablespoons chicken broth or water*
*1 tablespoon soy sauce*
*1 teaspoon vinegar*
*1 teaspoon sugar*
*2 teaspoons sesame oil*
*Salt and pepper to taste*

Shell and devein prawns. Rinse and pat dry.

In a bowl, mix prawns and marinade together. Let stand for 15 minutes.

Heat oil to 375°. Put in marinated prawns. Stir with a spatula until prawns just turn pink (not more than 1 minute). Drain. When oil is cool, clean and refrigerate for another use.

Stir-fry onion for 30 seconds. Add ginger and garlic. Stir-fry for another 30 seconds using a spatula to stir the ingredients to avoid burning, and then return the drained prawns to the wok. Add seasoning to the wok, stir-fry for 2 minutes and serve hot.

Serves: 4-6
Cooking time: 20 minutes

# Cantonese Steamed Prawns

Steaming prawns appears to be simple, and some gourmets may consider it too simple. However, the Cantonese consider this dish to be a gourmet item. Readers, please keep in mind that good-tasting food can be prepared in a simple way.

In Hong Kong, sight-seeing junks often have a kitchen in which they prepare steamed shrimp. They keep the shrimp in nets or baskets in the water so that they are fresh. Thus you can enjoy them as you watch the beautiful sunset in Aberdeen.

*1 pound extra large shrimp*
*(4-5 pieces to a pound size)*

*Sauce for dipping:*
*1/3 cup red Chinese vinegar*
*2 tablespoons soy sauce*
*1 teaspoon sesame oil or 1 teaspoon vegetable oil*
*1 teaspoon sugar*
*1 tablespoon ginger, peeled and thinly shredded*

*1/2 cup green onion, crushed and thinly shredded*

Remove legs and claws from shrimp. Wash and drain.

Place the shrimp on a round platter. Put 6-8 cups of water in the bottom of steamer. Set on high heat. When water is boiling vigorously, place steaming tray on top of steamer and place platter in steaming tray. Tightly cover. If steam is escaping, use a dampened towel to cover. Steam the prawns for 4-4½ minutes and remove.

Combine the sauce and green onion in a small bowl.

Shell the shrimp. Dip them in the sauce and eat them with the onion.

Serves: 2-4
Cooking time: 15 minutes

# Sea Bass with Aromatic Vegetables

Sea bass is the most versatile fish in Chinese cuisine. In Chinese fish markets you can buy the head only, the fillet only, or the bones only. The tail alone can make a delicacy. Also, Chinese eat sea bass slices with jook. You would marvel at Cantonese chefs' skill and imagination in presenting various parts of the sea bass.

*1 pound sea bass fillets (may substitute with sole or snapper)*
*1 teaspoon vegetable oil*
*Salt and pepper to taste*

Remove bone from fillet and slice ¼ inch thick by 2½ inches long, by 1 inch wide. Add oil, salt and pepper and mix well.

*2 teaspoons sherry*
*1 cup water or chicken broth*
*1 teaspoon sesame oil*
*1 teaspoon sugar*
*2 teaspoons oyster sauce*
*3½ teaspoons vegetable oil*

Heat wok over medium high heat for 30 seconds. Spread 3 teaspoons oil to cover the bottom of the wok and wait for 30 seconds. Place fillets in the wok in a thin layer. Saute 1 minute. Drop ½ teaspoon of oil around edge of the wok and wait 30 seconds. Turn the fillets and saute for 30 seconds. Sprinkle sherry around the edge of wok, followed by chicken broth, sesame oil, sugar and oyster sauce. Gently mix.

*Vegetables:*
*½ green pepper*
*½ red bell pepper*
*½ round onion*
*½ carrot, peeled and thinly sliced*

Cut peppers and onions in bite size pieces.

*1 tablespoon fungus*

Soak fungus in 2 cups warm water 20 minutes. Take out with your fingers and squeeze out excess water. Discard water. Chop fungus lightly.

*1 dozen Chinese pea pods*

Clean pods by removing tips on end and peeling off string.

Add vegetables except pea pods to wok and gently stir. Cook two minutes. Add pea pods for the last minute.

*1 tablespoon corn starch*
*2 tablespoons water*

Mix cornstarch and water. Make a well in the center of the wok, add cornstarch mixture and stir gently until thickened.

Serves: 4-6
Cooking time: 45 minutes

# *Scallops with Green Peas*

A light but delightful seafood dish with tender tips of broccoli or peas for weight watchers.

*1 pound scallops, fresh or frozen*

*Salt to taste*
*Dash pepper*
*4 tablespoons vegetable oil*
*1 tablespoon cornstarch*
*2 tablespoons straight sherry or brandy*
*½ egg white, lightly whipped*

*1 10-ounce package frozen green peas, thawed*
*½ cup chicken broth*

*Thickening base:*
*2 teaspoons cornstarch*
*4 teaspoons water*
*Salt and pepper to taste*
*Orange slices*

Thaw scallops if necessary, dry with a paper towel and slice to about ¼ inch thick.

Rub salt, pepper and 2 teaspoons oil into scallops. Mix cornstarch, sherry and egg white with scallops and let stand for ½ hour. Heat wok over medium-high heat for 1 minute. Spread 2 teaspoons oil in the bottom of the wok in as large an area as possible. Gently stir-fry the scallops on each side for about 2 minutes or until done. Add green peas and gently mix up everything. Add chicken broth and bring to a boil. Make a well in the center and stir in the thickening base when the broth comes to a hard boil. Salt and pepper to taste. Serve on a preheated platter decorated with orange slices.

Serves: 4
Cooking time: 15 minutes

冬菇斑片

# *Sea Bass Fillet with Mushrooms*

Sea Bass is a very interesting fish. It is in grouper family. There are approximately 400 varieties in this classification. Most groupers are dark or light pink in color; a few are gold in color. The largest grouper caught was recorded as weighing 116 pounds and being 8 feet long.

In China, when a proprietor is about to cut up a big fish, he puts up an announcement.

*2 pounds fresh sea bass fillet*

*Marinade:*
*1 egg white*
*1 tablespoon vegetable oil*
*2 teaspoons sesame oil*
*1 tablespoon cornstarch*
*4 tablespoons sherry*
*1 teaspoon sugar*
*1 inch crushed ginger (optional)*
*1 tablespoon soy sauce*

*1 tablespoon vegetable oil*
*2 teaspoons garlic, chopped*
*2 teaspoons ginger chopped*

*2 8 ounce cans button mushrooms, drained (may also use stems and pieces)*
*1 carrot, scraped*
*1 cup chicken broth*

*Thickening base:*
*1 tablespoon cornstarch*
*2 tablespoons water*

*Salt and pepper to taste*

*Pinch of parsley*

Cut fillets into slices approximately ¼ inch thick, 1 inch wide and 2 inches long.

Marinate the fillets for ½ hour.

Thinly slice mushrooms and carrot.

Heat wok over medium high heat for about 1 minute. Spread 1 tablespoon oil in the bottom of the wok to cover as large an area as possible. Add garlic and ginger and stir-fry for 10-15 seconds. Then add fish to the wok in 1 layer. If the wok is not large enough to contain 2 pounds of fish, you should cook a little at a time. Gently saute each side of the fish slices for 2 minutes. Then add mushrooms and carrots. Season with salt and pepper and gently mix everything. Add chicken broth. Make a well in the center, bring soup to a boil and stir in the thickening base. Gently mix everything together. Serve on preheated platter and garnish with a pinch of parsley.

Serves: 8-10
Cooking time: 30 minutes

# 白汁龍蝦

## *Lobster in Creamy White Sauce*

This Cantonese dish implements some Western cooking techniques. It is an East-meets-West dish: the lobster is cooked the Chinese way, and white cream sauce is adapted from the Western influence. It has great appeal for Westerners who enjoy eating lobster without the shell.

*½ pound lobster tail*

*2 teaspoons cornstarch*
*2 teaspoons water*
*2 teaspoons fresh ginger root, peeled and finely chopped (may substitute 2 teaspoons garlic, finely chopped)*
*2 teaspoons vegetable oil*

*1 teaspoon oil*

*4-6-ounce can Chinese straw mushrooms, drained (may substitute any canned mushrooms)*

*2 teaspoons white wine*
*½ cup chicken broth*

*1 teaspoon sugar*
*1 teaspoon sesame oil*
*Salt and pepper to taste*

*⅓ cup milk*
*1 egg white, slightly whipped*

*1 teaspoon cornstarch*
*2 teaspoons water*

Cut lobster tail lengthwise in half, remove shell. Cut each half into 4 to 5 chunks. Rinse and drain.

Place lobster meat in a bowl, add corn starch and water, mix well. Place the wok over medium high heat for 30 seconds. Spread 2 teaspoons of oil in the bottom of the wok and wait for another 30 seconds. Stir-fry ginger in the wok until it gives a fragrance. Add lobster meat to the wok in 1 layer for 1 minute.

Drop 1 more teaspoon of oil around the edge of the wok and saute the lobster meat for another minute. Turn meat over and saute for 1 more minute.

Combine the mushrooms in the wok. Gently mix.

Pour wine around edge of the wok, followed with chicken broth, and stir.

Add the sugar, sesame oil, salt and pepper. Stir until sauce comes to a boil.

Stir in the milk. Wait until barely boiling. Slowly stir in egg white.

In a small bowl, mix cornstarch and water. Slowly stir into sauce. Mix well and serve on a preheated platter.

Serves:
Cooking time: 15 minutes

# *Ginger-Onion Crab*

This is a very colorful Cantonese dish. By using the fresh ginger root and green onion, you get a very pungent flavor in the crab. This is a good dish to serve guests because it is very colorful. However, it should not be served with a very formal menu, because guests do have to eat the crab with their fingers. Toward the end of the dinner, you could offer a bowl of warm water with fresh lemon juice in it for guest to wash their hands.

*1 fresh crab 1½-2 pounds, cut up, cleaned and cracked*
*2 teaspoons vegetable oil*
*1 teaspoon garlic chopped*
*3 ounces ground pork*
*6 pieces green onion, cut in 2-inch segments*
*2 teaspoons ginger root, peeled and cut in thin slices*

*Seasoning:*
*1 tablespoon soy sauce*
*2 teaspoons bean sauce*
*1 teaspoon sugar*
*2 teaspoons sesame oil*
*2 teaspoons oyster sauce*
*1 cup chicken broth*

*2 teaspoons cornstarch*
*1 tablespoon water*

*1 egg yolk, lightly whipped*

Place wok over medium-high heat for 30 seconds. Spread oil in bottom of wok and wait for another 30 seconds. Quickly add garlic and pork. Stir-fry 30 seconds. Add crab and stir-fry for 2 minutes.

Add the green onion and ginger to the wok and stir-fry for 1-2 minutes. Add seasoning, cover and cook 2 more minutes.

Mix cornstarch and water in a small bowl.

Make a well in the wok and bring sauce to a boil. Add water and cornstarch mixture.

Add egg yolk to the sauce, stir well and serve.

Serves: 4-6
Cooking time: 30 Minutes

# *Shanghai Steamed Crab*

Steaming a crab seems to be very simple, and the Shanghainese people know how to use a live or fresh crab to prepare this dish in the most simple way and it is delicious. Shanghai cuisine is now becoming better known than it used to be, and this is a good dish for you to try.

*1 large crab (1½ to 2 pounds live or fresh crab)*

*Marinade:*
*2 tablespoons sherry*
*Salt and pepper to taste*
*1 square inch ginger root, crushed*

*Salt and pepper to taste*

Clean and crack the crab and cut in 6 to 8 segments.

Mix the crab in marinade. Let stand for 15 minutes.

Place the crab on a platter. In the wok, bring water to a hard boil. Place the steaming rack about 1½ inches above water to prevent water coming into contact with the crab while steaming. Place the crab on top of the rack. Tightly cover and steam for 6 minutes.

Use red Chinese vinegar as a dip. Add a few tablespoons of finely chopped ginger. Serve hot or cold.

Offer seafood fork and moist towel on the table. If the smell lingers on fingers, rub hand with juice of ½ lemon.

Serves: 2
Cooking time: 10 minutes

# 豉汁蒸蜆

## *Steamed Clams in Black Bean Sauce*

This Hong-Kong style dish has made its way to America, especially to those persons who enjoy Cantonese food. Steaming the meaty clams in the salty black bean sauce not only gives a delicious taste, but the green onion and red chili pepper also offer a strong contrast in color, which is the way a typical Chinese dish should be. A good Chinese dish should have four elements present: texture, aromatic effect, taste and beautiful color contrast.

*½ pound clams*
*2 tablespoons fermented, dried black beans*

*Seasoning:*
*2 teaspoons vegetable oil*
*1 teaspoon sesame oil*
*2 tablespoons white wine or straight sherry*
*1 teaspoon chopped garlic*
*Salt and pepper to taste*

*¼ cup green onions, chopped*
*1 small red chili pepper, coarsely chopped*

*If using live or fresh clams, select those with tightly closed shells.*

*Wash and drain clams. Place on a round platter.*

Soak black beans in 1 cup water for 10 minutes. With your fingers, pick out beans. Place in a small bowl. Combine seasoning, black beans and mash into a paste. Evenly spread the mixture on the clams.

In a steamer, add hot tap water and bring to a fast boil. (See note below). When vigorously steaming, place platter of clams on steaming rack and cover tightly. If steam is escaping, take a dampened towel and place it over the exit areas, so the steam will stay inside. Steam for 4 to 5 minutes.

Sprinkle the chopped onions and peppers on the clams as a garnish.

NOTE: The diameter of the steamer should be 2 to 3 inches larger than the platter, to facilitate handling of the hot platter. A 14-inch to 16-inch steamer is recommended for general kitchen use.

Serves: 2
Cooking time: 15 minutes

# 雞鴨類

# *Poultry*

# *How to Do a "Prepared Chicken"*

Remove giblets from chicken. Fill a large thick pot with enough water to cover the chicken at least 2 to 3 inches (but do not put chicken in at this point). Holding chicken by a wing or the neck, dip into the boiling water for approximately three seconds, then remove from water for approximately five seconds. Repeat this dipping procedured 4 to 5 times, so that the skin will not break and thus will retain the natural juices. Then immerse the whole chicken and bring water to boil. Reduce heat to simmer, uncovered, and cook for 20 to 25 minutes. To check for doneness, wait until the chicken floats, then prick it with a fork on the thigh. If juices that run out are not pink, the chicken is done. Cool chicken with tap water, dry with paper towel and rub 2 teaspoons vegetable oil on the skin. Refrigerate for 2 to 3 hours.

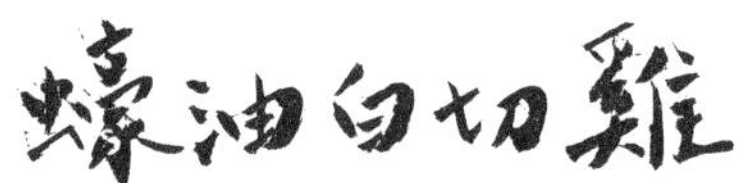

# *Boiled Chicken in Oyster Sauce*

This is a simple way of presenting a prepared chicken, with a tasty sauce, without much work. It's a fast dish for busy people, and a dish that can be done well in advance.

*1 medium-size fryer*

*Sauce:*
*3 tablespoons oyster sauce (prefer smooth-running, saucy type)*
*2 teaspoons soy sauce*
*1 teaspoon sesame oil*
*1 teaspoon vegetable oil*
*Dash white pepper*
*Salt, if desired*

*Pinch of parsley*

Follow instructions for making a "Prepared Chicken."

Cut chicken into pieces approximately 1½ inch by 2 inches, and place in platter with skin side up. For healthy eating, skin may be removed.

Mix sauce ingredients in a bowl. Evenly pour sauce over chicken. Garnish with pinch of parsley. Serve hot or cold.

Serves: 4-6
Cooking time: 60 minutes

## *Cutting Up Chicken*

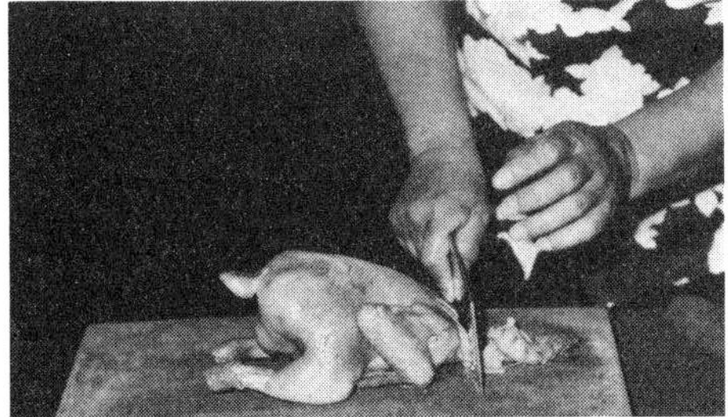
Cut off the neck and tail.

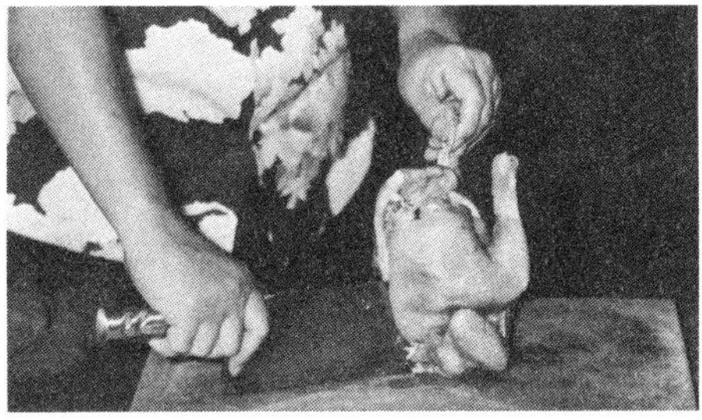
Hold the legs and cut the back in half.

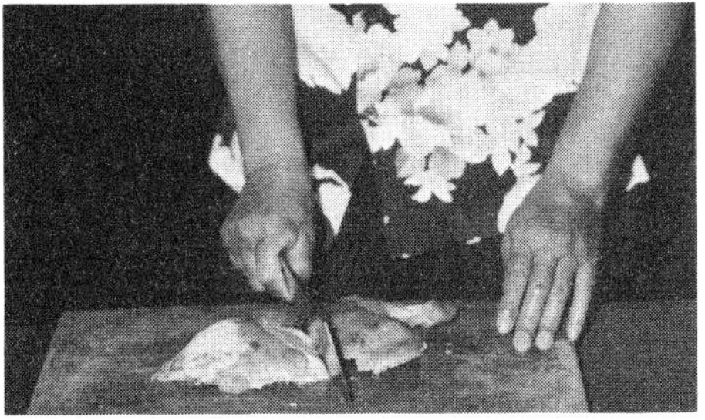
Cut back all the way and cut the breast in half.

From the half chicken cut off the wing.

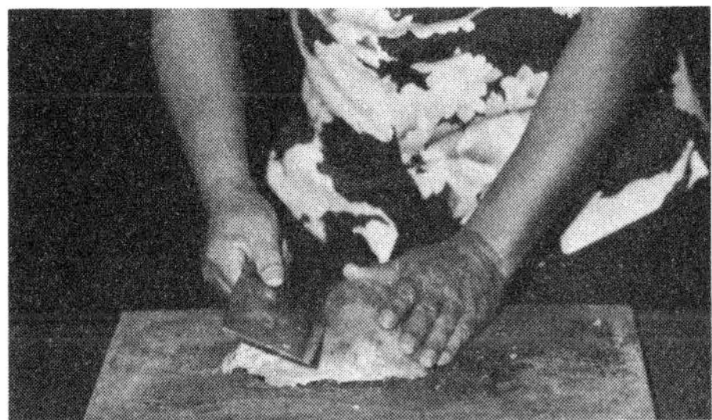
Cut off the leg and thigh in one piece.

With remaining part of chicken cut into pieces about 1 inch wide. Cut from back to front.

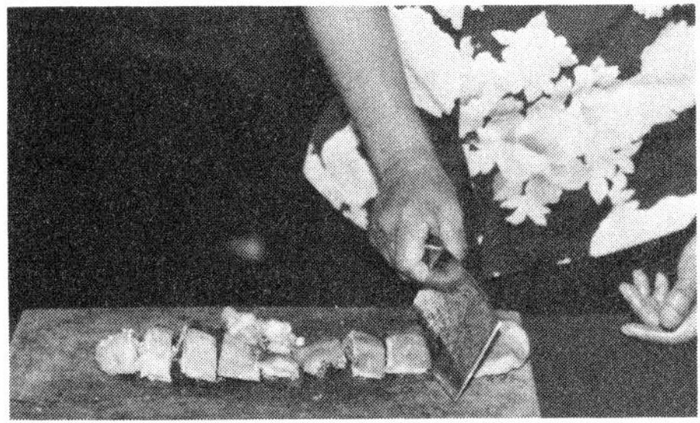
Cut thigh and leg into same size pieces

Arrange on a platter.

# *Cold Chicken in Ginger-Onion Sauce*

The theory of cooking the cold chicken at this time is the same theory as soy sauced chicken. It is the very clever way of the Cantonese people who would employ the heat from the water, or from the herb sauce, to slowly cook the chicken, so the chicken is juicy and very tender. This dish is a great favorite for home entertaining purposes.

*1 medium-size fryer chicken*

*Ginger Onion Sauce:*
*1½ cups chopped green onion*
*1 tablespoon peeled and chopped ginger root*
*1 teaspoon M.S.G. (Monosodium Glutamate) prefer used in this recipe*
*1 teaspoon salt*
*2 teaspoons of wine*
*⅔ cup vegetable oil*

*Note: Green onions and peeled ginger root may be chopped in a blender.*

Cook chicken and cut according to "Prepared Chicken" recipe.

Combine sauce ingredients (except oil) in a bowl, mix well. Let set for 15 minutes, then add oil. Place chicken on a platter. Just before serving, stir up the sauce, and spoon evenly over the chicken. Serve cold.

Serves: 4-6
Cooking time: 60 minutes

# *Chicken with Ham Hong Kong Style*

This is a great Hong Kong dish and has been adapted by the Cantonese to serve in dishes of romantic connotation. Usually, the ham is Virginia Ham which is rather salty. Combining the lightly seasoned chicken with the salty ham, you get a well blended flavor. This symbolizes the harmony between man and woman. You need each other to make a good thing out of life.

*1 medium-size fryer*

*½ pound fully cooked ham (or 2 packages luncheon ham)*

*Sauce:*
*1½ tablespoons oyster sauce*
*1 tablespoon soy sauce*
*1 teaspoon sesame oil*
*1 tablespoon brandy (optional)*
*Salt and pepper to taste*
*2 teaspoons vegetable oil*

*Sprig of parsley*

Cook chicken as directed in Ginger Onion Sauce recipe. Refrigeration process is optional, but I prefer to refrigerate for 2 hours.

Cut chicken in the same manner, and place on platter with skin side up. For healthy eating, skin may be removed.

Cut ham into thin slices. (Same size as the chicken, approximately 1 inch x 2 inches).

Pour sauce evenly over chicken pieces, just before serving. Place one piece of ham over each piece of chicken.

Garnish chicken and ham with parsley. Serve hot or cold.

Serves: 6-8
Cooking time: 1 hour

This dish may be completed well in advance. Cover with a dampened paper towel and refrigerate for hours before you serve. It is recommended for busy people and for serving at parties.

Chicken may be cut up with or without the bone, so if you desire a boneless chicken dish, after the chicken is cooked, de-bone the chicken and serve the chicken meat with ham.

# Cantonese Chicken in Oyster Sauce

This is a great dish one can prepare ahead. We suggest that you cook 3 or 4 chickens at one time. They will keep in the freezer for 3 or 4 months. Thaw them within 10 minutes of deep-frying time and you will have a delicious golden brown chicken in your favorite oyster sauce. This dish is also good for parties and for busy people.

*1 medium-size fryer*

*2 tablespoons soy sauce*

*4-6 cups vegetable oil*

*Pinch of salt*

*Sauce:*
*2 teaspoons vegetable oil*
*1 teaspoon chopped garlic*
*1 teaspoon chopped ginger*
*2 teaspoons brandy or whiskey*
*1 - 14½-ounce can or 2 cups chicken broth*
*2 tablespoons oyster sauce*
*2 teaspoons soy sauce*
*½ cup water*
*1 teaspoon sesame oil*
*Salt and pepper to taste*

*Thickening base:*
*2 tablespoons cornstarch*
*4 tablespoons water*

*¼ cup chopped green onion*

Follow instructions for "Prepared Chicken"

Cut chicken in half. Blot off excess water and refrigerate for one hour. Rub chicken thoroughly on all sides with 2 tablespoons soy sauce. Place chicken halves on a strainer and return to refrigerator for 1½ hours.

Heat oil to 375°. Deep fry one half of chicken at a time, placing the skin side down. Caution: Chicken may cause hot oil to splatter. Deep fry chicken for 5 minutes, or until the skin is golden brown. Remove and blot off excess oil.
Sprinkle with pinch of salt.
Cut chicken into 1-inch x 2-inch segments, and place in a bowl or deep platter, skin side up.

Place wok over medium-high heat for 30 seconds. Spread vegetable oil in the bottom. Stir-fry ginger and garlic to give fragrance. Sprinkle liquor along the edge of the wok, followed by chicken broth in the same manner. Add remaining sauce ingredients. Stir well and bring to a boil.

Mix thickening base in a small bowl until smooth.

When the sauce comes to a boil, slowly stir in the thickening base. Bring back to a boil.

Add green onion to sauce, mixing quickly. Pour sauce evenly over deep-fried chicken. Do not add the sauce to the chicken until just before serving.

Serves: 4-6
Cooking time: 60 minutes

## *Cold Chicken With Dips*

*3-3½ pound whole fryer*

*Dip sauce:*
*2 tablespoons Oyster sauce*
*1 tablespoon soy sauce*
*1 teaspoon sesame oil*
*Salt and pepper*

Follow instructions for making "Prepared Chicken."

Mix well all of the dip sauce ingredients in a small dip bowl.
Salt and pepper to taste.

# 雞炒麵

# *Chicken Chow Mein*

*1½ medium fryer chickens, cooked*

*2 packages (10 ounces) refrigerated chow mein noodles*

*1 tablespoon oil*

*1 can bean sprouts, drained*
*1 round onion*
*1 carrot*
*3 bunches chives, or 1 cup*
*2 stalks celery*
*5 green onions*

*Seasoning:*
*1 tablespoon oyster sauce*
*1 tablespoon soy sauce*
*2 teaspoons sesame oil*
*Salt and pepper to taste*

*Note: chicken need not be refrigerated again after it is cooked for this recipe.*

Remove skin and bones from chicken, shred meat. Use "Prepared Chicken" recipe for cooking.

Cut noodles in 2-inch lengths. Heat wok on medium heat for about 3 minutes, spread oil around sides of wok. Spread noodles in wok and slowly stir fry until hot.

Cut onion into halves and slice thinly.

Grate one carrot coarsely, cut the chives and cut the green onions in 2-inch lengths and celery julienne-style in thin diagonal strips.

Stir in vegetables with noodles, add chicken and stir fry for another 3-4 minutes or until hot. Add seasoning and stir-fry 2 more minutes. Add oyster sauce to taste.

Serves: 8-10
Cooking time: 1 hour

# Lemon Chicken Cantonese

This recipe became a runaway winner when the author wrote his column for the *Honolulu Advertiser.* They printed 400 copies of the recipe and asked readers to write in for it. The newspaper received 2100 letters requesting the recipe. They finally printed it in the column.

*1 pound chicken*

*Marinade:*
*1 teaspoon sugar*
*1 teaspoon sesame oil*
*2 teaspoons oyster sauce*
*2 teaspoons soy sauce*
*2 teaspoons cornstarch*
*Salt and pepper to taste*

*4-6 cups vegetable oil*

*Batter:*
*1 egg, lightly whipped*
*½ cup cornstarch*
*1 tablespoon water*
*2 teaspoons vegetable oil*

*Pinch of salt*

*Lemon sauce:*
*⅓ cup light brown sugar*
*⅓ cup cider vinegar*
*1 cup water*
*2 lemons, sliced (Discard both ends.)*
*¼ teaspoon yellow food coloring*

*Thickening base:*
*1 tablespoon cornstarch*

*2 tablespoons water*

*1 ripe tomato*

Remove meat from 1 small fryer or from breasts or thighs. Keep the pieces large.

Rinse chicken, drain and pat dry with absorbent towel. Marinate chicken for at least 5-10 minutes.

Heat oil to 375°- 400°.

Combine batter ingredients in a large bowl. Mix well. If a thinner batter is desired, add drops of water. If a thicker batter is desired, slowly add cornstarch.

Mix chicken in batter until well coated. Deep-fry chicken for 6-7 minutes, until golden brown and floating. If the wok is small, deep-fry chicken one small batch at a time.

Remove meat and blot off excess oil. Sprinkle with a pinch of salt. Cut chicken meat into 1-inch x 1½-inch long pieces. Place on platter.

Mix sauce ingredients well in a sauce pan. Gently bring the ingredients to a boil, keeping the mixture gently boiling for 10 minutes.

In a small bowl, combine corn starch and water. Mix well.

Bring sauce to a hard boil. Quickly stir in the thickening base and wait until it boils again. Remove from heat.

Right before serving, evenly pour the lemon sauce over the chicken. Serve immediately.

If you desire extra crispy chicken, deep-fry for 5 minutes, remove meat, let cool for 10-12 minutes, and deep fry for another 2-3 minutes.

Sauce can be done in advance, but can only be re-heated by double boiler method. Once the sauce is reboiled in the saucepan, it turns bitter. Ends of lemons also cause bitterness.

Cut tomato in half, then slice. Place half moon slices around the platter. This will create a striking color contrast effect.

Serves: 4-6<br>
Cooking time: 30 minutes

# 菠菜雞球

# *Mango Chicken in Hoisin Sauce*

*2 cups raw 1-inch chicken pieces*

*Marinade:*
*1 tablespoon cornstarch*
*1 tablespoon dry sherry*
*1 tablespoon oyster sauce*
*½ teaspoon sugar*
*½ teaspoon salt*
*Dash of white pepper*
*1 egg white*
*1 teaspoon vegetable oil*
*1 teaspoon soy sauce*
*½ teaspoon sesame oil*
*½-inch piece ginger root, crushed*

*¾ cup Chinese plum sauce*
*Juice from ½ lemon*
*½ cup Hoisin sauce*
*2 teaspoons sugar*

*2 teaspoons vegetable oil*

*½ cup 1-inch green pepper pieces*
*½ cup 1-inch onion pieces*
*½ cup 1-inch celery pieces*

*2 cups 1-inch mango pieces*
*½ cup 1-inch orange pieces*
*½ cup 1-inch Red Delicious apple pieces*

Combine marinade ingredients, add chicken and let stand 30 minutes.

Combine plum sauce, lemon juice, Hoisin sauce and sugar. Set aside.

Heat wok on high heat for 30 seconds. Spread oil over surface and heat for 30 more seconds until oil begins to smoke. Add chicken, spreading pieces thinly so they will brown evenly. Cook 3 minutes. Add vegetables; stir-fry gently for 2 minutes or until chicken is fully cooked, adding 1 or 2 tablespoons water if necessary to aid cooking. Stir in plum sauce mixture and cook for 30 more seconds. Turn off heat and stir in fruit. Serve hot.

Serves: 4-6
Cooking time: 1 hour, including marinating

豉油雞

# *Soyu Chicken*

This dish is a very clever example of Cantonese cooking. Actually it belongs in the category of roast meat, such as Peking Duck or Char Siu Pork. It is a great dish to do ahead of time as one can poach a half dozen chickens in the same sauce and freeze them for future quick meals. One should make at least three times the amount of the sauce given in the recipe, so that the chicken can be completely submerged in it.

Another classic way of doing this dish is to bring the sauce to a fast boil and submerge the chicken in the sauce. Bring it back to a fast boil for 5-7 minutes. Turn off the heat, cover tightly and let it stand for 30 minutes. This makes the chicken especially tender.

*1 fryer, medium size*

*Sauce:*
*6 cups of water*
*3 cups of light golden brown sugar*
*2 cups soy sauce*
*4 tablespoons of honey*

*2 tablespoons mixed Chinese Herbs (May be purchased from a Chinese herb store and may be stored for a year or two if sealed in a jar.)*

*If Chinese herbs are not available, you may substitute 1 dozen whole cloves, 2-3 star anise and 1 inch cinnamon bark.*

Remove the neck and the pieces from the cavity. Wash chicken inside and out and pat dry with a paper towel.

In a large pot combine the water, sugar, soy sauce, and honey; bring to a gentle boil.

Add the herbs to the pot and gently boil for 10 to 20 minutes.

Hold fryer by wings and dip in the sauce for 5 seconds, then remove from the sauce for 5 seconds and repeat the procedure 4 or 5 times. Leave the fryer in the sauce and bring the sauce to a boil Turn down to a simmer. Cook gently for 20-30 minutes. Turn the chicken once at midpoint.

To test for doneness, stick a fork into the chicken. If it is easy in and easy out and the juice does not look pink, then the chicken is done. Take out and let cool in the refrigerator a couple of hours before serving.

Quarter the chicken (use a Chinese knife so as not to splinter the bones). Cut in segments about 1 inch by 2 inches. Place on a platter with skin side up. Ladle a cup of sauce over the chicken. Garnish with parsley and serve.

When the chicken that has been set aside for future use is cool, rub each piece with 2 teaspoons of vegetable oil. Wrap chicken in aluminum foil. It can be kept in the freezer for 3 months.

Serves: 4-6
Cooking time: 40 minutes

## *Soyu Chicken with Vegetables*

*1 chicken, chopped*

*1 pound bok choy or broccoli, sliced and poached*
*2 cups bamboo shoots, sliced*
*½ cup cloud ear fungus, soaked*
*1 cup chicken broth*

*Seasoning:*
*2 tablespoons wine*
*1 teaspoon sugar*
*2 tablespoons oyster sauce*
*2 tablespoons soy sauce*
*1 teaspoon sesame oil*
*Salt to taste*

*Thickening base:*
*1 tablespoon cornstarch*
*2 tablespoons water*

Heat wok as usual. Add broccoli, bamboo shoots and fungus and stir fry a little until heated. Add chicken broth, let boil, then add in seasoning. When the sauce comes to a boil, add chicken and stir until all mixed. Let boil, then add thickening base. Cook until sauce thickens.

Serves: 8-10
Cooking time: 30 minutes

# 京式宫保雞

## *Kung Pao Chicken Peking Style*

Kung Pao was a person. Some say his last name is Ding. During the Dynastic era, many statesmen, poets and scholars were gourmets in their own right. It is said that Kung Pao directed his private chef to cook dishes in which the spicy, hot taste stands out. When ordering in a Chinese restaurant, you may expect all Kung Pao dishes to be hot. Those not versed in Mandarin or Northern cooking should ask the waiter for the hotness they would enjoy. Folks in the Western world are not the only ones not used to the hot, peppery flavor of Northern cuisine. Even the Cantonese have to be careful, lest they take a bite and have to rush for the water fountain. Happy crying.

*Meat from ½ chicken, deboned (or 4 large breasts, or 6 thighs or drums)*

*Marinade:*
*2 teaspoons cornstarch*
*1 egg white, lightly whipped*
*2 teaspoons soy sauce*
*Salt and pepper to taste*

*2 teaspoons vegetable oil*

*½ teaspoon chopped garlic*
*2-3 pieces ginger about the size of your thumbnail, peeled and thinly sliced*

*Vegetables:*
*1 cup celery, cut in ½-inch cubes*
*1 cup bamboo shoots, cut in ½ inch cubes*
*2 pieces of small, dried chili pepper, diced (or to taste, because this is very hot). To reduce hotness, discard the seed.*

*Seasoning:*
*1 teaspoon hot bean sauce (or any hot sauce)*

Cut chicken meat into ½-inch cubes. For healthy eating, skin may be discarded.

Combine the chicken and marinade in a large bowl. Let stand.

Heat wok on medium-high heat for 30 seconds. Spread oil in bottom of wok to cover a large area. Wait 30 more seconds. Stir-fry ginger and garlic for a few seconds until fragrant. Add chicken to the wok in a thin layer. Saute for one minute. Turn the chicken and saute for 2 more minutes. Then stir-fry chicken for 1 minute.

Add vegetables and stir-fry for 1 minute.

Add seasoning. Stir-fry for 1 more minute.

Add ½ of the peanuts to the wok. Transfer to a plate. Garnish with remaining peanuts.

*1 teaspoon sweet bean sauce*
*2 teaspoons white wine*
*1/3 cup water or chicken broth*
*Salt and pepper to taste*

*1/2 cup cashews or peanuts*

Serves: 4-6
Cooking time: 30 minutes

# *Egg Fu Young*

*4 eggs lightly whipped with fork*
*1 cup beansprouts, drained*
*1/2 small round onion, chopped*
*1/2 cup chives, chopped*
*1/2 medium-size ripe tomato, chopped*
*Salt and pepper to taste*

*2 teaspoons vegetable oil*

Mix all the ingredients except vegetable oil in a bowl. In a wok or heavy skillet over medium-high heat, spread vegetable oil. Drop the mixture from the bowl into the skillet 2 tablespoons at a time. Saute one side for about 1½ minutes until golden brown, then turn over and saute 1½ to 2 minutes or until it is done. Serve on a preheated platter.

Serves: 2
Cooking time: 15 minutes

# 雞球煲仔

## *Chicken Casserole Hong Kong Style*

This makes a good "down-home" family meal, but also can be "dressed up" for entertaining by simply adding a can of abalone (juice and all) sliced into thin pieces. Add to wok while cooking chicken. Change the name to "Abalone with Chicken Casserole." To adapt to Western tastes, debone the chicken first, for greater appeal.

It is good if the Chinese cabbage, or won bok, is very large, cut in half first, then cut 2 inches long, roughly separating the stem part and the leafy part. Line the bottom of the casserole with the stem part, then empty the contents of the wok directly onto the won bok. Place the leafy part of the won bok on top. Cover and gently boil 10 minutes. This is especially good when long rice is used, as the won bok is constantly offering water while it is cooking, and the long rice will constantly absorb the water, making it very tasty. While cooking the cassesrole on top of the stove, one should check occasionally to make sure there is enough sauce to keep it from burning. Add water or chicken broth if needed.

*¼ fryer or equivalent in chicken pieces (approximately 2 large chicken breasts, or 4-5 drums and thighs)*

Wash, drain and pat chicken dry. Cut in pieces approximately 1 inch wide by 2 inches long.

*Marinade:*
*1 teaspoon sugar*
*1 teaspoon soy sauce*
*1 teaspoon oyster sauce*
*Salt and pepper to taste*

Marinate chicken and set aside for 5 to 10 minutes.

*6 dried Chinese mushrooms*

Soak mushrooms in water for 20 minutes. Cut off stems and discard. Squeeze excess water from mushrooms and discard water.

*2 cups long rice*

Soak long rice in water for 20 minutes. Discard water.

*2 teaspoons vegetable oil*

Place wok over medium-high heat. Spread oil in the bottom. Saute the chicken 2 minutes per side. Add mushrooms and long rice, and stir to mix.

*Seasoning:*
*1 cup chicken broth*
*½ cup water*
*Salt & pepper to taste*

*Thickening base:*
*1 tablespoon cornstarch*
*3 tablespoons water*

*2 cups won bok cabbage or head cabbage*
*1/3 cup grated carrot*

Add broth, water, salt and pepper to the wok. Stir. Mix well. Bring the sauce to a boil.

In a small bowl, mix the thickening base until smooth. Wait until the sauce in the wok comes to a boil. Slowly stir in to form a thin gravy.

Cut won bok approximately 1½ inches wide x 2 inches long. Separate the stems and leaves. Place the stem part evenly in the bottom of the casserole. Empty the contents of the wok into the casserole and top with the won bok leaves. Cover and cook over medium high heat for 10 to 12 minutes.

If the sauce becomes too thick, add a little water.

Garnish the casserole with carrots. Place the casserole on a round platter and serve hot.

Serves: 4-6
Cooking time: 30 minutes

Note: This casserole is a very inexpensive one-dish meal since chicken is usually reasonable in price.

Chicken skin can be removed for healthy eating.

# 雞球龍蝦雀巢

## *Phoenix Nest*

*1 cup rice stick (rice vermicelli)*
*6 cups vegetable oil*
*1 medium-sized fryer chicken*

*Marinade for chicken:*
*Salt to taste*
*Dash white pepper*
*1 tablespoon cornstarch*
*1 tablespoon soy sauce*
*1 tablespoon white wine*
*1 teaspoon sugar*
*1½ inch ginger, crushed*
*1 egg white, lightly whipped*

*1 large lobster tail or 4 large prawns*

*Marinade for lobster:*
*Salt to taste*
*Dash pepper*
*½ tablespoon oil*
*1 tablespoon cornstarch*
*1 egg white, lightly whipped*

*1 small can straw mushrooms, drained*
*1 cup celery*
*1½ tablespoons vegetable oil*

*1 tablespoon chopped garlic*
*1½ teaspoons chopped ginger root*

*1 tablespoon cornstarch*
*2 tablespoons water*

*Seasoning:*
*2 tablespoons Mui Kew Lu or sherry*
*1 teaspoon sesame oil*
*1 tablespoon oyster sauce*
*2 teaspoons soy sauce*
*1 teaspoon sugar*

Use 2 large Jaw Lees for nest. Heat oil to 400°. Break up rice sticks and line one Jaw Lee, or Chinese wire basket. Place other Jaw Lee loosely on top of the rice sticks in the basket and deep-fry quickly to form nest.

Debone and cut the chicken meat into bite-size pieces.

Mix the marinade for the chicken, and then marinate the chicken meat in it for ½ hour.

Rinse lobster meat, cut lengthwise and then crosswise to make 6-8 bite-size pieces. Mix the marinade for the lobster and marinate the lobster for ½ hour.

Spread the lobster in the Jaw Lee basket and deep-fry 3 seconds and remove for 5 seconds; repeat this cycle 5 or 6 times. Follow the same cooking process for the chicken.

Peel celery with potato peeler and then cut in bite-size pieces. Heat wok to medium high heat; add ½ tablespoon oil. Add celery and mushrooms to the wok and stir-fry 2 minutes until celery is done. Remove from wok.

Add 2 to 3 teaspoons of oil around the edge of the wok. Add garlic and ginger root; stir-fry quickly Then add chicken and stir-fry for 4 sec-

*1 cup chicken broth*
*Dash pepper*
*Salt to taste*

onds. Add lobster and vegetables and stir-fry for 1 minute.

Add seasoning and thicken with cornstarch and water which has been mixed together. Bring to a rolling boil. Scoop the contents into the deep-fried nest and serve immediately.

Serves: 4-6
Cooking time: 1 hour

# *Chicken Fried Rice*

*2-3 teaspoons vegetable oil*
*2 eggs, scrambled*
*4-6 cups precooked rice*
*1 cup peas and carrots*
*2 cups cooked, diced chicken*

*Seasoning:*
*2 teaspoons sesame oil*
*1 tablespoon oyster sauce*
*1 tablespoon soy sauce*
*Dash pepper*
*Salt to taste*

*2 cups shredded lettuce*
*½ cup chopped green onion*

Heat wok to medium-high, add 2-3 teaspoons oil around edge of wok. Mix in precooked rice. Stir fry until hot. Then add eggs, peas, carrots and diced chicken. Combine ingredients thoroughly and stir-fry.

Add seasoning, mix well and add lettuce, green onion. Must serve immediately.

Serves: 4-6
Cooking time: 45 minutes

# 樟茶鴨

## *Smoked Tea Duck*

Smoked Tea Duck is Szechwan's answer to Peking Duck. Chefs from Szechwan province created this unique dish, with the emphasis on simplicity in seasoning, so that one can savor the true taste of the duck. By smoking properly, the duck will have much charisma, warmth, personality and sex appeal.

To smoke, we recommend that you use a 14-inch wok that is very inexpensive, because as the sugar melts on the tea, it creates a dark stain on the bottom of the wok. Camphor wood chips are chips used in Chinese furniture making. Their purpose in this recipe is to make a smoke of fragrant aroma for the duck.

Some people suggest that the bottom of the wok should be lined with aluminum foil. However, it depends upon the type of wok that you are using. If the heat can come through the foil and generate enough smoke to coat the duck, that's good, especially with expensive woks. But the better way is to go to a store and shop for the most inexpensive wok, however thin it is, so long as it will generate enough smoke. After you clean it up, it may not look too good but it can still be used. Or you may just want to use this wok for any other smoked dishes.

*1 4-4½-pound duck*

*8-10 cups water*
*2-2½ teaspoons red food coloring*

*6 pieces green onion (crushed)*
*½ cup tea leaves (your favorite tea)*
*½ cup uncooked rice*
*2 teaspoons brown sugar*
*½ cup camphor wood chips, optional, (may be purchased at herb stores in Chinatown)*

*Chinese buns or dinner rolls*

*Hoisin sauce (enough for dipping)*

*In Peking Duck chapter.*

Remove insides, the fat at the entrance of the cavity, and wing tips from duck. Cut off tail if preferred.

Place duck in a large pot. Add water. Make sure duck is completely submerged. Add coloring. Bring the duck to a boil, then reduce to gentle boil on medium heat for about 1 hour. Test doneness by sticking a fork into the thigh. If easy in and easy out, duck is tender and done. Drain and discard water. Empty the water from the cavity of the duck. Pat dry. Allow to cool.

Place the wok over medium-high heat for 1 minute. Stir-fry the tea leaves, rice, green onion, sugar and camphor wood, if any, for 1 minute.

Spread ingredients evenly on the bottom of the wok. Place 2 inexpensive chop sticks in the wok over the ingredients. Place the duck on the chop sticks. (The duck should be above the ingredients that will be causing the smoke.)

Wrap the inside of the wok lid with tin foil to prevent tea stain. Tightly cover. Smoke the duck 30-40 minutes on medium heat. It is advisable to check the duck once at midpoint, and turn it over to allow even smoking.

Remove the duck. Salt immediately on both sides, to taste. When cool enough, debone and cut into 1-inch x 1½-inch pieces.

May be served hot or cold.

Slice rolls open, leaving one edge joined together. Dip the duck in the sauce and place into the roll, and eat as you would a sandwich.

Serves: 6-8
Cooking time: 2 hours

# 荔枝鴨

## *Lichee Boneless Duck in Sweet and Sour Sauce*

This is a version of Cantonese cooking derived from the popular dish Lichee Chicken in Sweet-Sour Sauce. For healthy eating, the skin of the duck can be removed.

*2 duck breasts (approximately 8 ounces)*

*Marinade:*
*1 egg white, whipped*
*2 teaspoons cornstarch*
*1 teaspoon vegetable oil*
*2 teaspoons soy sauce*
*Salt and pepper to taste*

*Batter*
*1 egg, lightly whipped*
*2 teaspoons water*
*2 teaspoons oil*
*⅓ cup cornstarch*

*4 cups vegetable oil*

*Sauce:*
*⅓ cup water*
*⅓ cup apple cider vinegar*
*⅓ cup light golden brown sugar*
*¼ cup catsup*

*Thickening base:*
*1 teaspoon cornstarch*
*4 teaspoons water*

*1 large can lichee, drained*

Skin and dice the duck into ½-inch cubes

In a bowl, mix the duck meat to the marinade and then let it stand for 15 minutes.

Mix batter well in a bowl and add more water if necessary to your own desired consistency. Add duck meat to batter.

Heat oil to 350°. Deep fry the batter-coated duck meat for 6-7 minutes or until done. Drain the duck on absorbent paper. Cool and strain the oil for other use.

Mix the sauce well, then pour it in the wok and bring to a boil. Stir in the thickening base, and bring back to a boil. Quickly toss in the duck and lichee. Serve hot.

Serves: 4-6
Cooking time: 20 minutes

# 星州燒鴨

## *Singapore Style Roast Duck*

*1 4- to 4½-lb. duckling, fresh or frozen*
*1½ tablespoons honey*
*4 tablespoons apple cider vinegar*
*2 tablespoons oil*
*⅛ cup soy sauce*
*1½ teaspoons salt*

*1 bundle green onion*
*6 cloves of garlic*
*2 teaspoons salt*
*½ teaspoon 5 spice powder*

*Dips: Hoisin Sauce, Plum Sauce or Lemon Sauce*

Preheat oven to 450°. Cut off the neck skin, then dry duck with a paper towel thoroughly and rub the skin with honey, vinegar and soy sauce. Then sprinkle evenly with salt on all sides. Let set for 20 minutes. Brush with oil before roasting.

Preparation of cavity:
Crush onion and garlic, mix with 5 spice and salt and rub into the cavity of duck. Leave all of this mixture inside cavity.

Oven rack should be placed about ⅔ down from top of oven. Place the duck belly side up on rack in a roasting pan. Roast for 15 minutes at 450°, reduce heat to 400° and roast for another 45 minutes. Turn duck over and bake for another 20 minutes until tender and done. Cut duck (meat and bone) into pieces 2½-inches long, by 1-inch wide or serve it boneless by first de-boning and then cutting.

Serves: 4-6
Cooking time: 2 hours

四川脆皮鴨

# *Szechwan Crispy Duck*

Szechwan Crispy Duck is an easy alternative to the classic Peking duck. Unlike Peking duck, which requires a special oven 6 feet tall and 4 feet wide, Szechwan Crispy Duck can be prepared at home. It is an excellent dish for entertaining at home because it can be prepared in advance, thus enabling the host or hostess to spend more time with guests.

*1 4-5-pound duck*

*Marinade:*
*1 square inch ginger root*
*1 bundle green onions, cleaned and washed*
*1 cup soy sauce*
*½ cup Hoisin sauce*
*2 teaspoons sesame oil (optional)*
*2 teaspoons Szechwan peppercorns (oudie d'epice)*
*2-3 pieces or 2 teaspoons star anise*
*2 teaspoons light brown sugar*
*2 tablespoons white wine or straight sherry*

*4-6 cups vegetable oil*

If duck is frozen, thoroughly thaw, wash and clean inside and outside. Dry with absorbent towel. Remove giblets from cavity and discard the fat at the entrance of cavity. Remove skin from the neck.

Lightly crush ginger and green onions. Combine all of the marinade ingredients in a small pan, and mix well. Using vegetables as a brush, rub the duck inside and outside. Marinate duck for over 4 hours or preferable overnight. Turn the duck a few times during this process.

Fill a steamer with water and bring to a rapid boil. Lightly oil the steaming tray with a few teaspoons of vegetable oil. Drain and place the duck on the steaming tray. Cover and steam at medium-high heat for 1½ hours or 1 hour and 45 minutes. Check steamer and add more hot water if necessary. Remove duck and cool.

This process may be done two days in advance.

Use a deep wok or deep-fryer. Heat oil to 375°. If the duck is wet, dry off inside and outside with absorbent towel. Slowly place duck into the oil and deep fry for 5-6 minutes on each side. Take duck out and remove excess oil with absorbent towel.

Cut the duck into segments approximately 1 inch wide and 2 inches long. May be served in the same manner as Peking duck, using Hoisin sauce as a dip.

Serves: 8-10
Cooking time: 2 hours not including marinating time

## *Deep-Fried Chicken with Cashews*

*1 fryer or 4 chicken breasts, deboned*

*Marinade:*
*1 egg white*
*Dash of salt*
*Dash of white pepper*
*2 teaspoons oyster sauce*
*1 teaspoon sesame oil*
*2 teaspoons sherry*
*1 tablespoon cornstarch*

*2-3 cups boiling water*
*1½ cups cashews*

*4 cups oil*

Cut raw chicken meat into 1-inch-by-1½-inch pieces.

Marinate chicken pieces for ½ hour.

Bring water to boil, add cashews and cook for 10 seconds. Remove, drain, pat dry with paper towel and chop finely.

Heat wok until oil begins to smoke or reaches 350°. Dredge marinated chicken pieces in finely chopped cashews until thoroughly coated. Deep fry for approximately 3 minutes, stirring occasionally, until golden brown. Drain on paper towel. Pat dry. Salt and serve immediately.

Serves: 2-4
Cooking time: 45 minutes

*Peking Duck*

# Introduction to Peking Duck

Peking Duck is a classic dish. It is said to have evolved in the latter part of the Ching Dynasty (1644 - 1912 AD) and was originated by the master chefs at Court. To this day, one can understand how much research and effort have gone into making this dish fit for emperors and nobles. In Peking one can still see the thirty-six kitchens of the Summer Palace designed to serve the members of the Court of the Ching Dynasty. In the China National Museum in a glass display case is a hundred-year-old cookbook containing the original recipe for Peking Duck. It begins with the raising of the duck, the force-feeding and development to produce a bird befitting of this recipe.

The people of China consider the enjoyment of food as one of the greatest pleasures life can afford. Chefs from many different provinces are beginning to adapt to this method of roasting Peking Duck. Therefore, although Peking Duck was made popular in Peking, other regional cuisines are featuring this dish and Cantonese chefs are doing a great job.

In formal entertaining, the dish is carried out on a decorated tray by the head chef for approval by the host, and it is then shown to the guests for their admiration. On many occasions the Peking Duck is carved at the table in front of the guests. Carving is an art in itself.

One of the most popular ways of serving Peking Duck is to carve off the skin, cut green onion into 1-inch strips and dip them into a special sauce; and spread the sauce on a Chinese pancake. Then, one places one skin on the folded pancake and eats the delicacy like a sandwich. This is an unusual dish because eating with the hands is very rare in China. However, to make the skin so crispy that it will completely separate from the meat can only be accomplished in a professional kitchen, where the duck is either hung vertically inside a large oven, or roasted individually on an open fire.

Our recipes are home style and feature convenient ways of roasting the Peking Duck. As explained above, the skin will not separate from the meat unless a professional oven is used, so we have eliminated that one way of serving it. We have however added more new ways of enjoying this wonderful, gourmet dish. We offer Stir-Fried Boneless Peking Duck with Cashew Nuts, Peking Duck Salad, and a cold plate of boneless Peking Duck with pickled vegetables topped with golden brown slivered almonds. For these recipes we have even catered to the new trend of healthy eating, allowing the duck skin to be discarded and the succulent meat to be enjoyed boneless to eliminate much of the greasy effect.

Peking Duck meat in sweet and sour sauce will somewhat numb your taste buds. Therefore, this dish should be served toward the end of the dinner. Fried rice signals that the meal is coming to an end and also is very filling so that everyone feels that they have had enough to eat.

Clear soup refreshes the palate and leaves you full and content.

# *Eleven-Course Peking Duck Feast*



1. Light and Crispy Peking Duck Spring Rolls
   An all-time favorite hors d'oeuvre.
2. "Strange-Taste" Peking Duck
   A spicy Szechwan-style method of cooking. A wonderful dish for the cocktail hour.
3. Crunchy Peking Duck Salad
   This refreshing salad is mixed with deep fried snow-white long rice. It makes a delicious salad or entree.
4. Stir-Fried Peking Duck Meat with Celery and Young Corn
   A colorful stir-fry dish combining strips of duck meat with garden fresh aromatic vegetables for healthy eating.
5. Peking Duck Meat with Pickled Vegetables
   Duck meat and appetizing pickles tossed together and topped with crunchy almonds and sesame seeds.
6. Peking Duck with Chinese Pancakes
   Soft Chinese pancakes brushed with Hoisin sauce and wrapped around Peking Duck meat and skin with green onions.
7. Poached Head Lettuce in Oyster Sauce
   Lettuce poached in water until tender but crunchy, topped with tasty oyster sauce.
8. Peking Duck with Toasted Cashew Nuts
   Diced Peking Duck meat stir-fried with fresh vegetables and topped with toasted cashew nuts.
9. Deep Fried Golden Brown Peking Duck Meat in Sweet and Sour Sauce
   Lightly battered Peking Duck meat deep-fried to a golden brown and mixed with sweet and sour sauce.
10. Peking Duck Fried Rice
    Diced Peking Duck meat stir-fried with rice, scrambled eggs and green onions served in a bowl.
11. Peking Duck Soup
    A clear soup designed to create a refreshing and satisfied feeling after an elaborate dinner.

Start with golden brown, crispy spring rolls served as an appetizer, followed by a cold duck plate that is full of good fresh vegetables. For a light dish, serve Peking Duck with celery and corn – very tasty and also gives you the fiber needed in your diet.

All the above courses are light and you and your guests should be feeling satisfied, but not too full at this time. Poached head lettuce in oyster sauce will provide you with a comfortable, refreshed feeling so that you are ready to go on to the more filling dishes. If you wish to serve this feast, we suggest that you use other meat or seafood as a substitute for the duck to provide a variety.

北京鴨絲春卷

# Light and Crispy Peking Duck Spring Rolls

Spring rolls are an all-time favorite dish to start a meal. They complement wine and other alcoholic beverages. One may be able to pick up the skins or "pi" from Chinatown or gourmet stores. Usually spring rolls are made with pork or shrimp. This new creation is a very welcome item on the Peking Duck Feast.

*6 dried black mushrooms*

*1 tablespoon vegetable oil*
*Shredded meat from ½ Peking Duck*

*Vegetables:*
*2 cups green onions, cut in 2-inch lengths*
*2 stalks celery, cut in thin julienne*
*1½ cups bean sprouts*
*1 small carrot, peeled and shredded*
*1 cup bamboo shoots, shredded*

*Seasoning:*
*2 tablespoons dry sherry*
*Salt and pepper to taste*
*2 tablespoons cornstarch*
*2 teaspoons sesame oil*

*12 spring roll wrappers*
*1 egg, beaten with a fork*

*4-6 cups vegetable oil*

*Substitute for the duck:*
*2 cups thin strips of cooked pork or*
*2 cups shredded cooked chicken*
*or, one can omit the meat and make it a vegetarian spring roll by substituting 2 cup of chives, cut in 1-inch lengths, for the duck.*

Soak mushrooms in water for 20 mintes. Drain, remove and discard stems and cut in fine strips.

Set wok (or wide frying pan) over medium heat for ½ minute until hot. Add oil and swirl to coat sides. When oil is hot, add duck meat and cook 2 minutes.

Stir in vegetables mixed with the seasoning, and continue stir-frying 3 minutes longer. Bean sprouts should be slightly wilted, but still crunchy. Pour into a colander, drain and let cool in freezer for 1 hour.

To wrap, place wrapper with one point toward you. Moisten upper edges with egg. Use about 3-4 tablespoons of filling in the center of wrapper and fold bottom up over filling to cover. Fold over left and right corners so they meet in the center. Wrap, jellyroll style. Repeat process keeping all rolls under a dampened towel from the beginning to the end.

Heat oil in wok (or electric deep-fat fryer) to 375°. Put 5-6 rolls in oil and deep-fry for 2-3 minutes or until golden brown on all sides, turning occasionally. Let oil temperature return to 375° before frying next batch.

To serve: Cut rolls into thirds. Serve with Chinese mustard or sweet-sour sauce.

Yield: 3 dozen
Cooking time: 30 minutes

## *"Strange-Taste" Peking Duck*

"Strange-Taste" Peking Duck involves a Szechwan cooking method just like stir-frying and steaming. This dish is a popular Szechwan hors d'oeuvre. In Szechwan cooking the major taste is usually spicy, hot or salty, but this dish utilizes many seasonings. The taste comes out to be very pleasantly blended in contrast to its original taste. That's why it is called "strange-taste." However, some American people cannot get used to these names, so that some restaurants have changed its name and call it "wonderful-taste." This cooking method applies mostly to poultry.

*Meat from 1/2 Peking Duck*

*Seasoning:*
*1 teaspoon chili paste with garlic*
*1 tablespoon light golden brown sugar*
*1 1/2 tablespoons red Chinese vinegar*
*2 teaspoons soy sauce*
*2 teaspoons sesame oil*
*1 tablespoon white wine or straight sherry*
*Hot sauce to taste*
*Salt and pepper to taste*

*1 1/2 cup green onions*
*1 1/2 cup roasted peanuts*

*1 ripe tomato, cut in wedges*
*Parsley*

Cut duck in 1-inch squares.

Combine all seasoning ingredients and add to duck. Marinate 10 minutes.

Cut onion in 1 1/2-inch lengths.
Just before serving, combine duck with the green onions and 1 cup of the peanuts.

Garnish with remaining peanuts, tomato wedges and parsley.

Serves: 8-10
Cooking time: 15 minutes

北京鴨沙律

# *Crunchy Peking Duck Salad*

Although salad is not a Chinese dish, in China this dish is served as an entree and in America it is served as a salad.

*Meat from one Peking Duck*

*Marinade:*
*1 teaspoon sugar*
*1 teaspoon sesame oil*
*4 teaspoons oyster sauce (optional)*
*4 teaspoons soy sauce*
*2 teaspoons vegetable oil*
*2 tablespoons white wine or straight sherry*
*3 tablespoons Chinese red vinegar or Italian red wine vinegar*
*Salt and white pepper to taste*
*Hot sauce to taste*

*4 cups head lettuce*
*2 cups romaine lettuce*
*1 cup green onion*
*½ cup chives*
*2 cups celery*
*2 cups bean sprouts*
*½ cup Chinese or American parsley*

*Dressing:*
*1 teaspoon sugar*
*2 teaspoons sesame oil (optional)*
*2 teaspoons soy sauce*
*½ teaspoon hot sauce*
*½ teaspoon pepper*
*2 tablespoons oyster sauce*
*½ cup Chinese red vinegar*

*Substitute for the duck:*
*2 cups canned abalone, cut in 2-inch strips or*
*2 cups cooked chicken, cut in strips*

Cut the meat into 2-inch strips about ¼ inch thick.

Mix the marinade ingredients well. Add duck meat and let stand at least 15 minutes.

Slice the lettuce into strips about ¼ inch wide and 2 inches in length. Cut the green onion, celery, and chives into thin strips of about 1½ inches. Cut parsley into small pieces.

Put all vegetables in a large salad bowl and make dressing. Gently mix vegetables with the dressing. Add half of the peanuts with the cooked duck meat and gently mix again. Place on a platter, and garnish with the remaining peanuts and sesame seeds.

To keep the vegetables firm and fresh, it is better not to combine the salad with the dressing until just before serving.

Serves: 8-10
Cooking time: 30 minutes

# 香芹炒北京鴨絲

## *Stir-Fried Peking Duck Meat with Celery and Young Corn*

This is a very colorful dish. The red and green bell peppers, celery and young corn give a very colorful effect and it has a wonderful aroma. This is a dish that can be done in a short time.

*Meat from ½ Peking Duck*

*Marinade:*
*2 teaspoons granulated sugar*
*2 teaspoons brandy or straight sherry*
*2 teaspoons soy sauce*
*Salt and pepper to taste*
*Juice from ½ fresh lemon*

*Vegetables:*
*1 each green and red medium pepper*
*2 medium stalks celery*
*1 medium carrot*
*4 cups (2 cans) young corn*
*1 can whole mushrooms, drained*

*2 teaspoons oil*

*Seasoning:*
*1 tablespoon oyster sauce*
*2 tablespoons soy sauce*
*1 teaspoon sugar*
*2 teaspoons white wine*
*Salt and pepper to taste*

*Substitute for duck:*
*½ pound (30-35 per pound size) shrimp, shelled, butterflied and deveined. Marinate and deep-fry 30 seconds. Drain on absorbent paper and proceed as above.*

Slice duck meat into thin strips approximately 3 inches long and ¼ inch thick.

Mix the marinade ingredients in a large bowl. Add duck and let stand for 15 minutes.

Cut the peppers, celery and carrot into strips approximately ¼ inch thick and 3 inches long.

Heat wok over medium heat for about 1 minute. Add oil, and swirl pan to coat sides. Add all the vegetables. Stir-fry in the Cantonese style, using a Chinese spatula (wok cheun) and ladle (hok), for 5-10 seconds and let stand for another 15-20 seconds to absorb the heat. Repeat this procedure until the vegetables are done but still green and crisp. Add meat and seasoning. Stir-fry for 2 more minutes. Serve hot.

If the wok gets too dry, a tablespoon or so of water or chicken broth may be added to prevent burning.

Serves: 8-10
Cooking time: 20 minutes

# 涼拌北京鴨肉

## *Peking Duck Meat with Pickled Vegetables*

Mix the cooked Peking Duck meat and pickles and serve this dish about the middle of dinner to create an appetizing eye-appealing effect. The taste of the almonds go well with any cuisine.

*Meat from ½ Peking Duck*

*1 cup small sweet pickles*
*1 cup small dill pickles*
*1 medium-size carrot*
*1 jar marinated artichoke hearts cut in half*

*Sauce:*
*¼ cup juice from each of the pickles and the artichokes*
*1 teaspoon sesame oil*
*1 tablespoon oyster sauce*
*1 tablespoon red Chinese vinegar*
*2 teaspoons light golden brown sugar*

*½ cup toasted almonds*

*Substitute for duck:*
*3 cups roasted chicken cut in strips*

Cut duck meat in strips ¼ inch wide and 2½ inches long.

Cut pickles and carrots in strips same as duck above. Parboil carrots 5 minutes and let cool. Combine all of these ingredients.

Mix sauce ingredients in a bowl and combine with all other ingredients.

Serve at room temperature, garnished with the almonds.

Serves: 8-10
Cooking time: 10 minutes

家庭式北京鴨

# *Classic Peking Duck*
## *Home Style*

Roast Peking Duck is a challenge for the gourmet and is not for the cook who is looking for a fast-food dish. A little patience, however, is well rewarded and we guarantee admiration and respect from your guests. It also makes a special treat for your family. Happy cooking!

*1 4½-5½-pound duck*

*Sauce for cavity:*
*1 tablespoon white wine or straight sherry*
*1 tablespoon red bean curd, mashed*
*1 tablespoon Hoisin sauce*
*1 tablespoon bean sauce*
*2 teaspoons brown sugar*
*1 teaspoon sesame oil*
*½ teaspoon Chinese five-spice powder*

*6 green onions, cut in half*
*1 square inch ginger root, or ½ teaspoon ground ginger*
*1 cup Chinese or American parsley*

*10-12 cups boiling water*

*Sauce for coating skin of duck:*
*2 tablespoons white wine or straight sherry*
*1 tablespoon vinegar*
*⅓ cup honey*
*1½ cups water*
*½ teaspoon red food coloring*

*Serving the Duck:*
*1 Chinese knife, weighing approximately 14 ounces to 1 pound*

*6 green onions*

*5 teaspoons vegetable oil*

Thaw and wash duck. Pat dry with paper towel inside and out.

In a bowl, combine all the sauce for the cavity ingredients and mix well.

Lightly crush all vegetables and use as a brush to coat cavity of the duck with the sauce. Add vegetables to the cavity and use skewers to fasten the cavity.

Secure a string around each wing of the duck. Holding the duck by the string, ladle the hot boiling water over the duck for approximately 1 minute. Discard the water.

Combine sauce for skin coating ingredients in a wok, bring to a boil, and while the duck is still warm, slowly and thoroughly coat the duck with the mixture by ladling the sauce over the duck for about 1 minute.

Hang the duck in a well ventilated area and put an electric fan (medium speed) directly on the breast of the duck for 1½ hours. Place a pan underneath the duck to collect the drippings. Or put in refrigerator overnight to let it dry with breast up.

*Dip for the Duck:*
*2/3 cup Hoisin sauce*
*2/3 cup plum sauce*
*2 teaspoons light golden brown sugar*
*Juice from 1/2 fresh lemon*

Preheat oven to 400° for 10 minutes.
Line a roasting pan with aluminum foil and set a rack on top. Place duck on the rack and brush with 2 teaspoons oil. Roast the duck 30 minutes with the breast down. Reduce to 350°. Brush remaining oil over the duck and roast with the breast up for 45 to 55 minutes or until done. (To test whether the duck is done, prick a fork in the thigh. The fork should move in and out easily, and the juices should not be pink.) Turn duck over after 45 minutes and brush with 2 teaspoons of oil.

Remove the skewers and drain the duck. Cut the duck into pieces approximately 1 inch wide and 3 inches long. Arrange on a platter, skin side up. Serve as an entre itself.

Cut onions in half and then into 1½-inch lengths. Divide on two small plates.

Also the duck may be served with the following dip. Combine all of the ingredients listed for the dip in a bowl and mix well. Divide into 2 small bowls.

The duck may be eaten in Chinese pancakes or sesame seed buns cut in half. Using the green onion dipped into the sauce, brush over pancake or inside sesame rolls. Add duck meat to roll, and eat as you would a sandwich.

Serves: 8-10
Cooking time: 5 hours

## Special Notes on Preparing Classic Peking Duck



If Chinese ingredients are not available for the sauce for the cavity, you may use a few crushed cloves of garlic, 3 to 4 crushed star anise, 1 teaspoon five spice powder, and salt and pepper to taste. If you do not have hoisin or plum sauce for the dip for the duck, you may substitute a light touch of lemon or orange peel jam.

When cutting roast duck, you may follow the instructions for cutting chicken as illustrated by the photographs, or you may slice it in the traditional manner of slicing roast turkey. Roast duck is very easy to debone.

You may roast three or four ducks at one time and freeze those you do not intend to use immediately. They can be thawed and used for a number of dishes in this section.

For people on low sodium diets, omitting the salt in the cavity and the soyu sauce called for in the recipes in this chapter will not appreciably reduce the tastiness of these dishes.

# 北京鴨薄餅

## *Fancy Pancakes for Peking Duck*

This is a very traditional way to serve Peking Duck, with the green onion dipped in Hoisin sauce and brushed over the pancake. Add duck and roll it up. Enjoy it like a sandwich.

*¾ cup water*
*2 cups all-purpose flour*
*2 tablespoons sesame oil*

Bring water to a rolling boil. Sift flour into a mixing bowl and make a well in the center. Pour in the boiling water. Using a wooden spoon, stir until mixture forms a soft dough. Place dough on a lightly floured board and knead gently for 10 minutes, until smooth and elastic.

Roll dough into a circle approximately ¼ inch thick. Using a 2½-inch diameter cutter, cut out circles.

Lightly brush half the circles with sesame oil. Place plain circles on top and flatten each pair into 6-inch circles.

Place an ungreased skillet over high heat for approximately 1 minute.

Reduce heat to medium and fry pancakes individually. When they puff up and small bubbles appear, turn them over. Adjust heat so the pancakes have a light brown speckled appearance. This should take about 1 minute for each side.

When cooked, separate the halves. For a softer textured pancake, fold the circle in half and steam for approximately 3 minutes.

Pancakes can be made ahead of time. Wrap in plastic for refrigerating or freezing. The pancake can be reheated only once by steaming for 10-12 minutes, or until soft to the touch.

Makes 2 dozen pancakes
Cooking time: 40 minutes

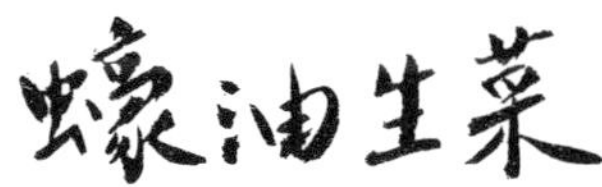

# *Poached Head Lettuce in Oyster Sauce*

Poached head lettuce is simple. It's appropriate to serve with an elaborate feast of rich dishes. With the light vegetable served between them, it gives the dinner a lighter feeling.

*2 large heads of lettuce*

*1 tablespoon vegetable oil*
*8-10 cups hot water*

*Sauce:*
*2 tablespoons oyster sauce*
*2 tablespoons soy sauce*
*2 teaspoons vegetable oil, optional*
*Salt and pepper to taste*

Clean and remove outer leaves of the lettuce and discard. Quarter lettuce and separate leaves.

Bring water and oil to a rolling boil. Put a small handful of lettuce leaves at a time into the boiling water for approximately 10 seconds. Remove and drain for 5 minutes. Leaves should be tender and crisp.

Pour sauce on the well drained lettuce. This may be served hot or cold.

Serves: 8-10
Cooking time: 10 minutes

# 腰果炒北京鴨丁

## *Peking Duck with Toasted Cashew Nuts*

This dish is in the same category as the all-time favorite Cantonese delight, Chicken with Cashews, except that this time the duck meat is roasted and stir-fried with vegetables and topped with crispy cashews. This is another great dish to serve with wine or any cocktail.

*Meat from ½ Peking Duck*

*2 teaspoons vegetable oil*
*2 teaspoons fresh ginger root, peeled, thinly sliced and cut in ¼-inch square pieces*

*1 each medium red and green bell peppers, diced*
*2 cups celery, diced*
*1 medium carrot, peeled, diced and parboiled 2 minutes*
*1 can or 1 cup whole mushrooms, drained*

*Seasoning:*
*2 teaspoons ground bean sauce*
*Salt and pepper to taste*

*1 cup cashews*

*Substitute for duck:*
*3 cups diced raw chicken or raw pork, stir-fried for 5 minutes or raw shrimp, shelled and diced and stir-fried for 2 minutes*

Dice duck meat.

Heat wok or a large heavy skillet over medium-high heat for 10 seconds. Spread oil to cover the bottom and wait for 30 seconds. Drop in ginger and stir-fry for a couple of seconds.

Add vegetables and stir-fry until vegetables are crisp. Add mushrooms last and continue stir-frying 1 more minute.

Add seasoning and stir well. Add duck meat and half of the cashews and stir-fry for 1 minute.

Put in a serving platter and garnish with the remaining cashews.

Serves: 8-10
Cooking time: 15 minutes

# 甜酸炸北京鴨球

## *Deep-Fried Golden Brown Peking Duck in Sweet and Sour Sauce*

A sweet-sour dish is a welcome item to many. Here, we are using a light batter to deep-fry the Peking Duck meat and mix with a reddish looking sweet-sour sauce. It makes a very delightful dish somewhat similar to the Cantonese sweet-sour pork.

*Meat from ½ Peking Duck*

*Marinade:*
*½ teaspoon sugar*
*½ teaspoon sesame oil*
*1 egg*
*2 teaspoons sherry*
*1 teaspoon cornstarch*
*1 teaspoon oil*
*1 teaspoon oyster sauce*
*1 teaspoon soy sauce*
*Salt and pepper to taste*

*Batter:*
*2 eggs*
*2 tablespoons cold water*
*2 teaspoons oil*
*⅔ cup cornstarch*

*4-6 cups vegetable oil*

*1 stalk celery*
*1 bell pepper*
*1 tomato*
*2 cups pineapple chunks*
*1 can lichee, drained*

*Sauce:*
*1 tablespoon cornstarch*
*2 tablespoons cold water*
*½ cup sugar*
*½ cup cider vinegar*
*½ cup water*

Cut duck meat in 1-inch cubes.

Mix the marinade ingredients in a bowl. Add duck and let marinate for at least ½ an hour.

Beat the eggs lightly with a fork, then combine with the water, oil and cornstarch to make a batter. Add a little more water if a thinner batter is desired.

Turn the duck meat into the bowl of batter. Using your hands, mix it well so that each piece of duck is well-coated. Pour oil into a wok set over medium-high heat. When the oil reaches 375°, add duck meat one piece at a time, until it is all in. Deep-fry for 3-5 minutes or until the duck meat is floating freely and has a rich brown color. When the cubes of duck meat are done, remove them from the oil and drain on absorbent paper.

Cut all vegetables into 1-inch cubes.

Mix the cornstarch and cold water in a small bowl. Place the rest of the sauce ingredients in a large sauce-pan and bring to a boil. Gradually stir in the cornstarch and water

*½ cup catsup (or to taste)*
*Hot sauce to taste*

*Toasted sesame seeds or almonds optional*
*Substitute for the duck:*
*1 pound raw chicken meat cut in cubes. Proceed as above. Cook for 7 minutes.*

mixture, and cook until it returns to a boil.

Combine the fried duck meat, vegetables, fruit and sauce, and cook for 30 seconds. Stir well so the sauce thoroughly covers the duck meat and vegetables. Transfer to a heated platter and serve at once.

Never combine the sauce with duck meat and vegetables until you are ready to serve. Garnish finished dish with sesame seeds or almonds.

Serves: 8-10
Cooking Time: 15 minutes.

I travel a lot in search of new recipes. Oddly enough, I just found my girl friend and I are the only people who look worse than our passport photos.

北京鴨炒飯

# *Peking Duck Fried Rice*

Fried rice is a good dish served toward the end of the meal. Especially at an elaborate dinner, we add a touch of finely chopped fresh pineapple, and place the fried rice in a pineapple bowl. A pineapple bowl is made by cutting a pineapple in half, and hollowing the inside. This makes an eye-appealing and attractive dish.

*½ cooked Peking Duck*

*4 teaspoons vegetable oil*
*2 eggs, slightly beaten*

*6 cups cooked rice, cooled*
*1 cup frozen green peas*

*Seasonings:*
*1 teaspoon sesame oil*
*1 tablespoon soy sauce*
*1 tablespoon soy sauce*
*1 tablespoon oyster sauce*
*Salt and white pepper to taste*

*1 small tomato, diced*
*2 cups head lettuce, shredded*
*½ cup green onions, chopped*

*Substitute for the duck:*
*2 cups cooked shrimp or*
*2 cups cooked pork or chicken*

Dice the duck meat.
Set wok (or large frying pan) over medium heat. Add 2 teaspoons oil, swirl around pan to coat sides. When oil is hot, add eggs and scramble. Remove from pan and set aside.

Add remaining 2 teaspoons oil. Heat and add rice. Stir-fry and when rice is hot, add duck meat, green peas, eggs and all of the seasonings. Stir-fry 3-4 minutes.

Add tomatoes, lettuce and onions, toss well and serve.

Serves: 8-10
Cooking time: 15 minutes

# 北京鴨骨湯

## *Peking Duck Soup*

This soup is clear. It's traditionally served at the beginning or at the ending of a meal. We suggest serving the soup at the end, to wash away any greasy effect one may have following the many courses served. It helps to create a light feeling instead of a heavy and full one.

*Bones from 1 Peking Duck*
*1 teaspoon vegetable oil*
*1 square inch fresh ginger, crushed*
*2 tablespoons brandy or straight sherry*
*12 cups water*

Heat a wok or pot over medium high heat for 30 seconds. Add oil and stir-fry ginger until it is fragrant. Add wine, water and bones. Bring to a rapid boil and reduce the heat to medium. Gently boil the bones, uncovered, until the water is reduced to 8 or 9 cups.

Drain the contents, discard the bones and, leaving the stock in the wok, scoop off the floating fat and scum, if any.

*1 or 2 cans chicken stock*
*1 cup water chestnuts, drained and sliced*
*1 can mushrooms, stems and pieces*
*1 medium carrot, peeled and thinly sliced*
*Salt and pepper to taste*
*½ teaspoon MSG, optional*

Combine all of these ingredients and continue cooking 3 minutes, or until carrots are tender.

*You may substitute chicken bones for the duck bones.*

Serves: 8-10
Cooking time: 1 hour

# 豬肉類

*Pork*

# 甜酸咕嚕肉

## *Sweet and Sour Pork*

This great Cantonese dish has become a runaway all-American favorite. Even the Mandarin restaurants are claiming that this is their specialty. This recipe would certainly give your family great satisfaction and would be appreciated by all your company. It should be served toward the latter part of the meal, as the combination of vinegar and sugar will numb your taste buds somewhat.

*1 pound pork butt, cut into 1-inch square pieces*

*Marinade:*
*1 teaspoon brown sugar*
*2 teaspoons soy sauce*
*2 teaspoons sherry*

*Batter:*
*2 eggs, lightly whipped*
*1 cup cornstarch*
*3 tablespoons water*

*4-5 cups vegetable oil for deep frying*

*Sauce:*
*⅔ cup water*
*⅔ cup apple cider vinegar*
*⅔ cup light brown sugar*
*⅓ cup catsup*
*Touch of hot sauce*
*½ square inch ginger root, crushed*

*Thickening base:*
*2 tablespoons cornstarch mixed with 4 tablespoons water*

*Optional vegetables:*
*½ round onion, cut bite-size*
*½ green bell pepper, cut bite-size*
*1 small tomato, cut bite-size*
*1 cup pineapple chunks*

Combine pork with marinade and set aside for 10 minutes.

Mix ingredients for batter in a large bowl. Coat the pork completely in the batter.

Heat oil in wok to 375 degrees. Drop pork pieces in 1 at a time, deep frying for 6-7 minutes or until golden brown and floating. Stir occasionally. When done, remove pork and drain on absorbent paper.

Remove oil from wok, add sauce ingredients and bring to a boil. Add thickener. Bring to boil and remove ginger.

Saute onion and pepper in a pan with a touch of vegetable oil, until tender and crisp.

Add pork, pineapple and vegetables to sauce, stir well and serve immediately.

Serves: 4-6
Cooking time: 60 minutes including marinating

甜酸排骨

# *Sweet and Sour Spareribs*

This great Cantonese dish is a sister dish of Sweet-Sour Pork. To those who enjoy bone chewing, this will give you great satisfaction.

*3 pounds spareribs*

*Marinade:*
*1 tablespoon soy sauce*
*2 teaspoons sugar*
*Salt and pepper*

*Batter:*
*2 eggs*
*1 cup corn starch*
*3 teaspoons oil*
*6 teaspoons water*

*4-6 cups vegetable oil*

*2 teaspoons vegetable oil*

*½ cup cider vinegar*
*½ cup light brown sugar*
*1 cup water (for stronger sauce, just add ½ cup)*
*½ cup catsup*
*Dash hot sauce to taste*
*½ square inch ginger root, smashed*

*1 medium onion, cut bite-size*
*1 cup cucumbers, sliced*
*2 cups fresh pineapple chunks*

*Thickening base:*
*1 tablespoon corn starch*
*1½ tablespoons water*

*Sesame seeds for garnish*

Cut spareribs in about 1½-inch pieces.

Marinate spareribs 30 minutes.

Prepare batter by mixing well. Adjust batter to your desired consistency by adding more water to make thinner, or more corn starch to make thicker.

Stir spareribs in batter until well coated.

Deep-fry about 1 pound of spareribs at a time, for 7 minutes at 350.° Drain and set aside.

Heat a clean wok to medium and add 2 teaspoons oil, spreading oil over the bottom with a spatula. Add vinegar, sugar, water, catsup, hot sauce and ginger, and bring to a boil.

Just before serving, saute onions for 2 minutes. Add to the sauce along with the pineapple and cucumbers.

Add thickening base and stir until thickened. Remove ginger from sauce.

Add meat and serve immediately.

Do not add anything to the sauce until you are ready to serve.

Garnish with sesame seeds.

Serves: 6-8
Cooking time: 30 minutes

The colors of this dish are beautifully balanced the way they are presented, but if you should want a touch of red color toward the holiday season, add 1 large ripe tomato cut into bite-size pieces.

To make sweet and sour shrimp, soak the shrimp (after you have them cleaned and deveined) in the basic fish marinade. Then the remaining steps are the same for both dishes, except deep-fry shrimp for 2-3 minutes.

# 燒烤排骨

## *Barbecued Spareribs*

This is a versatile Chinese dish because it can be served as finger food for your cocktail party or as an entree. You can roast a large quantity ahead of time and freeze it, and quickly heat it up in the oven. Then you have a rather fast dish. Also, because the color is red, in China people serve this dish on romantic occasions, such as weddings, anniversaries or engagement parties.

*2-3 pounds spareribs*

*Marinade:*
*1/4 cup sugar (light golden brown)*
*1 tablespoon salt*
*1/2 teaspoon five-spice powder*

*Red Chinese barbecue sauce*
*2 tablespoons wet bean curd (measure after smashing into a smooth paste)*
*1 tablespoon bean curd liquid*
*1 tablespoon sesame oil*
*1/2 teaspoon salt*
*1 tablespoon sugar*
*3 cloves garlic, crushed & finely chopped*
*1/4 teaspoon red coloring*
*1/4 cup ketchup*
*2 teaspoons honey*
*1/2 teaspoons MSG*

Mix all three spices and sprinkle evenly on both sides of meat. Put one piece of meat on top of the other until all are covered. Marinate for 4 hours. Strain off liquid and rub red sauce on. Let it set overnight or 4-8 hours.

Bake at 400° for first 15 minutes, then reduce heat to 350° and bake for 40 more minutes or until done. When the meat starts to recede from the bone, it is done. Be careful not to let the meat burn. Cut up meat between bones, and it makes good finger food.

Serves: 4-6
Cooking time: 60 minutes

# 核桃肉丁

## *Stir-Fried Diced Pork with Walnuts*

This Cantonese delight is very similar to Mandarin Diced Pork in Bean Sauce. Mandarin food uses different kinds of sauces, such as sweet bean sauce, hot bean sauce, and salty bean sauce. This dish simply eliminates the sauces, and creates a well blended flavor to suit the Cantonese palate. It's a good dish for entertaining.

*1 pound pork*

*Marinade:*
*2 teaspoons oyster sauce or soy sauce*
*2 teaspoons sherry*
*1 tablespoon corn starch*
*1 teaspoon sugar*
*1 egg white, lightly whipped*

*4 teaspoons vegetable oil*
*2 teaspoons chopped ginger or garlic*
*2 teaspoons white wine*

*½ red bell pepper, cut bite-sized*
*½ green bell pepper, cut bite-sized*
*½ white round onion, cut bite-sized*

*½ cup water chestnuts, diced or sliced*
*½ cup bamboo shoots, diced or sliced*
*½ cup peas and carrots*

*Seasoning:*
*2 teaspoons soy sauce*
*1 tablespoon oyster sauce*
*½ tablespoon sugar*
*1 teaspoon vegetable oil*
*Salt and pepper to taste*

*1 cup walnuts*

Dice pork into ½ inch square pieces.

In a large bowl, add marinade to pork and mix well. Let stand for 10 minutes.

Heat the wok over medium-high heat for 30 seconds. Spread 2 teaspoons oil to cover the bottom of the wok and wait for another 30 seconds. Add pork in the wok in a thin layer, and saute for 1 minute. Add 1 teaspoon of oil around the edge of wok, saute for another minute. Turn to the other side, saute for 1 more minute. Stir, and make a well at the bottom of the wok. Drop the remaining 1 teaspoon oil in the well. Stir in the ginger, wait until it gives a fragrance. Stir-fry the pork for 30 seconds. Add wine. Add bell peppers, and onion. Stir-fry for 2 minutes.

Add water chestnuts, bamboo shoot, peas and carrots to wok; stir-fry for 30 seconds.

Add seasoning and ½ cup of walnuts to wok and quickly toss.

Transfer contents to a serving platter and garnish with the remaining walnuts. Serve hot.

Serves: 4-6
Cooking time: 20 minutes

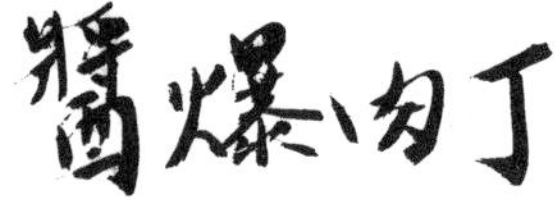

# *Bean Sauce Pork*

This is a great Szechwan dish. The bean sauce offers a delightful saltiness quite different from the taste of salt. As a rule, Northern dishes such as this one, are somewhat less colorful in eye appeal than Cantonese dishes, and cook a longer time too. Therefore the dishes are hotter in temperature than Cantonese.

*½-pound pork butt*
*Salt and pepper to taste*
*½ an egg white, lightly whipped*

*1 teaspoon fresh ginger root, peeled and cut into thin strips*
*2 teaspoons vegetable oil*

*1 teaspoon hot bean sauce*
*1 teaspoon sweet bean sauce*
*2 teaspoons soy sauce*
*2 teaspoons sesame oil*
*2 teaspoons red Chinese vinegar (or white vinegar)*
*1 teaspoon sugar*

*Vegetables:*
*1 cup celery*
*½ cup water chestnuts*
*2 or 3 pieces young corn*
*1 cup green bell pepper*

*6 pieces Chinese black mushrooms*

*½ cup peanuts or cashews*

Dice pork into pieces approximately ½ inch thick. Marinate the pork with egg white, salt and pepper for 10 minutes.

Place the wok over medium-high heat for 30 seconds. Spread oil in the wok and wait for another 30 seconds. Stir ginger strips 5-10 seconds. Add pork in a thin layer to the wok, and saute for 1 minute. Turn pork over and saute for another minute. Stir-fry for 1 minute.

Combine all the sauces, sesame oil, vinegar and sugar in the wok. Stir-fry for 2 minutes.

Soak mushrooms in warm water for 20 minutes. Squeeze water out, cut off and discard stems. Dice all vegetables in same size as pork, then stir-fry for 2-3 more minutes.

Mix ½ of the nuts in the wok. Serve on the platter with remaining nuts as a garnish.

Serves: 4-6
Cooking time: 20 minutes

鱼香茄子

# *Eggplant with Pork in Bean Sauce*

This is a popular dish in Szechwan cuisine. Although it is simple to make, it always offers a very good taste. The bean sauce may have to be obtained from a Chinese grocery store. It will keep for months in the refrigerator, and adds a very special flavor.

*6 ounces pork*
*Salt and pepper to taste*

You may use pork butt, shoulder, center cut or leg, cut in thin slices approximately 1/4 inch thick and 1 1/2 inch long. In a bowl, combine meat with salt and pepper, mix well.

*2 teaspoons vegetable oil*
*1 tablespoon chopped round onion*

Place wok over medium-high heat for 30 seconds. Spread oil in the bottom of the wok and wait for another 30 seconds. Stir-fry onion and pork for 1 minute.

*2 teaspoons straight sherry*
*2 teaspoons hot bean sauce*

Pour sherry around edge of the wok, and stir in hot bean sauce.

*1 1/2 pounds eggplant*

Wash and cut eggplant into strips 1/2 inch wide and 3 inches long.

*2 teaspoons soy sauce*
*1/2 cup chicken broth*
*2 teaspoons sesame oil*
*2 teaspoons red Chinese vinegar (or white vinegar)*

Add eggplant, soy sauce, chicken broth, sesame oil and vinegar to the wok, stir-fry 1 minute. Cover and cook 2 more minutes, or until the eggplant is soft and tender.

*1 tablespoon Chinese fungus*

Soak fungus in warm water for 20 minutes. Use fingers to pick out fungus and discard water.

*1/2 cup shredded bamboo shoots*

Add bamboo shoots and fungus, and stir-fry for 1 minute.

*1/2 cup green onion, cut in 1-inch lengths.*
*1 small red chili pepper, thinly sliced (optional)*
*Salt and pepper to taste.*

Add green onion, 1/2 of the red pepper, salt and pepper to the wok, mix well. Serve on a platter, and garnish with remaining red pepper.

Serves: 2-4
Cooking Time: 30 minutes

# *Szechwan Mu Sai Pork*

Mu Sai Pork is a popular dish in the Szechwan cuisine and is now served in Northern and Mandarin restaurants as well. In this book, for simplicity, all dishes which are not Mandarin, are classified as Cantonese. Of course, there are distinctions between the regional cuisines. Some people feel they should be classified into more than 30 separate schools of cooking, instead of just Mandarin and Cantonese.

You don't need chopsticks for this dish since it is one of the few dishes you eat like a sandwich because the meat is wrapped in a thin pancake.

*4-6 ounces lean pork (butt, center cut, leg portion)*
*2 teaspoons vegetable oil*
*Salt and pepper to taste*

Cut pork into thin strips approximately ¼ inch thick, and 1½ inch long. It will be helpful if you place the pork in the freezer to firm up the meat for easy cutting. Add salt and pepper to pork.

*2 teaspoons garlic (finely chopped)*

Heat wok on medium high heat. Add oil, spreading on the bottom. Wait 30 seconds, then saute the pork for 2 minutes. Add garlic to wok and stir-fry for 1 more minute.

*½ cup Chinese fungus*

Soak fungus in 3 cups of water for 20 minutes. Pick out with fingers and discard water. Chop very coarsely.

*1½ teaspoon Hoisin sauce*
*1 teaspoon ground bean sauce*
*4-6 ounces bamboo shoots, cut into thin strips*
*½ cup green onion, cut into 1-inch segments*
*2 eggs, scrambled*

Add the sauces to the wok. Mix well. Add the vegetables, fungus and scrambled eggs. Stir-fry to mix.

*Seasoning*
*2 teaspoons soy sauce*
*2 teaspoons white wine or straight sherry*
*⅓ cup water or chicken broth*
*1 teaspoon vinegar*

Add seasoning.
Stir-fry for 2 minutes.

*½ teaspoon sesame seeds*

Empty the contents onto a platter. Garnish with sesame seeds.

Some prefer this served on a Chinese pancake, placing the Mu Sai Pork in the center, rolled up like an envelope, and eaten as a sandwich. For Chinese pancake recipe, please refer to Peking Duck section.

Serves: 2-4
Cooking time: 20 minutes

Chinese cut pork into thin pieces before stir-frying. Americans cook pork chops in a thick piece. Both are good ways of cooking pork. Speaking of pork chops reminds me of my youth. When I was a child, I was so ugly my mother had to tie a piece of pork chop to my neck to get the family dog to play with me.

# 簡式薄餅

## *Easy Chinese Pancakes*

*2 cups sifted all-purpose flour*
*¾ cup boiling water*
*2 tablespoons sesame seed oil*
*2 tablespoons vegetable oil*

In a food processor, using the dough blade, combine the flour and boiling water. Process until dough forms a soft elastic ball. Let stand covered for 15 minutes.

On a lightly floured surface, roll dough into a circle ¼ inch thick. Cut 2-inch circles from this larger circle, and brush each small circle with sesame seed oil/vegetable oil mixture. Flatten this brushed circle into thin rounds approximately 5½ to 6 inches in diameter.

Pan fry each pancake in a greased skillet over high heat, turning as they puff up and small blisters begin to appear in the dough. Brown lightly, approximately one minute. Stack pancakes on a heated platter and serve immediately with Peking Duck.

TIPS FROM TITUS: You may be able to find frozen Chinese pancakes at a well-stocked Oriental grocery store in your area. Failing that, an acceptable substitute might be flour tortillas. A word of caution about this substitution: corn tortillas will not work in this recipe. Only flour tortillas come close to a reasonable substitute. Crepes and "swedish pancakes" would also work, but those would have to be made with care as the original recipes call for too much sugar.

扣肉

# *Kau Yuk*

Kau means "gently steaming" and Yuk is "pork". Kau Yuk is a dish that is served at the end of a meal. A touch of red food coloring is used to color the meat. The color itself stands for happiness so it is a Chinese tradition to serve Kau Yuk for an occasion to show happiness or to wish a happy life. So, you will find Kau Yuk served for birthdays, anniversaries and other special occasions. In a restaurant, the dish is served last with lots of tea. This is not a fast dish to prepare for it takes several stages. The meat has to be cooled off or drained thoroughly before going on to the next step.

*2½ pounds pork belly*
*2 tablespoons soy sauce*
*4 cups vegetable oil*
*1 bundle green onions*
*1-2 tablespoons oil*
*Chinese parsley (bundle) or cilantro*
*2 star anise*
*3-4 cloves of garlic, crushed*
*Chinese taro or potatoes*

*Sauce:*
*2-3 tablespoons sherry*
*1 tablespoon sesame oil*
*Dash white pepper*
*2 tablespoons mashed bean curd*
*1 teaspoon salt*
*1 tablespoon sugar*
*1 tablespoon oyster sauce*
*1½ cups water*
*½ teaspoon red Chinese food coloring*
*Parsley for garnish*

*Thickening base:*
*1½ tablespoons cornstarch*
*3 tablespoons water*

More than likely, you'll have to buy the pork belly for this dish in Chinatown. When you get it home, make a cut ½ inch deep around the bones and lift the bones out. In a large pot, gently boil the meat for 45 minutes. Then remove and run cold water over the meat for 7 minutes. Take out and drain. (Skin side should be warm to the touch). If the skin cools too much, the soy sauce will not stick. Prick the skin thoroughly with a fork. Rub the skin side only with about 2 tablespoons of soy sauce and let dry. Put the meat, skin side up, in a strainer and let all excess water drain off. Allow the meat to drain for about half an hour.

Caution: If you try to rush the draining process, you'll find that you'll have hot oil splattering in this next deep frying process.

Deep-fry the meat, skin side down, for 5 minutes in oil heated to 375°. Have a lid handy as a precaution in case the oil starts splattering. When it is done, the skin will be a golden brown color. Run cold tap water over the meat to cool it off completely.

While the meat is cooling, heat wok to medium high heat with 1-2 tablespoons oil. Add 1 bundle green onions, crushed (roots and all for we want them for aromatic effect. After cooking, all vegetables will be thrown away). Add the garlic cloves, peeled and chopped. Add crushed Chinese parsley bundle if you like, and the star anise. Stir fry briefly over medium high heat.

Cut meat into pieces which are approximately 2½ inches in length and ½ inch thick.

The traditional way would be to cut the potato or Chinese taro into the same size as the pork slices. Fry the potatoes in oil for 5 minutes. Remove and drain. Then make "sandwiches" of pork-taro-pork. Using 2 bowls, place the first sandwich into the bowl, skin side down; then the second. Continue placing the sandwiches in the bowl until the bowl is completely filled. Then steam for 45 minutes. This step is called "kau" or steaming.

When completed, put the second bowl over the first bowl and invert them so that the skin side is up. To serve, you pour the sauce, which you have boiled and thickened, over the pork.

If you wish to serve it family style, omit the kau step, then prepare the sauce as directed, add the meat and cook for 30 minutes. If the meat has been steamed, it's necessary to cook in the sauce for only about 15 minutes.

*This is a good party dish because you can refrigerate it for up to 3 days. However, it is not a dish that is served at a formal dinner.

## *Steamed Ground Pork With Salt Fish*

The zesty taste of this dish takes getting used to. It is an acquired taste, and is an excellent addition to your hot weather diet. This dish will make you popular with beer drinkers and cola manufacturers.

*2 ounces salted fish in oil*
*1 pound ground pork*
*10 water chestnuts, finely chopped*
*½ onion, finely chopped*
*½ cup finely chopped green onions*
*2 teaspoons finely chopped chung choy*
*1 egg, slightly beaten*
*2 teaspoons cornstarch*
*2 teaspoons oyster sauce*
*½ teaspoon sugar*
*½ teaspoon sesame oil*
*Dash of white pepper*

Drain salted fish and set aside. Combine remaining ingredients and let stand 30 minutes, and then put on a 9-inch plate. Arrange fish on top. Bring water to boil in steamer. Steam for 30 minutes or until done.

Serves: 4-6
Cooking time: 35 minutes

中国饅頭

# Chinese Buns

A simple recipe to make. It can replace Chinese pancakes for Kau Yuk, Peking Duck, or Pressed Duck.

*1/8 cup sugar*
*1 tablespoon shortening*
*1 cup cold water*

*3 cups flour*
*1½ teaspoons to 1 tablespoon baking powder*

Mix sugar, shortening and water together until well mixed.

Add flour and baking powder to the above mixture. Mix until it holds together into a dough, then place on floured board and knead until smooth.

Let set about 15 to 20 minutes. When dough rises, roll into a long piece and cut into about 15 to 18 pieces. Make a ball of each piece and flatten out to about 2 inches in diameter.

Brush with oil and fold in half. Let set for about 15-20 minutes. Steam for 20 minutes.

Yield: 15 to 18 buns

揚州炒飯



# *Young Chow Fried Rice Hong Kong Style*

Young Chow is a place in China known for its scenic beauty. In China, those who want "hand holding sessions" go down to the riverbank and hire a Chinese junk. The boat moves slowly just like a Sunday drive in America. When the couple pulls the curtains down they can "do their thing" in privacy. The boatman knows what to expect and while he waits for them he takes a weeping willow branch and attaches a string to fish for shrimp. During lunch or dinner they expect you to order from them. A frequent request is Young Chow Fried Rice.

You simply need 2 kinds of fully cooked meat, plus the shrimp. The Cantonese have adapted this dish, as have the chefs in Hong Kong. It can be served as a one-dish meal for lunch or dinner or can be served toward the end of a multi-course elaborate dinner to signify the ending, before sweets are served.

*4-6 cups cooked rice*

*2-3 teaspoons vegetable oil*

*½ cup Char Siu (Chinese red barbequed pork) or cooked ham, chopped*
*2 eggs, scrambled*
*½ cup cooked shrimp*
*½ cup peas and carrots*

*Seasoning:*
*3 teaspoons soy sauce*
*3 teaspoons oyster sauce*
*1 teaspoon sesame oil*
*Salt and pepper to taste*

*⅓ cup green onion, chopped*

*2 cups fresh bean sprouts or shredded lettuce (optional)*

Long grain rice which you cook yourself is preferable. When done, it should be relatively firm and not sticky. If a larger amount of cooked rice is used, it is best to cook the night before and refrigerate.

Heat wok on medium-high for 30 seconds. Spread oil in bottom of wok to cover a large area. Wait 30 more seconds. Stir-fry the rice in the wok until it is hot.

Combine ingredients and stir-fry for 2 more minutes until hot. Add seasoning. Stir well. Add vegetables to wok just before serving. Stir-fry and mix well for 10-15 seconds.

Serves: 4-6
Cooking time: 30 minutes

# 牛肉類

*Beef*

# *Mongolian Beef*

*1 pound or 1 medium flank steak*

*Marinade:*
*1 egg white, lightly whipped*
*1 teaspoon sugar*
*2 teaspoons cornstarch*
*2 teaspoons vegetable oil*
*½ teaspoon sesame oil*
*2 teaspoons soy sauce*
*2 teaspoons oyster sauce*
*Salt and pepper to taste*
*½ square inch fresh ginger root, crushed*
*2 teaspoons sherry*
*⅓ teaspoon baking soda (if used, meat must marinate 8 hours)*

*2 medium green peppers*
*½ carrot*

*2 cups oil for frying*
*⅓ layer Pai Mai Fun*
*4 teaspoons chili paste with garlic*
*2 teaspoons sesame oil*
*⅓ cup chicken broth*

Remove the thin membrane on both sides of the steak with a sharp knife. Then cut the steak along the grain into 3 to 4 long strips. Next cut the meat across the grain into pieces about ¼ inch thick, 1½ inches wide and 2 inches long.

Dry meat with a paper towel and place in a large bowl. Add all marinated ingredients and mix thoroughly. Let it stand for at least ½ hour and preferably overnight, if baking soda is used.

Cut the peppers and carrot in ½-inch strips.

In a wok, heat the 2 cups of oil. Fry Pai Mai Fun until crisp and drain. Remove all but 2 teaspoons of oil from the wok. Add steak and stir-fry until browned. Another teaspoon of oil can be added after about 20 seconds to hasten browning. Add vegetables and stir-fry until cooked but still crisp. Add chili paste and chicken broth. Cook 1 minute. Arrange Pai Mai Fun on top before serving.

Serves: 4
Cooking time: 45 minutes

# 蠔油牛肉

## *Beef with Oyster Sauce*

*½ pound beef, sliced thinly against the grain*

*Marinade:*
*½ egg white lightly whipped*
*2 tablespoons oyster sauce*
*2 teaspoons oil*
*Salt to taste*
*Dash white pepper*
*½ teaspoon sesame oil*
*2 teaspoons cornstarch*
*¼ teaspoon sugar*
*1 teaspoon water*

*2 tablespoons peanut oil*
*2 teaspoons chopped ginger or garlic*
*½ cup bamboo shoots*
*½ cup chicken broth*

*Seasoning:*
*1½ tablespoons oyster sauce*
*1 teaspoon soy sauce*
*3 tablespoons wine*

*Thickening base:*
*1½ teaspoons cornstarch*
*2 teaspoons water*

Cut away the fat and the thin membrane from all sides of steak with a sharp knife. Then cut the steak along the grain for 3 or 4 long strips. Cut across the grain into pieces 2 inches, and ¼ by 1½ inches wide

Mix marinade. Add beef and let marinate in refrigerator for ½ or 2 hours. When ready to cook, heat wok as usual, spreading oil in wok along sides. When heated, add ginger and beef pieces. Cook approximately 2 minutes on each side. Combine thin slices of chestnuts and bamboo shoots. Add chicken broth and seasoning, and return to a boil. Add the cornstarch mixture to thicken. Serve Immediately

Serves: 4-6
Cooking time: 45 minutes

# Beef Tomato

This is a popular everyday home dish. It is colorful and nutritious, and the vegetables – bell pepper and onion – add an aromatic effect. Every Chinese dish, whether for entertaining or home use, should contain four elements: good taste, proper texture, color contrast and aromatic effect. This favorite Cantonese entree exemplifies them all.

*1 pound or 1 medium-size flank steak*

*Marinade:*
*1 egg white, lightly whipped*
*1 teaspoon sugar*
*2 teaspoons corn starch*
*2 teaspoons vegetable oil*
*½ teaspoon sesame oil*
*2 teaspoons soy sauce*
*2 teaspoons oyster sauce*
*Salt and pepper to taste*
*½ square inch fresh ginger root, crushed*
*2 teaspoons sherry*
*⅓ teaspoon baking soda (if used must marinate meat at least 8 hours.)*

*2-3 teaspoons vegetable oil*
*1 teaspoon chopped ginger*
*1 teaspoon chopped garlic*

*½ small round onion - bite size pieces*
*½ green bell pepper – cut in bite size pieces*

*1 or 2 tomatoes – cut in bite sizes pieces.*

*Seasoning:*
*1 teaspoon sugar*
*2-3 tablespoons catsup*
*⅓-¼ cup chicken broth*

*1 egg yolk, lightly beaten*

Remove the thin membrane on both sides of the steak with a sharp knife. First cut the steak along the grain into 3-4 inch long strips then cut the meat across the grain into pieces about ¼ inch thick, 1½ inches wide and 2 inches long.

Dry the meat with an absorbent paper and place in a large bowl. Add all the marinade ingredients and mix thoroughly. Let stand for at least half an hour and preferably overnight, if baking soda is used.

Place wok over medium high heat for 30 seconds. Spread oil in the bottom of the wok, and quickly saute the ginger and garlic. Place beef in the wok in a thin layer. Saute for 1 minute, then turn the other side and saute for another minute. Stir, and add onion and bell pepper. Stir-fry for 1 minute, then add tomato.

Add seasoning to the wok, and stir-fry for 2 more minutes. Make a well at the bottom of the wok, and wait until the sauce comes to a boil. Slowly stir in the egg yolk and stir-fry for 30 seconds. Serve hot.

Serves: 4-6
Cooking time: 30 minutes

# 京式脆粉絲牛肉

## *Beef on Deep-Fried Rice Sticks Peking Style*

China is a vast country with a huge population to be fed. Throughout the centuries, from the Dynastic era to the present day, the majority of the Chinese have tried to save materials in cooking and this has long been a virtue among the Chinese folks. Chinese are so clever that they can make a piece of inexpensive flank steak delicious in the eyes of Westerners. They can transform it into meat that is tender and juicy, comparable to expensive cuts.

By marinating the beef in egg white and cornstarch and first sauteing it a minute or two on each side, then stir-frying it, you can create a tender and juicy effect, because the juice is sealed in by the thin paste of egg white and cornstarch. For home cooking all stir-fried dishes involving meat should be done this way, before any vegetables are added.

To create an extra tender effect in beef, to every pound of beef, one may add ¼ teaspoon baking soda, 2 teaspoons each of vegetable oil and water. Marinate overnight.

*1 pound flank steak*

*Marinade:*
*2 teaspoons soy sauce*
*2 teaspoons cornstarch*
*1 egg white, lightly whipped*
*Salt and pepper to taste*

*2 teaspoons vegetable oil*

*½ teaspoon garlic, chopped*

*½ green bell pepper, thinly sliced*
*½ red bell pepper, thinly sliced*
*1 small carrot, grated*

*Seasoning:*
*2 teaspoons white wine or straight sherry*
*2 teaspoons soy sauce*
*½ cup chicken broth*

Cut away the fat and the thin membrane from all sides of steak with a sharp knife. First cut the flank steak along the grain into 3 or 4 long strips. Cut across the grain into pieces 2 inches long, and ¼ inch by 1½ inches wide.

In a large bowl, combine the beef with the marinade. Let set.

Heat wok on medium-high heat for 30 seconds. Spread oil on the bottom of wok to cover a large area. Wait 30 more seconds.

Add garlic to wok, and quickly stir-fry for a couple of seconds. Add the beef, spreading in a thin layer to cook evenly. Cook for 1 minute or

*1 teaspoon sesame oil*
*1 teaspoon chili paste with garlic*

*1½ cup lightly crushed rice stick (Mai Fun)*
*2-4 cups vegetable oil*

*1 or 2 fresh chili peppers, thinly sliced*

until browned. Stir-fry for 1 more minute.

Stir-fry the vegetables for about one minute.

Add seasoning. Stir-fry and mix well with the beef and vegetables. Turn off heat.

Heat oil to 400-425°. Drop 1 pinch of Mai Fun at a time into hot oil. In 5-10 seconds, it should stop expanding. Take out. These could be done well in advance. Place the rice on a platter, and evenly spread the meat and vegetables on top.

Garnish with chili pepper (optional).

Deep fried Mai Fun can soften rather rapidly. Do not combine the meat with the Mai Fun until immediately before serving, so as to keep a nice, firm texture.

Serves: 4-6
Cooking time: 25 minutes

# *Beef Broccoli*

This is a great favorite among the Cantonese cuisine and it is enjoyed tremendously by the Westerners. In China, this is considered a dish for home use, rather than entertaining. To create special tenderness in the beef, add a pinch of baking soda and a few teaspoons (half and half) water and oil - and marinate over night. This method is an invention of the Cantonese people.

*1 pound or 1 medium-size flank steak*

*Marinade:*
*1 egg white, lightly whipped*
*1 teaspoon sugar*
*2 teapoons corn starch*
*2 teaspoons vegetable oil*
*½ teaspoon sesame oil*
*2 teaspoons soy sauce*
*2 teaspoons oyster sauce*
*Salt and pepper to taste*
*½ square inch fresh ginger root, crushed*
*2 teaspoons sherry*
*⅓ teaspoon baking soda (if used, must marinate meat at least 8 hours)*

*1-1½ pounds Chinese or American broccoli, cut into spears*
*4-5 cups water*
*2-3 teaspoons vegetable oil*
*1 tablespoon sugar*

*2-3 teaspoons vegetable oil*
*1 teaspoon chopped ginger*
*1 teaspoon chopped garlic*

*½ cup water chestnuts, sliced*
*½ cup bamboo shoot, thinly sliced*
*½ small red bell pepper, diced*

*Seasoning:*
*2 teaspoons sugar*

Remove the thin membrane on both sides of the steak and the fat with a sharp knife. First cut the steak along the grain in 3-4 inch pieces and then cut the meat across the grain into pieces about ¼ inch thick, 1½ inch wide and 2 inches long.

Dry the meat with absorbent paper and place in a large bowl. Add all the marinade ingredients and mix thoroughly. Let stand for at least half an hour, and preferably overnight if baking soda is used.

Cut stems off broccoli and peel. Cut in half, then slice diagonally in pieces. Cut bud part into spears 2-3 inches long. Bring water to a boil. Add oil and sugar and mix well. Place the broccoli in the water and cook for 2 minutes. Drain.

Place wok over medium high heat for 30 seconds. Spread oil over bottom of wok. Quickly saute ginger and garlic. Add beef to the wok in a thin layer. Saute for 1 minute, turn the other side and saute for another minute. Add broccoli and other vegetables and stir-fry 1 minute.

*2 teaspoons straight sherry*
*2 teaspoons soy sauce*
*2 teaspoons sesame oil*
*1 tablespoon oyster sauce*
*½ cup chicken broth*

*Salt and pepper to taste*

Add seasoning to wok, and stir-fry for 1 more minute. Serve hot.

Serves: 6-8
Cooking time: 30 minutes

# *Fresh Mushrooms with Boneless Chicken and Beef*

*4-6 ounces beef*
*1 chicken breast (4-6 ounces)*
*½ dozen mushrooms*
*4 teaspoons vegetable oil*
*2 cloves garlic, crushed*

*Seasoning:*
*1 tablespoon wine*
*1 tablespoon soy sauce*
*1 tablespoon oyster sauce*
*1 teaspoon sugar*
*1 teaspoon vinegar*
*Salt and pepper to taste*

*1 cup green onion, cut into strips*

Remove the fat and the thin membrane on both sides of the beef. Cut beef across the grain into pieces about 2½ inches long, 1½ inch wide and ¼ inch wide. Cut chicken meat about the same size as the beef. Cut mushrooms in half.

Heat wok on medium high for 1 minute. Pour 2 teaspoons of oil around edge of wok and add 2 cloves of crushed garlic. Add the chicken breast and stir fry for 2 minutes (1 minute on each side). Remove chicken from wok and place in bowl. Put aside.

Reheat wok on medium high. Pour 2 teaspoons oil around edge of wok. Place beef in wok and saute for 1 minute. Stir-fry. Add chicken and stir-fry 2 minutes and then add the seasoning ingredients and green onions. Stir fry for 10 seconds. Serve hot.

Serves: 4-6
Cooking time: 45 minutes

## Grilled Short Ribs

For picnicking, this is a dish you should try because you can get all the seasoning and marinating done at home, and just place the meat on the grill.

*2 pounds short ribs*

*Seasoning:*
*2 teaspoons salt*
*2 teaspoons sugar*
*½-1 teaspoon five spice powder*

*Marinade:*
*½ cup light brown sugar*
*1 cup soy sauce*
*2 cups water*
*Hot sauce to taste*
*1 tablespoon honey*
*½ square inch ginger, crushed*

Wash meat, drain and pat dry.

Combine the seasoning ingredients and put on the ribs. Let sit for 1 hour in refrigerator.

Combine marinade ingredients and marinate meat for 2 hours more.

Grill the meat to your own liking, over a medium-high heat. Brush with marinade and turn occasionally.

Serves: 2-4
Total preparation and cooking time: 3½ hours (Marinate for 2 hours)

## Steamed Beef

*1 pound flank beef steak*

*Marinade:*
*1 teaspoon chopped garlic*
*1 tablespoon soy sauce*
*1 tablespoon oyster flavored sauce*
*1 teaspoon sugar*
*1 teaspoon vinegar*
*Salt and pepper to taste*
*½ cup green onion*

Clean beef by removing membranes. Then cut the steak along the grain into 3 or 4 long strips. Cut across the grain into pieces 2 inches long and ¼ by 1½ inches wide. Marinate the beef for 15 minutes. Spread beef thinly on platter. Steam for 5 minutes Sprinkle on the chopped green onions. Let steam for another 15 to 20 seconds. Serve hot.

Serves: 4-6
Cooking time: 15 minutes

# 豆腐類

*Tofu*

# *Pork Tofu*

This is a popular home dish among the Cantonese people. The taste of pork is absorbed by the tofu. This dish is inexpensive to produce and very nutritious.

*12 ounces tofu (1 block, well drained)*

*½ pound lean pork: center cut, shoulder, leg or butt*

*Marinade:*
*1 teaspoon sugar*
*1 teaspoon sesame oil*
*2 teaspoons soy sauce*
*2 teaspoons oyster sauce*
*2 teaspoons cornstarch*
*1 tablespoon sherry*
*Dash pepper*

*3 teaspoons vegetable oil*

*Seasoning:*
*1 tablespoon soy sauce*
*1 teaspoon sugar*
*2 teaspoons cider vinegar*

*⅔ cup chicken broth*

*Thickening base:*
*1 tablespoon cornstarch*
*1½ tablespoons water*

*½ cup chives, cut 1-inch long*
*Salt and pepper to taste*

Cut tofu lengthwise in half, then cut crosswise in half. Slice into ½-inch-thick pieces.

Slice pork into 1½ by 2 inch pieces and ¼ inch thick.

Place the pork in a bowl and add marinade ingredients. Mix well. Let stand for 15 minutes.

Heat the wok for 30 seconds. Add 2 teaspoons oil and use a spatula to spread oil over the bottom. Add the pork in a single layer as much as possible. Saute for 1 minute. Around the edge of the wok, add 1 more teaspoon oil and saute 2 more minutes. Stir-fry for 1 more minute until pork is tenderly done. Add tofu and gently mix. Add seasonings and chicken broth. Stir. Make a well in the center of the wok and when the liquid is boiling, stir in the well mixed thickening base.

Add chives, toss and serve hot.

Serves: 4
Cooking time: 20 minutes

# 免治牛肉豆腐

## *Tofu with Ground Beef*

*12 ounces tofu (1 block, well drained)*

*½ pound lean ground beef*

*Marinade:*
*1 teaspoon sugar*
*1 teaspoon sesame oil*
*2 teaspoons soy sauce*
*2 teaspoons oyster sauce*
*2 teaspoons cornstarch*

*4 teaspoons vegetable oil*

*1 tablespoon sherry*
*⅔ cup chicken broth*

*½ small round onion, chopped*

*Thickening base:*
*1 teaspoons cornstarch*
*4 teaspoons water*

*Parsley for garnish*

*Salt and pepper to taste*

Cut tofu lengthwise in half, then cut crosswise in half, and slice into pieces ½ inch thick.

In a bowl, place the ground beef and mix in the marinade. Let set for 15 minutes.

Heat the wok over medium high heat for 1 minute. Spread 1 teaspoon oil over the bottom and wait for another 30 seconds until the oil is hot. Place the tofu in the wok and saute for 1 minute. Around the edge of the wok, add 1 more teaspoon of oil and saute for another minute. Turn the tofu over and cook 1 more minute. Place the tofu on a serving plate.

Heat a clean wok for 30 seconds. Add 2 teaspoons of oil and stir-fry the chopped onion until the aroma comes out. Add the beef and stir-fry to the doneness you prefer. Add sherry around the edge of wok, followed by the broth. Stir. Combine tofu with beef in wok. Make a well in the center and bring the sauce to a boil. Stir the thickening base, which has been well mixed, in the well and bring to a boil. Transfer to a plate and top with sprigs of Chinese parsley.

Serves: 4
Cooking time: 20 minutes

# 荳腐蝦米

## *Tofu with Dried Shrimp*

This home-cooked dish is a clever way that the Cantonese people use tofu, which in itself tastes somewhat bland. Tofu and dried shrimp are a perfect combination for a dish. This can be served cold as an appetizer or as a side dish.

*12 ounces tofu (1 block, well drained)*

*3 tablespoons small dried shrimp*

*Seasoning:*
*1 tablespoon oyster sauce, optional*
*2 tablespoons soy sauce*
*1 teaspoon granulated sugar*
*2 teaspoons sesame oil*
*2 teaspoons cider vinegar*

*1 tablespoon salted turnip, finely chopped*
*½ cup chopped green onions*

*Salt and pepper to taste*

Cut tofu lengthwise in half. Then cut crosswise in half, and slice into pieces ½ inch thick.

Soak dried shrimp in warm tap water for 45 minutes. Drain and discard water.

In a small bowl, mix together all the seasoning ingredients. Place the tofu on a serving plate. Pour the seasonings over the tofu, then sprinkle the turnip, shrimp and green onion evenly on top.

Serves: 4
Cooking time: 20 minutes

# *Tofu with Crab Meat in Creamy White Sauce*

The capitol of Kwongtung Province, Canton has been exposed to many foreign embassies and foreign people. Many Westerners stayed in the city for work and visiting, therefore the Cantonese chefs had the opportunity to absorb some of the good points of Western cooking brought in by the visitors. White sauce is indeed a creation of East and West. This dish has good visual appeal when a touch of red from the crabmeat floats in the white sauce.

*12 ounces tofu (1 block, well drained)*

*Thickening base:*
*2 teaspoons cornstarch*
*4 teaspoons water*

*2 teaspoons vegetable oil*

*1 package (4-8 ounces) cooked frozen crab meat, thawed*
*½ medium-size green bell pepper, cut bite size*
*½ small red bell pepper, cut bite-size*

*1 tablespoon straight sherry*

*⅔ cup chicken broth*
*¼ cup cream*

*1 egg white whipped*

*Salt and pepper to taste*

Cut tofu lengthwise in half, then cut crosswise in half. Slice into pieces ½ inch thick.

Mix thickening base well in a small bowl.

Heat wok. Add 1 teaspoon oil and heat for 30 seconds. Spread oil over bottom with a spatula. Stir-fry the bell peppers for 1½ to 2 minutes until tender and crisp. Put on a plate. Spread the other teaspoon of oil in the wok and stir-fry the crab meat for 1 minute. Around the edge of the wok, pour in 1 tablespoon straight sherry. Stir and then add chicken broth and bring to a boil. Add the cream and quickly stir in egg white. Add tofu and bellpeppers, gently mix and cook for 1 minute. Serve hot.

Note: This recipe may be made using shrimp, scallops or fish fillet.

Serves: 4
Cooking time: 15 minutes

# 豆腐雙冬

## *Black Mushrooms with Tofu*

Dried black mushrooms are one of the major ingredients in vegetarian dishes. Once they are soaked and the water is squeezed out, they will absorb the sauce they are cooked with, thereby becoming a very tasty dried vegetable which at the same time gives a delightful aroma. Combining the mushrooms with bean curd, you will have both the good taste and the wonderful fragrance.

*1 ounce dried black mushrooms*
*2 cups water*

*10 ounces winter melon*

*4-6 ounces tofu*

*2 cloves garlic, chopped*
*3 thin pieces ginger root, peeled*
*1 tablespoon sherry*
*½ cup chicken broth*

*Seasoning:*
*1 tablespoon oyster sauce*
*2 teaspoons soy sauce*
*½ teaspoon sugar*
*1 teaspoon sesame oil*

*Thickening base:*
*1 tablespoon cornstarch*
*1½ tablespoons water*

*½ cup green onion, chopped*

*Salt and pepper to taste*

Soak mushrooms in water for 20 minutes. Cut and discard the stems. Tightly squeeze out the water. Peel and cut the melon 1½ inches by 2 inches. Rinse and cut the tofu in four equal pieces. Mix melon and tofu well in a bowl.

Stir-fry ginger and garlic with a drop of oil until fragrant. Pour sherry around edge of the wok. Follow with winter melon and tofu and stir-fry for 2 minutes. Add mushrooms and chicken broth. Simmer until melon is tender. Mix in seasoning. Add thickening base and bring to a boil. Toss in green onion just before serving. Serve hot.

Serves: 6
Cooking time: 30 minutes

# *Tofu With Mushrooms*

This is a very popular vegetarian dish that people enjoy cooking at home. Tofu is very nutritious, and the best vegetarian dishes are actually not masterpieces of chefs in great restaurants, but oftentimes come from the temples, perfected by the monks. This dish is perfect for people who enjoy cooking vegetable dishes.

*2 teaspoons vegetable oil*
*1 teaspoon chopped garlic*
*1 teaspoon bean sauce*

*1 medium size can straw mushrooms, drained*

*1 block tofu (the hard kind), cut into 6-8 equal slices*

*Seasoning:*
*2 teaspoons white wine*
*1 teaspoon sugar*
*1 tablespoon soy sauce*
*2 teaspoons oyster sauce*
*2 teaspoons red Chinese vinegar (or white vinegar)*
*Salt and pepper to taste*

*½ cup chicken broth or water*

*½ cup green onion, cut in 1-inch pieces*
*1 cup bean sprouts*

*1½ teaspoons cornstarch*
*2 teaspoons water*

Place wok over medium-high heat for 30 seconds. Spread oil in bottom of wok and wait for another 30 seconds. Quickly stir-fry garlic and bean sauce.

Add straw mushrooms and stir-fry for 1 minute. Add tofu. Gently mix and cook for 1 minute.

Add seasoning to the wok. Gently mix.

Add chicken broth around the edge of the wok.

Add onion and bean sprouts to the wok. Gently mix.

Mix cornstarch and water in a small bowl. Make a well in the bottom of the wok and stir in the mixture until it comes to a boil. Gently mix the contents in the wok. Serve hot.

Serves: 4-6
Cooking time: 15 minutes

# 甜酸荳腐

## *Tofu in Sweet and Sour Sauce*

This is not a traditional Chinese dish, as tofu is not popularly used in sweet and sour sauce. However, through kitchen-tested recipes such as this, we are using oriental ingredients adapted to the Western palate.

*12 ounces tofu (1 block, well drained)*

*2-3 teaspoons vegetable oil*

*2 teaspoons garlic, finely chopped*
*2 teaspoons ginger, peeled and finely chopped, optional*

*Sweet and Sour Sauce:*
*½ cup cider vinegar*
*½ cup water*
*½ cup light golden brown sugar*
*¼ cup catsup*
*Hot sauce to taste*

*Thickening base:*
*1 tablespoon cornstarch*
*2 tablespoons water*

*Salt and pepper to taste*

Cut tofu lengthwise in half, then cut crosswise in half. Slice into ½ inch thick pieces.

Heat the wok over medium-high heat for 1 minute. Spread 2-3 teaspoons oil around the edge of the wok and use the spreader to cover the oil over a large area. Stir in the ginger and garlic. Mix in tofu by gently stirring.

In a small saucepan, mix all the sauce ingredients and bring to a gentle boil.

Mix thickening base well in a small bowl.

Add the thickening base to the sauce pan while stirring and bring back to a boil. This can be made in advance.

Pour the sweet and sour sauce over the tofu. Serve immediately.

Serves: 4
Cooking time: 20 minutes

# 微波爐類

*Microwave*

獅子頭

# *Lion's Head*

Lion's Head is a northern Chinese dish, using meat balls which are not commonly used in Chinese cooking.

*1 pound lean ground pork*
*2 teaspoons garlic, finely chopped*
*1 teaspoon ginger root, finely chopped*
*1 tablespoon oyster sauce*
*2 tablespoons straight sherry*
*1 tablespoons soy sauce*
*1 egg, beaten*

*1 pound bok choy (Chinese cabbage) or celery cabbage*
*2 teaspoons oil*

*Salt and pepper to taste*

Combine all the ingredients except bok choy in a large bowl and mix well. Divide the mixture into 10 portions to form 10 meatballs.

Cut cabbage lengthwise into 3 sections, then slice crosswise into 4-inch sections. Mix cabbage and oil.

Arrange cabbage in heatproof dish, leaving center open. Cover with plastic wrap, leaving small vent. Cook on high for 1 minute. Then uncover. Arrange meatballs evenly spaced on cooked bok choy, leaving center of dish open. Tightly cover and cook on high for 5 minutes. Serve hot.

Serves: 4-6
Cooking time: 12 minutes

# 微波爐蒸肉餅

## *Pork Hash*

This Cantonese dish usually is done in a steamer. To adapt to the fast-paced living style, one can simply use the microwave oven to steam this dish and have the same effect in taste as if it were done traditionally in a steamer or wok.

*½ pound ground pork*

*Vegetables:*
*½ cup green onions, chopped*
*½ cup water chestnuts, chopped*
*½ cup bamboo shoots, chopped*

*Seasoning:*
*2 teaspoons soy sauce*
*2 teaspoons oyster sauce*
*2 teaspoons sesame oil*
*1 teaspoon sugar*
*2 teaspoons cornstarch*
*Salt and pepper to taste*

*1 egg, lightly whipped*

Mix pork with vegetables, seasoning and egg and place in microwave container. Cover and cook for total 4 minutes. In about 2 minutes, stir. Use carousel to keep dish turning if necessary.

Serves: 2-4
Cooking time: 4 minutes

# 微波爐焗白豬肉

## *White Turnips With Pork Or Beef*

In recent years, the Chinese have been adapting many of their recipes for cooking in the microwave oven. And as with cooks everywhere, the microwave is great for quick heating and it allows green vegetables to retain their color. The following recipe can use turnips or daikon.

*½ pound pork butt or flank steak*
*2 teaspoons soy sauce*

*Vegetables:*
*½ cup bamboo shoots, thinly sliced*
*2 carrots, thinly sliced*
*6 button mushrooms*
*½ pound white turnip, bite size*
*1 can young corn, drained (optional)*

*Seasoning:*
*3 teaspoons oyster sauce*
*3 teaspoons soy sauce*

*Salt and pepper to taste*

*½ cup chicken broth*

Thinly slice the meat 1-inch wide by 1½ inches long by ¼ inch thick, marinate meat with soy sauce.

Mix vegetables with meat.

Add seasoning to meat and vegetables.

Wet bottom of microwave dish with chicken broth, put ingredients in dish and try to keep meat near sides of dish. Cover with plastic wrap and vent wrap to let steam escape. Cook for 8 minutes.

Serves: 4-6
Cooking time: 8 minutes

# *Steamed Fish in Black Bean Sauce*

The microwave oven used for steaming is probably the greatest contribution for Chinese cuisine. It can make a very fast, yet tasty dish when working people come home and desire a fast and simple, tasty dish.

*1 fresh fish (1½-pound whole fish, such as sea bass, snapper, scrod, haddock)*

*Salt to taste*

*1 tablespoon fermented, salted black beans*

*Seasoning:*
*1 tablespoon vegetable oil*
*2 tablespoons cooking sherry*
*2 tablespoons soy sauce*

*½ cup green onion*
*3 thin slices ginger, peeled and cut into thin strips*
*Parsley, optional*

Slit fish lengthwise into 2 pieces. Make 2 or 3 deep crosscuts in skin of each piece on both sides. Rub each fish piece on both sides with a touch of salt.

Soak fermented beans in 2 cups of warm tap water for 15 minutes. Drain and mash. Discard water.

Combine the seasoning in a bowl with the fermented beans. Place fish, skin side up, in a large heatproof dish. Pour black bean mixture evenly over the fish. Top with onions and ginger. Cover fish tightly with plastic wrap. Cook in microwave on high for 6 minutes or until done. Serve hot and garnish with parsley if desired.

Serves: 4-6
Cooking time 15 minutes

# *Steamed Chicken with Black Mushrooms*

This popular Cantonese home-style dish now can be done in the microwave oven with a lot less effort. It is a tasty dish.

*1 dozen Chinese mushrooms*

*1 pound raw chicken, skinned and boned*

*2 lean lop chong (Chinese sausage), sliced*

*Seasoning:*
*1 tablespoon soy sauce*
*1 tablespoon oyster sauce*
*2 tablespoons cooking sherry*
*½ teaspoon sugar*
*2 teaspoons vegetable oil*
*1 inch ginger root, very thinly sliced*

*Salt and pepper to taste*

Soak mushrooms in warm tap water for ½ hour. Cut and discard the stems. Tightly squeeze out the water.

Slice chicken into thin pieces, 1-inch by 1½ inch in size.

Mix all the ingredients together. Arrange evenly in heatproof dish, leaving center open. Cover with plastic wrap, leaving small vent. Cook on high for 2 minutes. Stir, leaving center open. Re-cover, leaving small vent. Cook on high for 2 minutes more. Let stand for 3 minutes, in or outside the oven. Serve hot.

Serves: 4-6
Cooking time: 8 minutes

微波爐芥蘭

## *Chinese or American Broccoli*

Chinese broccoli is very plentiful in the southern part of China where Cantonese food originated. Both American or Chinese broccoli can be cooked in the microwave oven for 2-3 minutes for a fast vegetable dish.

*1-1½ pounds Chinese or American broccoli*

*Seasoning:*
*½ tablespoon vegetable oil*
*2 tablespoons soy sauce*
*Salt and pepper to taste*

*2-3 tablespoons chicken broth*

Slice broccoli at an angle.

In a glass microwave dish, place vegetable oil, soy sauce, salt, pepper and chicken broth, mix well, add broccoli, cover and cook for 2½ minutes.

Serves: 4-6
Cooking Time: 2½ minutes

## *Fresh Bok Choy (Chinese White Stem Cabbage)*

*1 pound fresh bok choy*

*Seasoning:*
*1 tablespoon soy sauce*
*½ teaspoon sugar*
*2 teaspoons vegetable oil*
*2 teaspoons water*

*Garnish:*
*Parsley*
*Chopped scallions*

*Salt and pepper to taste*

Cut stem lengthwise in half, then cut crosswise into 1½ inch-long pieces at an angle.

Place the stem part in a heatproof glass plate. Cover with plastic wrap, leaving small vent. Cook on high for 2 minutes, add in the leafy part, and mix well with the seasoning. Give dish a quarter turn, cook on high for 2 more minutes. Serve hot.

Garnish with parsley and chopped scallions.

Serves: 4-6
Cooking time: 4 minutes

# 微波爐煑鮮菜

## *Fresh Broccoli*

*1 pound fresh broccoli*

*Seasoning:*
*1 tablespoon soy sauce*
*2 teaspoons sugar*
*2 teaspoons vegetable oil*
*2 teaspoons water*

*Garnish:*
*Tomato slices or parsley sprigs*

*Salt and pepper to taste*

Remove lower leaves, and cut lower stems 1½ inches on the diagonal. Break tops apart to form bite size florets.

In large heatproof glass plate, mix in seasoning and broccoli. Cover with plastic wrap, leaving small vent. Cook on high for 2 minutes and give dish a quarter turn, then cook on high for 2 more minutes.

Garnish and serve hot.

Serves: 4-6
Cooking time: 4 minutes

## *Tender Asparagus*

*1 pound fresh asparagus*

*Seasoning:*
*1 tablespoon soy sauce*
*½ teaspoon sugar*
*2 teaspoons vegetable oil*
*2 teaspoons water*

*Garnish:*
*Pimento strips or parsley sprigs*

*Salt and pepper to taste*

Cut off or snap and discard tough ends of asparagus. Cut the stalks diagonally, into 1½-inch pieces.

In a large heatproof glass dish, mix seasoning and asparagus. Cover with plastic wrap, leaving small vent, and cook on high for 2 minutes. Then give dish a quarter turn, cook on high for another 1 minute. Garnish and serve hot or cold.

Serves: 4-6
Cooking Time: 4 minutes

微波爐焗鮮菇

## Fresh Mushrooms

Cooking fresh mushrooms with a touch of Chinese seasoning in a microwave oven can have amazing results in terms of time and effort saved.

*1 pound fresh mushrooms, halved*

*Seasoning:*
*2 tablespoons soy sauce*
*2 teaspoons water*
*2 teaspoons vegetable oil*
*½ teaspoon sugar*
*2 teaspoons garlic, chopped*

*Garnish:*
*Chopped scallions or sprigs of parsley*

*Salt and pepper to taste*

*Note: This recipe may be also used with broccoli, asparagus, and bok choy.*

Place mushrooms on a heatproof glass plate, mix in seasoning, cook on high for 2 minutes, and stir. Cover optional. Give dish a quarter turn and cook on high for 1 more minute. Remove dish from oven. Let stand a few minutes

Serve cold or hot. Garnish with a few scallions or sprigs of parsley.

Serves:4-6
Cooking time: 3 minutes

## Mixed Fresh Vegetables

*½ pound fresh broccoli*

*1 medium size carrot*

*1 8-ounce tray mushrooms*

*Seasoning:*
*1 tablespoon soy sauce*
*½ teaspoon sugar*
*2 teaspoons vegetable oil*
*2 teaspoons water*

*Salt and pepper to taste*

Cut the broccoli into flowerets and slice the carrots thinly. The mushrooms may be used whole or cut in half.

In a heatproof glass plate, mix vegetable and seasonings, leaving small vent. Cover with plastic wrap. Cook on high for 2 minutes. Give dish a quarter turn, then cook on high for 2 more minutes. Serve hot.

Serves: 6-8
Cooking time: 4 minutes

# 微波爐焗豆腐

## *Bean Curd Casserole*

Casserole cooking, Chinese style, has been popular in recent years. Though not necessarily an expensive dish, it sure makes a one-dish meal that is terrific for working people.

*1 pound tofu (bean curd)*

*Thickening base:*
*2 teaspoons cornstarch*
*1 tablespoon water*

*½ pound lean ground pork*
*3 tablespoons soy sauce*
*2 tablespoons cooking sherry*
*½ teaspoon sugar*

*2 teaspoons vegetable oil*

*Salt and pepper to taste*

Cut tofu lengthwise in half, then cut crosswise in half, and slice into ½-inch thick pieces

Mix thickening base and then combine ground pork, soy sauce, sherry, sugar, and thickening base and mix well. Spread oil in a large heatproof dish. Spread pork in an even layer, leaving center open. Cook on high for 3 minutes, stir. Cook for 1 more minute, and then stir. Mix with tofu, cover with plastic wrap and cook on high for 3 minutes. Serve hot.

Serves: 4-6
Cooking time: 7 minutes

微波爐焗蛋花湯

# *Egg Drop Soup*

Egg Drop Soup is another Chinese soup easily adapted to the Western microwave cooking. This popular dish can be done with little effort, yet can be enjoyed by many.

*1 tablespoon fungus*

*2 cans chicken broth or 4 cups home-made stock*
*1 cup water*

*½ cup water chestnuts, diced*
*½ cup bamboo shoots, sliced*

*2 eggs, well beaten*

*Garnish:*
*1 green onion, chopped*

*Salt and pepper to taste*

Soak fungus in 2 cups warm water for 20 minutes. Remove fungus with your fingers and discard water. Chop fungus lightly.

Combine chicken broth and water in a heat-proof bowl. Cover and heat on high for 8 minutes or until it comes to a boil.

Add water chestnuts, bamboo shoots, fungus, and heat on high for 2 minutes, or until it again returns to a boil.

Remove soup from the microwave, and slowly stir in the beaten eggs, using the heat of the broth to cook the whipped eggs.

Pour into individual serving bowls and garnish.

Serves: 4-6
Cooking time: 10 minutes

# *Egg Flower Soup*

*2 cans chicken broth or 4 cups homemade stock*
*1 cup water*
*2 eggs, well beaten*
*1 small can mushrooms (pieces and stems)*
*1 cup frozen green peas*

*Garnish:*
*Green onions, chopped parsley*

*Salt and pepper to taste*

Combine chicken broth and water in heatproof bowl. Cover, leaving small vent. Heat on high for 8 minutes or until boiling. Mix in all ingredients except eggs. Heat on high for 2 more minutes until boiling. Slowly stir in beaten eggs, using heat of broth to cook the whipped eggs. Garnish with chopped green onions.

Serves: 4-6
Cooking time: 10 minutes

# *Steamed Eggs*

The microwave oven can certainly be utilized to make this Chinese dish. It is not only fast, but a tasty dish which can be done with little effort.

*6 eggs, beaten*
*½ tablespoon vegetable oil*
*2 tablespoons cooking sherry*
*2 teaspoons soy sauce*
*1 cup green onion, chopped*

*Salt and pepper to taste*

Beat eggs and mix with rest of the ingredients. Pour in a heatproof bowl (cover optional). Cook on low for 8 minutes. Give dish a quarter turn. Cook on high for 5 minutes until texture is custard-like.

Serves: 4-6
Cooking time: 30 minutes

微波爐焗粟米羹

# Creamed Corn Soup

This is a hearty home-style soup utilizing the microwave oven. It's fast and tasty. Although creamed corn is not a traditional Chinese food, many people who live in America like it very much.

*2 cans chicken broth or 4 cups home-made stock*
*1 cup water*
*1 can cream-style corn*
*1 cup fully cooked ham, diced*

*Thickening base:*
*1½ tablespoon cornstarch*
*4 tablespoons water*

*½ tablespoon brandy*

*Salt and pepper to taste*

Mix together ⅔-cup ham, water, chicken broth and corn in a large heatproof bowl, and cover, leaving small vent. Cook on high for 6 minutes or until boiling.

Add thickening base and stir well. Re-cover, leaving small vent, and cook on high for 3 more minutes until boiling.

Let stand for 5 minutes and drop in brandy.

Garnish with ⅓ cup of ham.

Serves: 6-8
Cooking time: 9 minutes

# 蔬菜類

*Vegetables*

# 浸西洋菜

## *Poached Watercress*

Watercress can be used in salads but this poaching method makes the vegetable tender and nutritious; a fast dish for busy people who need a green vegetable on their dining table.

*2 bunches watercress, washed*
*8-10 cups hot water*

*Seasoning:*
*2 teaspoons oil*
*2 teaspoons sesame oil*
*2-3 teaspoons dry sherry*
*3 teaspoons soy sauce*
*3 teaspoons oyster sauce*

*1 teaspoon toasted sesame seeds*

*Salt and pepper to taste*

Fill pot with water. Bring to a rapid boil. Grasp bunch of watercress by stems and dip leafy portion completely into water for 3 seconds. Remove and shake cool for 5 seconds. Repeat this cycle 5 times or until done to taste. Repeat with second bunch. Drain and cut cooked leafy portion into 1½-inch segments. Stems can be reserved for soup later. Pour seasoning over watercress and sprinkle with sesame seeds. Serve hot or cold.

Serves: 4-6
Cooking time: 10 minutes

浸鮮露筍

# Poached Asparagus

*1 pound fresh asparagus*
*4-6 cups water*
*Seasoning:*
*1 tablespoon soy sauce*
*1 tablespoon oyster sauce*
*1 tablespoon vegetable oil*
*2 teaspoons sesame oil (optional)*
*Salt and pepper to taste*

Bring water to a boil. Place asparagus in boiling water for 3 minutes. Stir. Remove from boiling water. Drain well. Sprinkle seasoning over asparagus. Serve hot or cold.

Serves: 4-6
Cooking time: 15 minutes

# Poached Broccoli Deluxe

*3 cans or 6 cups chicken broth*
*1 pound broccoli*

*Seasoning:*
*2-3 teaspoons oyster sauce*
*1-2 teaspoons sesame oil*
*2-3 teaspoons sherry*
*2-3 tablespoons soy sauce*
*Dash white pepper*
*Salt to taste*

*2 teaspoons toasted sesame seeds*

*Note: Broccoli may be substituted with choy sum*

Bring chicken broth to boil and add broccoli, cook for 2 to 3 minutes. Remove broccoli, arrange on serving platter. Save broth for soup, such as egg flower soup.

Distribute seasoning ingredients evenly over broccoli.

Dust with toasted sesame seeds

Serves: 4-6
Cooking time: 15 minutes

# 清炒瓜菜

## *Stir-Fried Vegetables – Broccoli and Carrots*

*1 pound fresh broccoli*
*1 medium-size carrot*
*2-3 teaspoons vegetable oil*

*2 teaspoons chopped garlic*
*2 teaspoons white wine*
*1 tablespoon soy sauce*
*1 tablespoon oyster sauce*
*1 teaspoon sugar*
*2 teaspoons sesame oil*
*Salt and pepper to taste*

*Asparagus may be substituted for broccoli*

Peel and cut broccoli in flowerets. Clean and slice carrots.

Bring water to a boil. Place broccoli and carrots in boiling water for 30 seconds. Stir constantly. Remove from boiling water and drain well for about 5 minutes. Set aside.

Thoroughly heat wok on medium-high heat for 1 minute. Place around edge of wok 2-3 teaspoons oil and distribute on all sides of wok. Stir 2 teaspoons chopped garlic in wok. Add carrots and broccoli to wok for 2 minutes. Stir and add 2 teaspoons wine around edge of wok. While vegetables are in wok, saute with soy sauce and oyster sauce. Stir-fry with seasoning for 30 seconds and serve hot.

Serves: 4-6
Cooking time: 15 minutes

# *Stir-Fried Chinese Pea Pods*

For those who can get fresh pea pods, this makes a very fast stir-fry dish, as it requires only a couple of minutes of actual cooking time.

*½ pound Chinese pea pods*

*1 5 ounce can water chestnuts or*
*1 can of bamboo shoots*

*1 tablespoon vegetable oil*
*2 teaspoons chopped garlic*
*2 tablespoons soy sauce*
*2 tablespoons oyster sauce*
*1 teaspoon sherry*
*1 teaspoon sugar*

*Salt and pepper to taste*

De-vein and clean pea pods. Drain and slice the water chestnuts.

Heat wok on medium-high heat for 1 minute. Place around edge of wok 1 tablespoon of oil, and distribute on all sides of wok. Stir in 2 teaspoons chopped garlic. Add the pea pods and stir-fry for 1 minute. Add water chestnuts or bamboo shoots. Add soy and oyster sauces, sherry, and sugar, saute one minute.

Serves: 4-6
Cooking time: 15 minutes

# 蠔油鮮蔬

## *Mixed Vegetables in Oyster Sauce*

High quality oyster sauce enhances the taste of vegetable dishes. Generally speaking, plain vegetables do not offer much of a taste to suit the palate of the gourmet. But that can be changed with the proper use of Chinese sauce.

*½ pound broccoli*
*½ pound cauliflower*
*1 can baby corn (6-8 ounces)*

*6 cups boiling water*
*1 tablespoon sugar*
*1 tablespoon salt*
*2 teaspoons oil*

*2 cloves garlic, finely chopped*
*⅓ cup green onion, chopped*

*Seasoning:*
*1 tablespoon sherry*
*⅓ cup chicken broth*
*1 tablespoon soy sauce*
*2 tablespoons oyster sauce*

*1 small carrot, thinly sliced*

*Salt and pepper to taste*

Trim and cut broccoli and cauliflower into small florets. Parboil in the water with salt, sugar and oil for 1 minute. Drain.

Stir-fry garlic and onion for 30 seconds. Stir-fry remaining vegetables in the wok, for 2 minutes. Add sherry and chicken broth, and then the rest of the seasoning. Heat through, turn onto warm plate.

Serves: 4-6
Cooking time: 15 minutes

# Assorted Vegetables in Turmeric Sauce

Vegetarian dishes that skillfully utilize sauces eliminate the common notion that vegetarian dishes are bland, and this is a good example.

*1 tray (or 8 ounces) fresh mushrooms*
*1 medium-size carrot, sliced*
*½ pound broccoli*
*½ pound cauliflower*

*6-8 cups water*
*2 teaspoons vegetable oil*
*1 teaspoon sugar*

*Turmeric Sauce:*
*¾ cup chicken broth*
*¾ cup milk*
*¾ cup coconut milk*
*3½ tablespoons turmeric powder*

*Thickening base:*
*2 tablespoons cornstarch*
*3 tablespoons water*

*2 teaspoons ginger, chopped (optional)*
*⅓ cup green onion cut in 1-inch pieces*
*2-3 teaspoons sherry*

*Salt and pepper to taste*

Clean and trim carrot, broccoli and cauliflower and cut into small pieces.

Parboil all vegetables with sugar and oil for 1 minute. Drain.

In small bowl, mix cornstarch, water and turmeric powder.

In a small saucepan, pour chicken broth, milk and coconut milk and bring to a boil. Gently stir in the thickening base to form the gravy.

Stir-fry ginger and chive with a drop of oil until it gives aroma. Stir-fry-carrot, broccoli and cauliflour for 1 minute. Add fresh mushrooms, and stir-fry for another minute Around the edge of the wok, add sherry. Pour the tumeric sauce into the wok and stir. Serve hot in a bowl.

Serves: 6
Cooking times: 15 minutes

# 白汁鮮蔬

## *Mixed Vegetables in White Sauce*

White sauce is not really a traditional Chinese sauce. It is an adaption by the Cantonese of the Western way of cooking. Canton, since the old days, has been a city exposed to many westerners. Cantonese are great adapters. So they cook these vegetables and add the white sauce to it. It makes a delightful dish of East-meets-West.

*½ pound fresh asparagus*
*½ pound fresh cauliflower*

*Water for poaching:*
*4-6 cups water*
*1 tablespoon sugar*

*1 can (6-8 ounces) button mushrooms, drained*

*2 teaspoons vegetable oil*
*1 tablespoon chopped fresh ginger*
*2 teaspoons chopped garlic*
*1 tablespoon sherry*
*1 cup chicken broth or water*

*Seasoning:*
*2 teaspoons sugar*
*1 teaspoon sesame oil*
*½ teaspoon MSG*

*¼ cup cream*

*Thickening base:*
*1 tablespoon cornstarch*
*1½ tablespoons water*

*Salt and pepper to taste*

Wash and slice asparagus diagonally ¼ inch thick. Wash and break cauliflower into florets.

Put ingredients for poaching in water and bring to a boil. Poach asparagus and cauliflower for 1 minute, drain.

Mix cornstarch and water well in a small bowl.

Stir-fry garlic and ginger in 2 teaspoons of vegetable oil until fragrant, then stir-fry all the vegetables for 2 minutes. Sprinkle in the sherry followed by chicken broth. Stir and add all the seasoning except the cream. When the sauce comes to a boil, mix in cream. Stir in thickening base. Serve hot.

Serves: 6
Cooking time: 15 minutes

清炒鮮蔬

# *Stir-Fried Mixed Vegetables*

Zucchini, although it is an Italian squash, is available in most markets. It takes little work and fits into the Chinese stir-fry method of cooking very well.

*½ pound fresh zucchini*
*1 medium-size carrot*
*1 cup bamboo shoots, sliced*
*1 medium-size can button mushrooms, drained*
*2-3 teaspoons vegetable oil*

*Seasoning:*
*1 tablespoon soy sauce*
*1 tablespoon oyster sauce*
*2 teaspoons sesame oil*
*½ cup chicken broth*

*1 cup green onions, cut into 1½-inch pieces*

Cut zucchini in half, then thinly slice. Clean and slice carrots into thin pieces.

Heat wok thoroughly on medium high heat for 1 minute. Distribute 2-3 teaspoons oil on all sides of wok. Add zucchini, carrots, bamboo shoots and mushrooms and cook for 2 minutes. Add seasonings and broth and saute 2 more minutes.

Add half of the onions. Quickly mix and place in serving bowl and top with remaining onions.

Serves: 4-6
Cooking time: 15 minutes

# Young Corn With Carrots

*4-5 small cloves garlic*

*2 teaspoons vegetable oil*

*1 medium-size carrot*
*1 can button mushrooms (4-8 ounces), drained*
*1 can young corn (8-12 ounces), drained*

*Seasoning:*
*2 teaspoons sesame oil*
*2 teaspoons soy sauce*
*2 teaspoons oyster sauce*
*Salt and pepper to taste*

*⅓ cup chicken broth*

*½ cup green onion cut in 1-inch pieces*

Place wok over medium-high heat for 30 seconds. Spread oil in the bottom of wok and wait for another 30 seconds. Quickly stir-fry garlic that has been chopped fine.

Add thinly sliced carrots, mushrooms and corn to the wok, and stir-fry for 3 minutes. Add seasoning to the wok, stir well. Add chicken broth to wok and stir-fry for 2 more minutes. Add green onion cut into 1-inch pieces, mix and serve hot.

Serves: 2-4
Cooking time: 15 minutes

四川茄子

# *Szechwan Eggplant*

*2 pounds long eggplant*
*1/4 cup Chinese fungus*

*4 teaspoons vegetable oil*
*1 tablespoon minced garlic*
*1 tablespoon sherry*

*1 cup chicken broth*
*2 tablespoons red Chinese vinegar*
*2 teaspoons soy sauce*
*1 cup shredded bamboo shoots*
*4 teaspoons chili paste with garlic*
*1 teaspoon sesame oil*
*2 teaspoons sugar*
*1 1/2 cup green onion strips*
*1 tablespoon cornstarch*
*2 tablespoons water*

Cut eggplants into 3-inch sticks. Soak fungus in 2 cups water for 20 minutes, remove and squeeze out excess water.

Heat wok over medium-high heat and sprinkle 2 teaspoons of the oil around the edge. Add eggplant and garlic and stir-fry for 1 minute. Sprinkle sherry around edges of wok, and cook for 1 more minute. Stir in chicken broth, vinegar, soy sauce, bamboo shoots, chili paste, sesame oil, sugar and fungus. Cover and cook until eggplants are tender – about 7 minutes. Stir in green onions. Stir in cornstarch with water, add to wok and cook briefly until thickened. Sprinkle with remaining 2 teaspoons oil to give eggplants a shiny appearance.

Serves: 6-8
Cooking Time: 45 minutes

Caution: This recipe is spicy hot.

# Poached Bok Choy Cabbage

Chinese vegetables are more readily available in supermarkets nowadays. The white stem cabbage, or, as it is sometimes called, the spoon cabbage, is among the more common ones. This vegetable is very nutritious. A simple poaching will retain the vitamins in the vegetables.

*1 pound bok choy cabbage*

*4-6 cups water*

*Seasoning:*
*1 tablespoon soy sauce*
*1 tablespoon oyster sauce*
*1 tablespoon vegetable oil*
*1 teaspoon sesame oil*
*1 teaspoon wine or sherry*

*Salt and pepper to taste*

Cut cabbage stalks in half, separating the stem from the leafy part of the cabbage. Then cut in 1½-inch slices.

Bring water to a boil. Place the stems of the cabbage in the boiling water for approximately 2 minutes. Then add the leafy part of the cabbage for 1 minute. Stir occasionally. Remove from boiling water and drain well. (About 5 minutes to drain completely). Sprinkle seasoning over the top and serve hot or cold.

Serves: 4-6
Cooking time: 10 minutes

*Noodles*

# 豬肉炒麵

## *Pork With Noodles*

*½ pound pork pieces*
*2-3 teaspoons oil*

*2 12-ounce packages Chow Mein noodles*
*1 bell pepper cut into 1-inch pieces*
*1 onion cut into 1-inch pieces*
*1 carrot sliced very thin*
*2 cloves finely chopped garlic*
*1 cup cleaned, de-stringed snow peas*

*Seasoning:*
*2 teaspoons sherry*
*1½ cans chicken broth (3 cups)*
*Dash salt, pepper*
*1 teaspoon sesame oil*
*2 tablespoons oyster sauce*
*2 teaspoons soy sauce*

*Thickening base:*
*1½ tablespoons corn starch*
*3 tablespoons water*

*Cilantro*

Slice pork thinly.
Bring wok to medium-high heat. Add 1 teaspoon oil around edge. Lower heat; noodles burn easily. Brown noodles 2-3 minutes each side. Remove and place on heated serving platter.

Heat wok and add teaspoon of oil. Stir-fry pork for 3 minutes. Add garlic, onion, green pepper, carrot. Stir fry for 1 more minute. Place snow peas in wok and stir. Add, sherry and chicken broth followed by the remaining seasoning ingredients.

Mix well. Bring liquid back to boil, then add thickening base. Return to boil; pour over noodles and garnish with cilantro. Serve immediately.

Serves: 4-6
Cooking time: 45 minutes

# 排骨炒麵

# *Sparerib Chow Mein*

*2 pounds spareribs*
*2 tablespoons vegetable oil*
*Salt and pepper to taste*

*3 packages chow mein noodles (about 2 pounds)*

*Topping:*
*1 bundle broccoli (or to make a more fancy topping, use mushrooms, young corn, Chinese fungus, etc.)*

*3 cups chicken broth, heated*

*Seasoning:*
*2-3 tablespoons wine*
*Dash white pepper*
*½ tablespoon sesame oil*
*3 tablespoons soy sauce*
*3 tablespoons oyster sauce*
*2 teaspoons light brown sugar*
*Salt to taste*
*Tabasco sauce to taste*

*Thickening base:*
*1 tablespoon cornstarch*
*2 tablespoons water*
*½ bundle green onions*
*1 cup cilantro, cut in 2-inch pieces*

*Tips from Titus: Optional ingredients in the recipe are sesame oil and hot sauce. Vegetables for this recipe can be prepared the night before.*

Cut spareribs into bite-size pieces (with cleaver – chop through bone.)

Heat wok to medium high. Add 2 teaspoons oil around the edge of wok. Saute noodles on one side; shake loose to heat all noodles. Then turn over and shake loose again. Heat about 5-7 minutes. Add salt and pepper and a little oil. Remove from wok. Place hot noodles on serving tray in cone shaped mound.

Cut off top of broccoli. Peel stems with potato peeler lightly. Then cut stem diagonally. Parboil. Vegetables can be prepared the night before.

Heat wok to medium high. Spread 2 teaspoons oil around edge of wok. Stir-fry spareribs 5 minutes. Add chicken broth and all of the seasoning to the wok. Cook two minutes more, or until the spareribs are done. Bring sauce to boil. Add vegetables.

Mix thickening base in small bowl. Add this to wok. Bring to boil. Cut onions into 1½ inch strips. Add to mixture after thickened. Pour over noodles and serve.

Use cilantro as garnish.

Serves: 8 to 10
Cooking Time: 40 minutes

# Cantonese Crab Meat Chow Mein

Chow mein means "stir-fried noodle." This noodle dish has plenty of sauce in it, so the taste of the meat and crab and vegetables combine with the sauce and are absorbed by the noodle, making it a very tasty entree. For a formal dinner, noodles are served, just one or two dishes before the end of the meal.

*1 pound Chinese noodles (Chow Mein-the kind that is ready to eat)**
*4 teaspoons vegetable oil*

*Vegetables:*
*½ white onion, cut bite-size*
*½ green bell pepper, cut bite-size*
*½ red bell pepper, cut bite-size*
*1 4-6 ounce can straw mushrooms, drained well*

*½ cooked chicken, cut bite-size*
*4-6 ounces cooked ham, cut bite-size*
*4-6 ounces crab meat (canned or cooked)*

*2-3 teaspoons white wine*
*1 can or 2 cups chicken broth*

*Seasonings:*
*2 teaspoons sugar*
*2 teaspoons sesame oil*
*1½ tablespoons oyster sauce*
*2 teaspoons soy sauce*

*Thickening base:*
*2 tablespoons cornstarch*
*4 tablespoons water*

*Tips from Titus: These noodles are briefly precooked and can be bought from noodle makers or in the freezer section of some supermarkets. If not available, canned ones may be used but don't stir-fry.

Place wok over medium-high heat for 30 seconds. Spread 2 teaspoons oil in the bottom of the wok to cover as large an area as possible and wait another 30 seconds. Stir-fry the noodles 2-3 minutes, or until hot. Remove the noodles and place on a platter.

Spread 2 teaspoons oil in wok. Wait 30 seconds. Stir-fry all vegetables except straw mushrooms, for 1 minute. Add straw mushrooms and stir-fry for 1 more minute.

Combine meats and add to vegetables. Stir-fry for 1 minute.

Pour the wine around the edge of the wok, followed by the chicken broth. Stir.

Combine seasoning and add to wok. Stir to mix.

Mix cornstarch and water well in a small bowl, until smooth.

Make a well at the bottom of the wok. Wait until the sauce comes to a boil. Slowly stir in the thickening base. Wait until it boils again, and quickly stir together all contents in the wok. Transfer this mixture onto the noodles. Serve hot.

Serves: 4-6
Cooking time: 20 minutes

# *E Mein with Ham*

*1 E Mein*
*2 teaspoons oil*
*1 teaspoon salt*

*2 teaspoons oil*

*Vegetables:*
*2 cups fresh mushrooms thinly sliced*
*1 cup green onion cut in 1-inch lengths*

*Seasoning:*
*1 tablespoon oyster sauce*
*2 teaspoons soy sauce*
*1 teaspoon sugar*

*Salt and pepper to taste*

*1 cup fully cooked ham, cut in thin strips*

In the wok, bring 4-6 cups of water to a boil. Add oil and salt to the water. Submerge the E Mein in the water 10 seconds, and then drain.

Heat another wok and spread 1 teaspoon of oil in it. Place the E Mein evenly in the wok and saute over low heat for 1 minute. Around the edge of the wok, add 1 teaspoon of oil and saute for 1 minute. Place E Mein on a plate.

Starting with a clean wok, stir-fry vegetables for 2 minutes until tender yet crisp. Combine E Mein and vegetables in wok and stir well. Add seasoning and ham and stir-fry until hot. Serve immediately.

Serves: 2
Cooking time: 15 minutes

# 三絲乾撈麵

## *Sam See Gon Low Mein*

Sam See means three different meats cut in strips. Gon means without sauce. Low means stir-fried and mein means noodle. One can actually cook it in the morning, and serve it in the evening. You must keep in mind to add the fresh vegetables just before it is served.

*1 pound Chinese noodles (Chow mein)*

*2-3 teaspoons vegetable oil*

*Seasoning:*
*1 teaspoon sugar*
*2 teaspoons straight sherry*
*2 teaspoons soy sauce*
*2 teaspoons oyster sauce*
*Salt & pepper to taste*

*Meats:*
*4-6 ounces cooked chicken, shredded*
*3-4 ounces cooked ham, shredded*
*2-3 ounces barbequed pork (char siu), shredded*

*Vegetables:*
*½ white onion, sliced*
*1-1½ cup bean sprouts*
*½ cup carrot, peeled and grated*

Place wok over medium-high heat for 30 seconds. Spread the oil in the bottom of the wok, to cover as large an area as possible, and wait another 30 seconds. Stir-fry the noodles for about 2 minutes, or until hot.

Add seasoning mixture to the noodles in the wok and stir-fry for one minute.

Combine meats and add to wok. Stir-fry to mix.

Add onion, bean sprouts, and half the carrots to the wok. Stir-fry for 2 more minutes. Serve hot. Use remaining carrots for garnish.

Serves: 4-6
Cooking time: 20 minutes

星州炒米

# *Singapore Noodles with Curry*

*2 layers rice sticks or Pai Mai Fun*

*1 large onion*
*4 cups won bok (Chinese cabbage) or head cabbage*
*2 tablespoons vegetable oil*

*Curry powder to taste; approximately 2 tablespoons*

*3 eggs scrambled*
*½ pound char siu, shredded*

*Seasoning:*
*2 teaspoons sesame oil*
*1 tablespoon sherry*
*1 tablespoon soy sauce*
*Dash white pepper*
*Salt to taste*

*½ tablespoon toasted sesame seeds*

While you soak the rice sticks in water for 15 minutes until they are soft, you can slice the onion and won bok quite thin.

Heat the wok and spread 2 tablespoons oil in it. When it is hot, stir-fry the rice sticks. Add curry powder and eggs and stir-fry 2 minutes. Then add the vegetables and stir-fry for 3 minutes.

Add the seasoning and then toss together the rice sticks, vegetables and seasoning in the wok. Pour in char siu.
Add the toasted sesame seeds as a topping and serve.

Serves: 4-6
Cooking time: 30 minutes

# Stir-Fry Vegetables E Mein

E fu is a title of an official somewhat like a mayor in America. There was the mayor in that E city. He was a gourmet and he instructed his home chef to make the raw noodle first, then deep-fry it into the shape of a piece of round cake. Thus this special noodle was named in his honor. It is a good dish as a mid-day snack or toward the end of an elaborate multi-course dinner. E Mein has to be purchased in Chinatown.

*2 cakes E Mein*

*4 teaspoons vegetable oil*

*Vegetables:*
*2 cups bean sprouts*
*1 cup chives, cut 1 inch in length*
*2 teaspoons soy sauce*
*1 teaspoon sugar*

*Salt and pepper to taste*

In the wok, bring 4-6 cups water to a boil. Immerse the E Mein in the hot water for 10 seconds until the cake just barely softens. Drain.

Heat the wok, spread 1 teaspoon oil, place the E Mein evenly in the wok over low heat and saute for 1 minute. Around edge of wok, add 1 teaspoon of oil and saute for 2 more minutes. Turn the E Mein over and saute other side 2 minutes. Remove from wok and place on a heated round platter.

In the same wok spread 2 teaspoons oil and stir-fry vegetables until they are crisp and tender. Add soy sauce, sugar, salt and pepper to taste. Mix well, and place on top of E Mein.

Serves: 2
Cooking time: 15 minutes

# 甜品類

*Desserts*

雜果甜荳腐

# *Tofu with Fruit Cocktail*

Dessert is not a part of a Chinese meal when eating at home. However, sweets are served in restaurants, after a banquet. Chinese eat sweets, maybe in between lunch and dinner or as a midnight snack. They are most frequently used during festivities. This dessert dish makes a very good ending to a meal. Although it is not tradition, it certainly complements a meal, because it is simple to make and very light.

*12 ounces of tofu (approximately 1 block), well drained*

*1 can fruit cocktail*
*Pineapple jam*

*1/3 cup dry-roasted crushed peanuts*

Cut tofu into cubes.

In a bowl, gently combine the fruit cocktail, including all the syrup, and the diced tofu. Let chill in the refrigerator. Serve in a dessert bowl. Top each serving with 2 teaspoons pineapple jam and finally sprinkle with crushed peanuts.

Serves: 6-8
Cooking time: 8 minutes

# *Strawberries with Tofu Dip*

This is more a Western idea than traditional Chinese cooking. This recipe is a creation of Chinese people who live in America. But what a refreshing creation!

*2 baskets fresh strawberries, halved*

*Juice from 1 lemon*

*12 ounces of tofu (select tender, soft type)*
*5 tablespoons white granulated sugar*
*1 teaspoon almond extract*

Combine all the ingredients except half of the lemon juice in a dessert bowl. Sprinkle the other half of the lemon juice over the mixture.

Serves: 6-8
Cooking time: 15 minutes

# 低熱量杏仁荳腐

## *Low-Calorie Almond Float*

This almond float can be done with or without a microwave oven. It's a dessert popularly served at Chinese restaurants from coast to coast. Now you can enjoy it in your own home and with little time spent. It is not a traditional Chinese dish, but it sure is a great combination of the "East-meets-West" method of cooking.

*2 tablespoons unflavored gelatin*
*1 cup plus 2 tablespoons water*
*2 tablespoons granulated white sugar*
*1 tablespoon almond extract*
*1 cup milk, evaporated or homogenized*
*1 small can mandarin oranges*
*1 large can lichee (may substitute fruit cocktail)*

*4-6 red cherries, with stems*

Dissolve gelatin in 2 tablespoons of water. Stir together gelatin mixture and sugar into 1 cup of boiling water until dissolved. Cool to room temperature. Add milk and almond extract to gelatin mixture. Gently stir well. Pour into an 8-inch-by-8-inch pan and chill in the refrigerator until firm. Dice the gelatin and add oranges and lichee, including the liquid. Gently mix. Spoon fruits and gelatin into individual serving bowls. Add a cherry with stem as garnish.

Serves: 4-6
Cooking time: 7 minutes

# 中式白雪餅

## *Chinese Almond Snow Cookies*

Although this is not a traditional Chinese cookie, like almond cookies, it is a creation of East meets West. After all, almond is a Chinese flavoring. In the old days we described a beautiful Chinese girl by saying her eyes were in the shape of almonds. So snow cookie, may be foreign in its origin, but it is readily acceptable and enjoyed by the Chinese and Westerner alike.

*1 cup butter*
*1 cup confectioner's sugar, sifted*
*2 teaspoons vanilla extract*
*½ teaspoon almond extract*

*2 cups all purpose flour*
*½ teaspoon salt*
*¼ teaspoon ground cinnamon*

*1 cup chopped almonds*
*¼ cup coconut, shredded*

*Confectioner's sugar*

Cream butter and sugar. Beat in the vanilla and almond extract.

Sift together flour, salt and cinnamon and add to the creamed mixture.

Stir in the almonds and coconut.

Form dough into 1-inch balls and place 2 inches apart on an ungreased cookie sheet. Bake at 350° for 15-18 minutes.

Let cool, then dust by rolling them twice in sifted confectioner's sugar. (½ teaspoon of cinnamon may be added to the sugar).

Yields 5 dozen cookies
Cooking time: 45 minutes

中国薑餅

# *Sweet Chinese Ginger Cookies*

Ginger is a Chinese vegetable, mostly used to increase the aromatic effect in stir-frying, steaming, etc. It is used at times for food and for medical purposes, as it would, reportedly, keep one from catching cold. Using ginger in cookies seems to be a new and sophisticated idea. Try it for yourself.

*½ cup butter*
*½ cup shortening*
*1¾ cups brown sugar, packed*
*½ teaspoon almond extract*

*1½ cups all-purpose flour*
*½ teaspoon baking soda*
*¼ teaspoon salt*
*¼ cup water*

*1 cup almonds, chopped*
*¼ cup crystalized ginger, finely chopped*

Cream butter, shortening and brown sugar.
Beat in the almond extract.

Sift flour, baking soda and salt. Add to the creamed mixture. Blend in the water.

Stir in the almonds and ginger.

Form dough into 1-inch balls and flatten with the palm of your hand to about ¼ inch thick. Place 2 inches apart on an ungreased cookie sheet.

Bake at 350° for 12-14 minutes.

Yields 5 dozen cookies
Cooking time: 45 minutes

# *Lichee Banana Orange Dessert Topping*

*3-4 pitted canned or fresh lichee*
*1 banana peeled*
*1 orange, peeled and seeded*
*¼ teaspoon almond extract*
*½ cup coconut milk*
*1 jigger rum, optional*

Combine all ingredients in blender or food processor. Remove to a bowl and refrigerate. Top fruit desserts and puddings. An ideal way to top off a delicious Chinese meal.

# Sesame Cookies

How simple and delightful is this cookie. We feel sure that your family and your company will be delighted by its taste.

*1 cup butter*
*¾ cup sugar*
*1 teaspoon vanilla extract*

*2 cups flour*
*1 teaspoon baking soda*
*1 cup corn flakes, crushed*

*1 egg, separated*
*3 tablespoons sesame seeds*

Cream butter and sugar together. Beat in the vanilla extract.

Sift together flour and baking soda and add to the creamed mixture. Add the corn flakes.

Form into 1-inch balls and place 3 inches apart on an ungreased cookie sheet. Flatten to ¼-inch thickness with the palm of your hand.

Brush egg yolk over formed dough. Sprinkle ¼ teaspoon sesame seeds over each cookie and press in firmly. Brush over top with beaten egg white.

Bake at 350° 12-15 minutes.

Yields 25-36 cookies
Cooking time: 45 minutes

# *Slivered Almond-Topped Chinese Cookies*

Chinese are great pastry makers. There are so many varieties of cookies in China. In fact, during the old days, before marriage, the groom's family was supposed to send hundreds of pounds of cookies to the bride's family. In turn, the bride's family would distribute the cookies to those who sent a wedding gift to the family.

*½ cup shortening*
*½ cup sugar*
*½ cup brown sugar, packed*
*1 egg*
*1 tablespoon soy sauce*

*½ teaspoon almond extract*

*1⅔ cups all-purpose flour*
*1½ teaspoons baking powder*
*½ teaspoon baking soda*

*Almond topping:*
*½ cup slivered almonds (2 ounces)*
*2 teaspoons sugar*
*1 teaspoon soy sauce*

Cream shortening and the sugars. Beat in egg, soy sauce and almond extract.

Sift together flour, baking powder and baking soda and add to the creamed mixture.

Form dough into 1-inch balls, and dip the top into the almond topping mixture. Place 2 inches apart on an ungreased cookie sheet.

Bake at 350° for 12-15 minutes.

Yields: 4 dozen cookies
Cooking time: 45 minutes

正宗杏仁餅

# *Chinese Almond Cookies*

This probably is one of the better known Chinese cookies in America. It is simple, yet has great appeal to young and old alike. Try this recipe and include it in your Christmas cookie-giving. You will have a delightful result.

*1½ cups shortening*
*1 cup sugar*
*1 egg*
*1 teaspoon almond extract*

*3 cups all-purpose flour*
*1 teaspoon baking soda*
*½ teaspoon salt*

*¼ cup coconut*
*¼ cup almonds, finely chopped*

*Blanched almonds or red food coloring*

*1 egg white*
*1 teaspoon sugar*

Cream shortening and sugar well together. Beat in the egg and almond extract.

Sift flour, baking soda and salt and add to the creamed mixture.

Stir in the coconut and almonds.

Form dough into 1-inch balls and place 2 inches apart on an ungreased cookie sheet. Press thumb gently in the center of each ball. Fill depression with an almond, or touch it with the end of a chopstick that has been dipped in red food coloring.

Before baking, whip the egg white slightly with a fork or wire whisk, add sugar and mix well. Brush the mixture on top of cookie dough.

Bake at 350° for 20 minutes.

Yield: 4-5 dozen cookies
Cooking time: 1 hour

# Chinese Banana Tea Muffins

There are many types of bananas. If you can find the Chinese banana, it will give the muffins a special taste. However, any banana will do the job. The banana is featured in the poems written by the poets. Raindrops on the leaves of banana trees are so poetic that Chinese writers and painters have been using it as the themes for many of their creations. We have now adapted that creation into the culinary arts.

*1¾ cups all purpose flour*
*1 teaspoon baking powder*
*1 teaspoon baking soda*
*¾ teaspoon salt*

*½ cup shortening*
*1⅓ cups sugar*
*2 eggs*
*1 teaspoon vanilla*

*1 cup mashed Chinese bananas*
*½ cup buttermilk**

*2 tablespoons sesame seeds*
*¼ cup coconut, shredded*

**If you do not have buttermilk, add ½ tablespoon of vinegar to 4 ounces of milk and let it sit for 10 minutes before you add it to the bananas.*

Heat oven to 350°

Sift flour, baking soda, baking powder and salt and set aside.

Cream shortening and sugar. Beat in eggs, one at a time. Add the vanilla extract.

Mix mashed bananas and milk well in a small bowl.

Add the sifted dry ingredients alternately with the banana mixture, to the creamed mixture, starting and ending with the dry ingredients.

Stir in the sesame seeds and coconut.

Fill 24 muffin tins, lined with paper cups, ⅔ full. Bake for 25 minutes, or until a toothpick inserted in the center comes out clean.

Serves: 10 to 12
Cooking time: 1 hour

牛油蛋糕

# Steamed Butter Cake

This is, again, a recipe of East-meets-West, as butter is not commonly used among the Chinese people, except by those who live in the cities and are more educated in the Western way of living.

*½ cup butter*
*¾ cup sugar*
*2 eggs*

*1 cup all purpose flour*
*¼ cup milk*

*1 teaspoon lemon juice*
*2 teaspoons sherry*

*2 teaspoons sesame or vegetable oil*

*1 tablespoon melted butter*

Cream butter and sugar well together. Beat in eggs, one at a time.

Blend flour and milk alternately into the creamed mixture, starting and ending with the flour.

Add lemon juice and sherry.

Grease bottom of an 8-inch round cake pan with the oil. Pour in the batter.

Steam in a wok or a steamer for 30 minutes or until a toothpick inserted in the center comes out clean.

Cool slightly, brush top with melted butter, and serve.

Serves: 6 to 8
Cooking time: 45 minutes

# 醬芥類

*Dips and Sauces*

# *Dips, Sauces and Zesty Accompaniments*

Many of the dips and sauces below are tasty accompaniment to the recipes in this book. In and of themselves, they are adaptations of traditional sauces and dips. Like so much else, these recipes are meant to be used as guides. Go ahead and experiment. A good practice is to make up the sauce of your choice, then make a note in this book as to how you would like to modify it for the next time.

## *Titus Chan's Mild Dipping Sauce*

*¼ cup soy sauce*
*¼ cup Chicken Stock*
*2 teaspoons sugar*
*1 stalk scallion, finely minced*
*4-6 radishes, grated*
*3-4 drops of sesame seed oil*

Combine all ingredients in a bottle, shake well, and refrigerate overnight, if possible. Serve in small dishes as an accompaniment to simple stir-fried dishes, steamed dishes and deep-fried or dry-braised dishes.

## *Chinese Hot Mustard*

*4-6 tablespoons dry mustard powder*
*Water to moisten mustard into a paste*
*Vegetable oil*

Combine dry mustard powder and water in a small bowl, mixing until mustard becomes paste-like in consistency. Add a dash of vegetable oil to promote sheen. Prepare hot mustard several hours before intended use in order for the mustard to develop its full flavor.

## *Five Spice Salt*

*4 tablespoons table salt or course salt*
*⅓ teaspoon Chinese Five Spice Powder*

Combine salt and Chinese Five Spice Powder in a frying pan over medium heat for one minute. Stir often. Transfer to serving dish or place in airtight jar to be used as needed.

## Garlic Ginger Oil

*½ cup vegetable oil*
*6-8 cloves garlic, peeled and minced*
*4-6 teaspoons ginger, peeled and chopped*
*2 teaspoons sesame seed oil*
*3 stalks scallions, minced*
*Dash of Chinese five spice powder*
*Dash of salt*
*Dash of sugar*
*Splash of sherry*

Combine all ingredients in a jar. Shake vigorously, and store in refrigerator overnight. Set out and let it return to room temperature before serving. Excellent with blanched, boiled and steamed fish, fowl and vegetables.

## Sesame Lime Red Chili Dip

*Juice of two limes*
*3 teaspoons sesame seeds, toasted*
*1 teaspoon red chili oil*
*1 teaspoon soy sauce*
*½ teaspoon sugar*
*1 sprig of mint or ¼ teaspoon dried mint flakes*

Combine all ingredients in small serving dish. Mix well.

This is especially good with fish and fowl dishes.

## Spicy Fire Sauce

*4 tablespoons soy sauce*
*1½ teaspoons chili flavored oil*
*1½ teaspoons sweet rice vinegar*
*2 cloves garlic, minced*
*2 stalks green onions, minced*
*Dash of sesame seed oil*
*Dash toasted sesame seeds*
*Hot sauce to taste*

Combine all ingredients and serve as an alternative dip to mustard or chili oil.

Especially good with cooling summer dishes.

## Satay Sauce (Spicy Peanut Sauce)

*3 tablespoons creamy or crunchy peanut butter*

Mix all ingredients together. Use as a dipping sauce or as a marinade for

*2 tablespoons soy sauce*
*1 teaspoon hot chili oil*
*1 teaspoon rice vinegar*
*1 teaspoon sesame seed oil*
*1 teaspoon minced fresh ginger*
*1 teaspoon sugar*
*1 stalk green onion, minced*
*1 clove garlic, minced*

beef, chicken, pork or lamb en brochette.

## *Basic Marinade*

(For ½ pound poultry or meat)

*¼ teaspoon sesame oil*
*¼ teaspoon brown sugar*
*Dash white pepper*
*2 teaspoons vegetable oil*
**2 teaspoons oyster sauce*
**2 teaspoons soy sauce*
*2 teaspoons cornstarch*
*¼ egg white, beaten*
*2 teaspoons sherry*
*⅓ to ½ square inch fresh ginger, crushed*

**Eliminate when using with sea foods.*

Mix ingredients. Let sit for ½ hour to 2 hours.

## *Basic Sweet-Sour Sauce*

(For ½ pound meat, shrimp or as a sauce for appetizers)

*⅓ cup water*
*⅓ cup apple cider vinegar*
*⅓ cup light golden brown sugar*
*¼ cup catsup*
*½ square inch ginger, crushed (optional)*
*Hot sauce to taste*

*Thickening Base:*
*2 teaspoons cornstarch*
*1 tablespoon water*

Bring sauce items to a boil.

In a small bowl combine cornstarch with water. Stir into the boiling sauce and wait until it comes back to a boil.

# *Red Chinese Barbeque Sauce*

*2 tablespoons wet bean curd*
*1 tablespoon bean curd liquid*
*1 tablespoon sesame oil*
*½ teaspoon salt*
*1 tablespoon sugar*
*3 cloves garlic*
*¼ teaspoon red coloring*
*¼ cup catsup*
*2 teaspoons honey*
*½ teaspoon MSG*

Measure the wet bean curd after mashing it into a smooth paste. Crush and finely chop the garlic cloves. Mix all the ingredients together in a bowl and store in the refrigerator.

*Menus*

# *How to Order Chinese Food*

Many times I have seen Americans start the dinner with won ton soup, followed by crispy spring rolls or crispy won ton. For them, a typical main course for the evening would be sweet and sour pork, beef broccoli, chicken cashew, fried rice, etc. There is nothing wrong with ordering your own favorite dishes, but after reading our book and trying some of our recipes, I suggest a more sophisticated approach in ordering.

Light-tasting foods should begin the meal, such as a clear soup, and steamed or poached dishes, such as fish. Won ton soup is made out of noodles and is usually on the salty side. As a result, you drink much hot tea, and the noodles swell up in your stomach, giving you a false sense of fullness. You no longer can fully appreciate the delicate taste of light dishes such as steamed sea bass or stir-fried lobster tail. When ordering soup, you should avoid ordering any accompanying Cantonese dishes having the word "war." "War" means a dish contained in a bowl of soup. This way you won't end up with two soups in one evening.

The heavier-tasting dishes, such as the dry-braised ones involving hot and spicy sauces, and heavy meat dishes, such as the Cantonese fatty Kau Yuk, should be taken later in the meal.

Chinese food is traditionally ordered to share – not just to order for oneself. Many waiters have seen the situation in which a group of four walk in and all order their own serving of sweet and sour pork. It is not only proper, but more fun and congenial to order "family style." The larger the number of dishes, the more variety; hence, more enjoyment. When going to a Chinese restaurant, the more people you have in your party, the better opportunity you have to experience the many gourmet dishes.

Unlike continental cuisine, in general, Chinese foods don't have "go-together dishes" such as mashed potatoes and roast beef. However, the choices can compliment each other if the menu consists of a variety, such as meats, seafood, poultry and vegetable dishes, so you have a balanced diet while you're enjoying the meal. Vegetable dishes are good to serve in between heavy meat dishes. Green vegetables offer you high vitamin value.

A Chinese Fire Pot specialty house will serve fire pot, or fondu types of meals only. A Chinese seafood specialty house serves mainly seafood. Some seafood specialty houses have fresh seafood, so you can select your own. Some even keep live fish, crab, shrimp, lobster and clams for you to choose from. The author recommends when in the mood for seafood, the latter kind of establishment will provide the best in dining pleasure.

# *Presidential Dinner in Peking*

This Presidential dinner was given in honor of President Reagan by the government of the People's Republic of China at the Great Hall of People in Peking on April 27, 1984.

The centerpiece was a large circle of assorted fresh flowers. In the center of the flowers was a nine-tiered pagoda, carved from a large carrot. This was surrounded by eight cranes carved from daikon.

## *State Dinner Given to President Reagan at the Great Hall of People in Peking, April 27, 1984*

Assorted Cold-Cut Hors D'Oeuvres in Decorated Trays

冷盤

Tender Bamboo Shoot Tips with Pea Leaves Soup

豆苗竹蓀湯

Braised Abalone Fillet with Shark's Fin

魚翅鮑脯

Roasted Calf and Sea Crab

烤仔牛肉及烤海蟹

Stir-Fried Meaty Clam and Kung Pao Phoenix from Chong Bak Mountain

清炒扇貝及宮爆飛龍

Vegetarian Spring Bamboo Tips with Vegetarian Delicacies

春筍三素

Boneless Duck Slices with Bean Sauce

醬爆鴨片

Sweet Almond Soup as Dessert

杏仁酪

Assorted Dim Sum and Fresh Fruits as Dessert

点心水菓

Soup for Today

例湯

Tender Beef Slices in Black Pepper Sauce

黑椒牛柳

Stir-Fried Spareribs

生炒排骨

Shrimp Chunk in a Bird's Nest

雀巢蝦球

Stir-Fried Fresh Fish Fillet with Tender Tips of Vegetable

菜遠青衣球

Sea Catch in Soup

海鮮羹

Deep Fried Skin-Crisp Chicken

炸子雞

Beef Slices Flavored with Tea Leaves

沙茶牛

Fresh Hot Salty Shrimps

椒鹽大蝦

Fish Ball with Green Fresh Vegetables

菜遠青衣球

Steamed Fresh Sea Catch

清蒸海上鮮

## *Meal for Ten Persons*
## *featuring low calorie, light seafood*

Assorted Seafood in Thick Soup
海鮮羹
Chunky Fresh Salad With Shrimp
明蝦大沙律
Golden Brown Crispy Fried Chicken
炸子雞
Beef Steak, Cantonese Style
中式牛柳
Steamed Fresh Catch of the Day
清蒸海上鮮
Three Seafood Delicacies Served in a Bird's Nest
雀巢三鮮
Classic Peking Duck
北京片皮鴨
Abalone Fillets with Fresh Mushrooms
鮑甫燴冬菇
Scallops with Crispy Mashed Chinese Taro
荔茸酥帶子

Meaty Lobster Salad

龍蝦沙律

Two Hot Entrees

兩大熱葷

Deep Fried Crispy Shrimp Balls

脆皮蝦棗

Tender Beef Slices in a Bird's Nest

鷹巢牛肉絲

Colorful Dried Scallops in Thick Soup

鳳凰瑤柱羹

Golden Brown Skin-Crisp Chicken in Brown Sauce

當紅炸子雞

Sauteed Peking Spareribs

京都焗肉排

Sea Cucumber with Tender Hearts of Fresh Vegetables

海參扒菜胆

Steamed Fresh Sea Bass

清蒸游水斑

Roasted E-Mein

干燒伊麵

Dessert

甜品

Braised Shark's Fin with Three-Meat Shreds
普天同慶
Assorted Shrimp Ball Platter
金碧輝煌
Golden Brown Skin-Crisp Fried Chicken
鴻運當頭
Abalone with Two Kinds of Garden Fresh Vegetables
富貴有餘
Stewed Stuffed Fresh Mushrooms
金錢滿掌
Fruit with Whole Duck
百子千孫
Sweet and Sour Pork
左右逢源

Pot Roast Chicken, Hong Kong Style

香港式焗雞

Stir-Fried Colorful Fresh Sea Bass Meaty Slices

翡翠石斑球

Stir-Fried Boneless Duck Served in Bird's Nest of Taro

雀巢鴨柳絲

Roasted E-Mein

干燒伊府麵

Almond Tofu

杏仁豆腐

Fresh Fruits (In Season)

新鮮時菓

# *Dinner for a Romantic Occasion*

Fish in Hot Sauce
干燒青魚

Duck Smoked with Tea Leaves
樟茶鴨子

Twice-Cooked Pork Slices
回鍋肉

Beef in Small Bamboo Steamer
小笼牛肉

Shark's Fin with Three Shreds
三絲魚翅

Fresh Vegetables with Dried Scallops
搖蚌時菜

Bean Curd with Pepper and Chili
麻婆豆腐

Fruit in Rice Wine
酒糟果子羹

Lightly Stewed Oysters with Angel's Hair

蠔豉發菜

King Clam Meat Tenderly Parboiled in Oil

油泡象拔蚌

Bird's Nest Soup Topped with Shrimp Meat

蝦肉燕窩湯

Golden Brown Crispy Chicken with Shrimp Chips

當紅炸子雞

Classic Peking Duck

北京片皮鴨

Chopped Boneless Duck Wrapped in Lettuce Leaves

鴨肉生菜包

Deep Fried Pork Chops in Sweet and Sour Sauce

京都鴛鴦扒

Stewed Abalone with Mushrooms Nestled in a Bed of Fresh Vegetables

冬菇鮑魚扒時菜

Sauteed Fresh Squid in Peppery Salt

椒鹽吊片

Sweet and Sour Pork

咕嚕肉

Fried Rice, Young Chow Style

楊州炒飯

Red Bean Paste in Sweet Soup

紅豆砂糖水

# *Szechwan Cuisine Graduation Banquet*

Assorted Hors D'Oeuvres on a Decorated Tray
什景拼盤錦

Stir-Fried Shrimp with Szechwan Pepper
四川椒蝦

Three Seafood Delicacy Combination Served on a Sizzling Platter
鐵板三鮮

Smoked Tea Duck
樟茶全鴨

Steamed Yellow Fish
松鼠黄魚

Chinese Fire Pot, Dong Bor Style
東坡砂鍋

Fresh Mushrooms with Garden Vegetables in a Creamy Sauce
奶油口磨菜花

Baked Whole Chicken Wrapped in Clay
富貴雞

Chinese Fire Pot with Assorted Meat and Chrysanthemums
菊花火鍋

White Fungus in Sweet Soup
冰糖銀耳

Fresh Fruits
水菓

Foochow "Buddha Jump Over the Wall" Soup

福州佛跳牆

Sauteed Frog's Legs with Fragrant Oil

香油石磷腿

Stir-Fried Tender Slices of Conch

清炒香螺片

Venison Delicacy, Peking Style

靈芝隱玉蟬

Tender Bamboo Shoots with Pea Leaves

豆苗燴竹蟶

Lotus Seeds in Sugar Sweet Crystal Soup as Dessert

冰糖銀耳建蓮

Assorted Dim Sum and Fresh Fruits as Dessert

点心水菓

# *A Cantonese Banquet for All Special Occasions*

Decorated Cold Chicken Platter

金鳮冷盤

Four Small Side Dishes

四小碟

Shrimp in Two Flavors

双色虾仁

Turnip with Snow Peas

紅羅雪衣

Chicken with Broccoli

玉樹鳮

Chicken Cutlets and Beef Fillets

鳮牛柳

Prawns with Three Kinds of Sauce

三色明虾

Roasted Stuffed Duck

片皮填鴨

Abalone with Four Delicacies

鮑魚四宝

Ham with Shark's Fin

火腿魚翅

White Custard Cream

銀耳奶露

Dim Sum: Four Kinds of Pastry

四色点心

Fresh Fruits (in Season)

应時鮮菓

Shark's Fin with Tender Shreds of Chicken

滑雞絲生翅

Succulent Lobster Chunks in Cantonese Sauce

上湯焗龍蝦

Skin-Crisp Deep-Fried Chicken

當紅炸子雞

Lo Hon Braised Whole Duck

羅漢扒大鴨

Assorted Sea Treasures in Bird's Nest of Taro

雀巢海中宝

Red-Cook Pair of Pigeons

紅燒双乳鴿

Chinese Style Saute Tender Beef Fillet

中式煎牛柳

Steamed Assorted Fresh Catch of the Day

清蒸海上鮮

Meaty Shrimp Fried Rice, Young Chow Style

楊州炒飯

Rice Pudding

西米布甸

# *Banquet for Chinese New Year for 10-12 Persons*

Tender Boneless Chicken Served in a Bird's Nest

金銀滿屋

Diced Succulent Shrimp Topped with Cashews

菓樹銀花

Shark's Fin with Crab Meat

鴻圖大展

Abalone Fillet with Mixed Tender Hearts of Fresh Vegetables

包保發財

Golden-Brown Skin-Crisp Fried Chicken

鴻運當頭

Light Stewed Oysters with Angel's Hair

發財好市

Braised Whole Duck with Fresh Fruits

全家滿福

Steamed Fresh Fish, Cantonese Style

有餘有剩

Fortune Fried Rice

鴻運炒飯

Salt-Baked Whole Chicken, Tong Kong Style
東江鹽焗雞

Deep-Fried Pork Chops in Sweet and Sour Sauce
京都酥排骨

Stuffed Tofu in Brown Sauce
紅燒釀豆腐

Beef Slice Stir-Fried with Tender Tips of Vegetables
菜遠牛肉

Kau Yuk with Preserved Vegetables
梅菜扣肉

Meaty Crab with Fresh Ginger Strips
薑絲肉蚧

Poached Fresh Shrimp
白灼蝦

Steamed Fresh Fish
清蒸海鮮

Deep Fried Whole Sea Bass in Brown Sauce
紅燒大石斑

Lo Hon Vegetarian Delight with Quail Eggs
羅漢扒鵪鶉蛋

Sauteed Ginger-Onion Meaty Lobster Chunks
薑葱焗龍蝦

Creamy Chicken Nestled in a Bed of Tender Hearts of Fresh Vegetables
奶油菜胆雞

Light Stewing Drunken Duck, Toy Shan Style
台山醉扣鴨

Phoenix City Sauteed Milk
鳳城炒鮮奶

Double-Colored Stir-Fried Fresh Scallops
金銀炒帶子

Assorted Sea Treasures in Thick Soup
山珍海味羹

## *Economical Delicious Seafood Dinner*

Assorted Seafood in Soup, White Cloud Mountain Style

雲山海鮮羹

Mussels Lightly Parboiled in Oil

油泡桂花蚌

Succulent Lobster with Chopped Fresh Garlic

蒜茸焗龍蝦

Stir-Fried Shrimp in Black Bean Sauce

豉汁炒大蝦

Stir-Fried Squid Served on a Sizzling Platter

鐵板鴛鴦魷

Poached Chinese Broccoli in Oyster Sauce

蠔油芥蘭

Steamed Fresh Fish

清蒸海上鮮

# *Three Chinese Firepot Dinners*

Chinese Firepot with Assorted Meat and Fresh Vegetables

合時禦寒生鍋

Chinese Firepot with Assorted Lamb Cuts

涮羊肉鍋

Chinese Firepot Featuring Chrysanthemum and Assorted Seafoods

菊花火鍋

Five Cold Dishes
五樣冷盤

White Fungus with Mushroom Soup
磨菇湯

Fried Sesame Chicken
芝麻炒雞

Deep Fried Pork Slices with Bean Sprouts
綠豆芽炒肉片

Abalone and Cane Shoots
竹片炒鮑魚

Prawn with Snow Flakes
雪花大虾

Three Delicacy Combination
炒三鮮

Moon Cake
月餅

Hors D'Oeuvres in Small Basket
小花篮冷盆

Lo Han Shrimps
羅漢虾仁

Fried Sliced Fish
錦綉魚絲

Crystal Chicken Slices
透明鷄脯

Beef with Seasoned Orange Peel
陳皮牛肉

Abalone Fillet
明珠酥鮑

Mandarin Fish with Roast Pork
叉燒桂魚

Crispy Chicken Luyang Style
綠楊酥鷄

Assorted Dry Bean Curd Shreds
什錦干絲

Assorted Delicacies
一品西施

Assorted Snacks
花色点心

Fresh Fruits (in Season)
应時鮮菓

Assorted Cold Hors D'Oeuvres Platter
金魚冷盆

Six Small Side Dishes
六小盤

Stewed Oxen Tails
烩虎尾

Chicken with Chinese Fruit
佛手雞

Sea Cucumber with Scallion
葱扒海参

Shredded Turnip Cake
羅白絲餅

Boiled Dry Bean Curd Shreds
煮干絲

Stewed Turtle with Brown Sauce
紅燉水魚

Duck's Leg Wrapped in Lotus Leaf
荷葉包鴨腿

Ham and Pigeon Soup
火腿斑鴿湯

Thousand Layer Cake
千層油糕

Assorted Cold Hors D'Oeuvres Platter
七彩冷拼盤

Sauteed Milk with Four Delicacies
四宝炒牛奶

Chicken Flavored in Shao-Xing Wine
名牌花雕鸡

Sauteed Shrimp
油泡鮮虾仁

Perch Balls with Green Vegetables
翡翠鲈魚球

Bird's Nest with Lobster and Pigeon Eggs
月影龍宮燕(窩)

Stuffed Crab
金錢鑲宝盒

Fried Rice
香油炒飯

Dim Sum: Two Kinds of Sweet Pastry
双甜点

Dim Sum: Two Kinds of Salty Pastry
双咸点

Assorted Cold Hors D'Oeuvres Platter

像生冷拼盤

Braised Crab with Shark's Fin

蚧肉烩魚翅

Chicken with Ham and Broccoli

金华玉樹鸡

Roasted Goose

掛炉烤鵝

Sauteed Shrimp

油泡鮮虾肉

Braised Bear's Paw with Brown Sauce

紅扒熊掌

Steamed Mandarin Fish

清蒸桂魚

Fried Rice, Guangzhou Style

广州炒飯

Dim Sum: Four Kinds of Salty Pastry

四种咸点

Dim Sum: Two Kinds of Sweet Pastry

二种甜点

# *An Elaborate Feast in Hong Kong*

Roasted Suckling Pig

金陵乳豬全体

Dried Scallops with Angel's Hair

發財瑤柱甫

Stir-Fried Lobster with Szechwan Peppercorns

川椒龍蝦球

Braised Shark's Fin

紅燒大鮑翅

Large Oysters Braised with Thick Slices of Abalone Fillet

蠔皇鮮網鮑片

Double King-Sized Pigeons with Mui Kwe Lo Wine

玫瑰双鴿皇

Eight Treasures Steamed in Soup with Whole Winter Melon

八宝冬瓜盅

Steamed Fresh Sea Bass

清蒸大海斑

Crab Meat and Assorted Seafood on Rice

蟹肉海鮮飯

Golden Brown Sauteed Pot Stickers

高湯煎粉果

Bird's Nest in a Coconut Shell

椰盅炖燕窩

Four Kinds of Pastry and Dim Sum

精美四式点

Assorted Fresh Fruits on Decorated Tray

合時鮮菓盆

# *Cooking Tips*

# Cooking Tips

STARTING THE WOK

Place the wok over medium-high heat, and wait 30 seconds for it to warm up. Add 2 to 3 teaspoons of vegetable oil and spread over the bottom to cover as much area as possible. Wait another 30-40 seconds until wok is hot. Then anything you put in the wok will not stick.

ON STIR-FRYING

When the wok is hot, place your meat in the wok in as thin a layer as possible. Let it saute for about 1 minute then add 1 more teaspoon of oil around the edge of the wok, to let the oil seep in between the meat and the wok. This will create a nice browning effect. Wait another minute, turn the meat over, saute for 1 or 2 minutes, then stir-fry. The meat will have a nice browned effect which is very appetizing. In the case of fish, turning and stir-frying should be done very carefully so as to maintain the texture.

BASIC MARINADE FOR BEEF.

In addition to the basic marinade per half a pound of beef, add 1 teaspoon of vegetable oil and water, 1/3 teaspoon baking soda, and let marinate overnight. This will create an extra tender effect on beef, and for beef only. Before marinating the beef, it should always be cut across the grain. Remove the thin membranes and fat before you cut. For slicing either beef or pork it will be helpful if you freeze it at least 20-30 minutes, until firm for easy slicing.

TO MARINATE FISH

From the basic marinade, you omit the soy sauce and oyster sauce, to allow the natural color of the seafood to show. Since the meat of the fish will flake very easily, the pieces should be cut twice as large as pork or beef: about 1½ inches wide, 2 inches long and ½ inch thick. Beef and pork should be cut 1 inch wide by 1¼ inches long and ¼ inch thick.

Beaten egg white and cornstarch mixed with soy sauce and oil will create a thin paste. When sauteing the meat, these ingredients make a protective coating to seal in the juices. Be careful not to use too much egg white, since egg white burns rather easily.

Marinade is used to make the food tasty and juicy. For half a pound of fish, one can use 1 square inch of fresh ginger root well crushed. Place it on your palm, and pour the wine in your palm, and tightly squeeze, using your hand to mix the fish with the marinade. The ginger will eliminate the fishy smell.

As a whole, marinating may take a little time. In China, even for home cooking, people do take the time to create tender, juicy and tasty meat and fish. The perfect marinating time would be around half an hour to 2 hours. If you marinate more than 30 minutes, the meat should be returned to the refrigerator. While you are marinating the meat you can make other preparations.

TO PREPARE THE INGREDIENTS

We suggest the reader first read through the recipe, then start to work with the meat if it needs time to marinate. Then work with the dried ingredients such as fungus, or black mushrooms, as it takes time for them to soften. Then parboil your vegetables, and add the garlic and onion if any. All the ingredients you need for that dish should be completely ready before you start using the wok, especially in the case of stir-fried dishes. Green vegetables may be overcooked and fresh bean sprouts may lose their texture in no time unless everything for the dish is ready to be put in the wok.

ON MSG

A lot of people have expressed a desire not to use MSG, but the author feels for certain dishes it enhances the taste tremendously if the proper amount is used. Cold Chicken in Ginger-Onion Sauce and some of the soups are examples. The author has been a professional cook and chef in leading hotels and restaurants; and in commercial work he does use a proper amount of MSG, but he feels the readers should use their own discretion, as everyone has their own needs.

TIME

In our book, when we quote the time, we are estimating the time an average cook can accomplish the dish including soaking and/or marinating, to the finished product. However, everybody has their own speed in doing things, so the timing listed on the recipe will more or less serve as a guide. Some of the ingredients can be prepared in advance, especially for those who have little time for food preparation. For instance, after a vegetable is parboiled, immediately rinse it with cold water, let it cool as if you were cooling off a hard-boiled egg, then refrigerate. It is good for up to 2 days. Meat can be sliced the night before it's used, but do not marinate, unless it is beef. All chopped ginger or garlic can be done the night before.

SERVINGS

In this book we have a number of servings. When we say 4 to 6, we simply mean that specific dish has 4 to 6 servings. You should have at least 3 or 4 other dishes in order to have enough food for 4 to 6 people. A traditional Chinese meal involves 3 to 5 different dishes to serve 4, 5 or 6 people.

TIME-SAVING IDEAS

We are concerned about working people whose time is needed for other activities than cooking. We have suggested a lot of do-ahead dishes. For instance, instead of doing one chicken for deep frying, one may cook 4 chickens in the pot. Use 1 and freeze 3. When you need to use it, simply thaw it. Deep-fry the chicken 5 to 7 minutes, then you have a lot of time. Such is the case of roasting a Peking Duck, home-style. One can roast 4 ducks at one time. This will save you a lot of cleaning and energy. Use 1 and freeze the other 3.

## SAUCES AND SAUCE-MAKING

With most of the Cantonese dishes, especially stir-fried dishes, after chicken broth or water is used, the Cantonese like to make a thin sauce very much like American gravy to end the dish. To make the gravy, stir together 1 tablespoon of cornstarch and 2 tablespoons of water. Just before you are ready to serve the dish, make a well at the center of the wok and slowly stir in the thickener until the gravy comes back to a boil. For eye appeal, the Chinese like to add 1 or 2 teaspoons of vegetable oil for a shiny appearance.

## USING OIL

Traditionally, Chinese like to use peanut oil because it offers a better smell. However, for healthy eating, any vegetable oil that you prefer to use can do the job. For making sauces, such as ginger-onion sauce, or the sauce for steamed fish, Chinese prefer to have the oil cooked until it barely begins to smoke. They believe this smells better, and creates a tenderizing effect in the dish. Sesame oil in this book is mainly for a touch of aromatic effect, and may be considered optional. In Northern food dishes, sesame oil is used in much greater amounts, like the spicy hot ingredients, and is the characteristic of the Northern dishes. Chinese cooks do not use sesame oil for deep-frying, like the Korean cooks do.

## USE OF THE WOK

Nowadays, wok cooking has become so popular, and not only just for oriental cooking. Many people use it for other kinds of cooking, including continental dishes. You can cook your stew in the wok, or scramble your eggs for breakfast. Some woks are round-bottomed, some are flat. Both are functional. Unless it is a flat-bottom wok – and the flat area is equivalent to the diameter of the largest burner on the stove, so that the wok can set firmly on the stove – we strongly recommend that you buy a ring or a base made out of metal. You place the ring over the heat, then place the wok on the ring. If the ring has holes around it, one should cover the ring with foil to avoid the heat escaping when it is used over an electric stove. One should place the ring on the largest burner so you don't create a ring on the enamel of your stove.

The same rules should be followed on a gas stove, except that when using a ring with holes in it, the ring should *not* be covered with foil, as you need the air for proper cooking.

## VEGETABLE CUTTING

To cut vegetables that have a stem, such as Chinese and American broccoli, celery, carrots – vegetables that have a solid body – we suggest you cut them on a slant. This exposure of a larger surface helps them cook quickly and retains their beautiful color. 

PARBOILING VEGETABLES

Traditionally, Chinese parboil their vegetables in water, then discard the water. Parboiling before stir-frying helps to maintain a tender, yet crisp, effect. For green vegetables, say half a pound of broccoli or asparagus, one can parboil in 6 cups of water, keeping the water boiling hard. When the water is not boiling, the green vegetables may turn yellow. One may add 2 teaspoons of brown sugar, or a pinch of salt combined with 1 tablespoon oil, or use ¼ teaspoon baking soda (practically all professional Chinese use this method). However, the author prefers using the first two ways for home cooking. Time for parboiling should be between 30 seconds to 1 minute. Remove vegetables from water immediately. If you are not ready to finish the dish immediately, you should cool it in cold water to stop the cooking. This is especially true with green vegetables. Allowing green vegetables to turn yellow is one of the greatest sins on earth to the Chinese.

COMBINING INGREDIENTS

One should be very careful when combining ingredients, such as in the recipes for Shrimp with Cashew Nuts, or Chicken with Walnuts. All ingredient such as, nuts, bamboo shoots, water chestnuts, celery or green pepper do not offer juices; but, if you add tomato, it offers so much juice, that the whole dish will lose the crispy, crunchy effect that characterizes the dish. Dishes involving nuts should use half the amount of nuts called for mixed in with other ingredients, and the remainder should be used as a topping, so as to maintain the crispness. Aromatic vegetables such as celery, bell pepper or round onion, should be stir-fried with a touch of oil, but never with any water or sauces, unless the deep-frying period is over. This way we can get the most fragrance from the vegetables.

USE OF WINE

Using wine in stir-fried dishes simply increases the aromatic effect for the whole dish. The technique is to pour the wine around the edge of the wok, so that the heat transforms the wine into a form of gas. The alcohol evaporates, and the smell lingers on. We recommend you preheat a serving platter by placing it in the oven, or run hot water from the tap on both sides, and dry it with a towel. The aromatic effect of the whole dish lasts longer if the serving platter is hot. In the case of stir-frying, after the wine is added, one should follow with chicken broth in the same manner as the wine procedure, by pouring around the edge of the wok. It helps to retain the smell.

Straight sherry or white wine seems to work well with Chinese cooking. For expensive gourmet dishes moderately priced brandy may be used. For soup for 10, drop 2 teaspoons of brandy or whiskey in the soup in the serving bowl and do not stir until you are serving into individual bowls. This helps the aromatic effect tremendously. For Chinese cooking, this aromatic effect is essential.

MUI KWE LU

Mui Kwe Lu is a desirable wine for gourmet cooking. Simply use half of the amount called for in the recipes. Mui Kwe means *roses* in Chinese. Lu means *the dew.* It is very expensive. Although you can drink it, we recommend you don't because we feel after one glass of Mui Kwe Lu you can't make it to your car before you lie down. Happy dreams.

GRAVY MAKING

If black beans and yellow beans are used when making gravy for Lobster in Black Bean Sauce, add a whipped egg while making the gravy. It will add body. For healthy eating, skin the poultry and remove the fat of meat. However, those materials do offer a good taste. We suggest the readers use their own discretion.

FIBRE FOOD

The Chinese like their vegetables tender and so remove much of the fiber. For instance, if the celery is not too old, do not remove the long strings. Fiber is important in our diet.

HOT AND SPICY FOOD

For Cantonese food, most of the time the use of hot chili pepper is for decorative purposes. It is characteristic of Cantonese food to emphasize eye appeal and decoration; whereas the Northern or Mandarin food is more spicy and hot in taste and temperature. We recommend the degree of hotness should be strictly personal, so you can enjoy the food instead of wondering how hot it's supposed to be.

FOR AROMATIC EFFECT

For adding the aromatic effect to stir-fried dishes, we have the following suggestions. For beef, use chopped garlic as the base, then add chopped ginger or chopped onion. For seafood, we suggest diced white part of the green onion as the base, then combine with either chopped garlic or ginger. For poultry and pork, we suggest ginger as the base. Add garlic or the white of the green onion. A few teaspoons of white wine around the edge of the wok would also enhance the aroma.

COOKING VEGETABLES

Fresh vegetables, such as watercress, bean sprouts or Chinese pea pods, are very easily overcooked, so you should be very careful not to overcook or you will lose a lot of food and create some unnecessary sauce in the wok. Ingredients such as bamboo shoots, water chestnuts, black mushrooms and fungus need to be cooked a minute or two, only until they're hot.

CHINESE VEGETABLES

Chinese broccoli is a very tasty dish that has a slight touch of bitterness. It offers the jade green look for eye appeal. It's good either poached or stir-fried. Chinese Choy Sum, like broccoli, can be either poached or stir-fried, and both can be added to stir-fried dishes for beautiful color, and for nutrition, because green vegetables contain more vitamins than white vegetables. Chinese broccoli is called *gai lan.* Choy sum means *the heart of the vegetable.* The former has white flowers, and the latter has yellow flowers. All flowers are edible. These two vegetables may have to be found in Chinatown only. Asparagus can often be substituted for broccoli.

Bok Choy is also called *spoon cabbage.* When using this vegetable, one should cook the stem part a few minutes earlier, then add the leaves, so that the vegetable is done at the same time. The stem part should be cut in a diagonal shape to enable it to absorb the heat faster.

Gai Choy, the mustard green, should be treated like bok choy, as the stem is firm. Both vegetables are very good as a part of any stir-fried dish. They are more often found in some of the supermarkets on the West coast.

Seequar is Chinese okra. "See" means *string,* "quar" means *melon* – so some call it string melon. It's good to use for stir-fry or for soup. The seed of bitter melon is not edible. To reduce the bitter taste, one should parboil it in salt water, then rinse with cold water. It goes well with black beans.

FRESH GINGER ROOT

Fresh ginger root occupies an important place in Chinese cooking. It has the pungency to refresh the meat or fish when it has been refrigerated for some time. Though it is an optional item, we do not recommend that you substitute ginger powder.

CONDIMENTS

There are a few sauces that will enhance the taste of your dishes. Red Chinese vinegar is always good for noodles in any form. Mushroom soyu, although you may have to obtain it in Chinatown, is good to use as a dip. Fish sauce may be used as a soy sauce and as a dip. Oyster sauce is good for practically any kind of Cantonese dish as a dip. You should use the smooth-running oyster-flavored type, instead of the thick, lumpy, and overly salty kind. For both Cantonese and Northern food, Hoisin sauce or plum sauces, or a combination of both, would be very good for roast meat, such as the classic Peking Duck of the North, and the Skin Crisp Golden Brown Roast Pork of the South. Mustard is also good to serve.

## CHICKEN BROTH

Generally speaking, Chinese try to save all the bones and scraps from the meat, whether pork, beef or chicken. Add the green onion stems and roots, and the parsley roots, to the broth and boil it for a couple of hours, strain and season. Using a can of chicken broth takes only the knowledge of opening the can, so that's why we use chicken broth all the time.

## SEASONING

Soy sauce does add taste to Chinese food. There are several types of soya sauce. One type is called light soy sauce. It is light in color and salty. You use a small amount for marinating. It should not cause the food to turn too dark. Another type is called dark soy. It is darker and heavier than the ordinary kind you find in supermarkets, and is mainly used for creating a pleasant dark brown color in food, such as Black Mushrooms with Abalone. Unless dark soy is specifically called for in our recipes, use it with care. Mushroom Shoya is in the dark soy category. It is good to use for specified dishes, and is good for dipping for general dishes.

Wine is considered a good seasoning. White wine or brandy can be used.

Chicken broth is a good item to enhace the taste of Chinese food. We recommend that you the canned liquid and not the bouillon cubes or powder. Beef broth is recommended as a substitute.

Oyster sauce generally used in Cantonese dishes must be of the smooth kind. It is somewhat on the salty side. People on low-sodium diets should not use it too much.

Sesame oil adds a touch of fragrance. When you cannot find it, simply omit it.

White pepper is good because if some of the people who are not versed in Chinese cooking see black pepper floating in the soup or in the sauce, they may be suspicious and not eat.

Cornstarch is used as a thickening agent. Different brands of cornstarch give different degrees of thickness. But this should not cause any concern, as our recipes are catered for home and party cooking and not for professional use in the strict sense. Flour or other forms of thickening may be used without hesitation. Comparatively speaking, cornstarch offers a somewhat shiny effect, and the power of thickening lasts somewhat longer than the other type. For Cantonese, cooking, you simply add less chicken broth than is called for in the recipe. For Northern cooking, you simply cook the ingredients longer, uncovered, so that part of the sauce evaporates. Cornstarch, when used to marinate meat, will form a protective shield to create a tender effect when the meat is cooked. However, for healthy eating, this also may be eliminated.

SUGAR

In this book, when we refer to sugar, we are speaking in a general way. However, in making Sweet and Sour Sauce, or Lemon Chicken, we prefer light golden brown sugar. To make Almond Float, we prefer white granulated sugar. For general cooking, it's up to you.

HORS D'OEUVRES

We recommend that you prepare hors d'oeuvres sparingly for your guests unless you intend to feature heavy pupus (Hawaiian for *hors d'oeuvres*). We want the people to have an appetite to fully appreciate the dinner that is to come. Just before a dinner that you have devoted some care to, we recommend you do not drink cold soft drinks half an hour before, nor during the mealtime, as the sweetness would overpower your taste buds so you cannot fully appreciate the delicate flavor that we have carefully worked out in the recipes throughout the book.

THOUGHTS ON DEEP FRYING.

For a 14-inch wok, 4 cups of oil is a good amount for deep frying. A 16-inch wok uses 6 cups of oil.

You should deep-fry small portions of food at a time.

Whenever possible, food should be at room temperature before deep-frying. If the material to be deep-fried is taken directly from the refrigerator, the temperature of the oil will be cooled down after the first batch. You should cover the oil and let the temperature rise to 375°.

If you do not have an automatic wok or deep-fryer, it is sometimes difficult to tell when the oil is at the proper temperature. A deep-fat frying thermometer is a wonderful investment. When bubbles the size of green peas appear when food is added, the proper temperature has been reached.

When deep-frying, one should use a wire basket and turn objects over a few times.

When the objects are finished deep-frying, take them out immediately and place on absorbent paper to absorb the excess oil.

If the food is to be served without any sauce, lightly sprinkle with salt for an extra-salty effect.

Some dishes, like Crispy Lemon Chicken and Crispy Pressed Duck, should be deep-fried twice. For example, if the total deep-frying time is 8 minutes, first deep-fry for 4 minutes, take out and drain for 10 minutes then fry an additional additional 4 minutes. This will ensure the crispy effect.

As I have said earlier, when you are deep-frying, the temperature should be approximately 375°. Before doing the actual deep-frying, one should keep the oil hot by using medium heat; you will be saving a lot of time since you are not starting with cool oil.

If objects for deep-frying are to be coated with flour, be sure to coat both sides and allow to stand for 10 or 15 minutes before deep-frying. It will also help if you sprinkle both sides with water, just before deep-frying. This will help stick the flour to the food and keep the oil cleaner.

If you are cooking large batches, strain the oil occasionally so that any flour that has settled to the bottom can be discarded.

After deep-frying, the oil may be reused several times, by adding fresh oil on a ratio of one to four. Use cheese cloth to strain the oil, cool and refrigerate in a covered jar.

These thoughts are good for all types of cooking – not just for Chinese cooking.

# *Proper Order For Serving A Chinese Dinner*

It is often said that after eating a Chinese dinner, within a short time you'll feel hungry again!

This is partly true, because Chinese food uses more vegetables and less meat, therefore, you won't have the same lasting effect as if you'd eaten a 12-ounce steak and a baked potato. However, by serving the dishes in the proper order, you can somewhat eliminate this problem.

To enjoy Chinese food to its full capacity, dishes must be served with the light-tasting dishes first, followed by the more pungent, heavy courses, and ending with a clear soup that leaves a pleasant and refreshed feeling.

Poached fish, therefore, should be served during the early part of the meal and shrimp around mid-point. Courses with heavy sauces, such as sweet and sour sauce and fatty dishes are always offered at the latter part of the meal. A good example would be Kau Yok, a fatty pork in heavy, salty sauce.

Salty and heavy food tends to make you thirsty, and drinking tea creates a false feeling of fullness early in the meal. Also pungent sauces tend to numb the taste buds, thus the subtle flavors of the lighter dishes would be lost if they followed such courses. Vegetable dishes should be alternated with ones containing meat to give variety and to refresh the taste buds.

An excellent light course to be served between dishes is poached lettuce in oyster sauce. It is a pleasant change and gives you the chance to relax before going on to the heavier dishes.

Either fried rice or noodles are served to signify that the meal is coming to an end.

Thick soups, such as Shark's Fin or Bird's Nest soup, are served at the beginning of a meal. Clear soup is served at the end of the dinner to cleanse the palate of any greasy taste, and to leave a light satisfied feeling.

The Chinese have no salads as such, although pickled vegetables are served with Northern Chinese cuisine. They are usually offered near the beginning of the meal.

Dessert is not served after the meal. Sweets are eaten as an afternoon snack, or most frequently during festivities, particularly Chinese New Year, the Moon Festival, the Dragon Boat Race and the Lantern Festival.

Fortune cookies are defined by the author as "an American invention, made in Japan."

A Ch'ing dynasty feast (Mon Han Feast) consists of a banquet of 30-40 dishes for lunch, 40-50 dishes for dinner and 20-30 dishes for midnight snack, over a period of three days! There are about three or four highly competent restaurants in Hong Kong, which given months of advanced notice, can present such a feast. The menu that is listed may be ordered in full, or in part, depending upon the number of persons in your party.

Peking Duck must be ordered in advance. You can have several varieties prepared from the same duck. The traditional way is for the duck skin to be wrapped in a Chinese pancake and eaten like a sandwich. Another way is duck meat with cashew nuts, stir-fried with pickled vegetables.

Other dishes can be ordered on the spot, even though not listed in your regular menu. Dishes listed in the regular menu are usually suited to fast, mass-produced cooking, in order to serve the crowd in the dining room.

The dishes we have listed are served in areas where there are better Chinese restaurants, such as New York, the West Coast and Honolulu. In Hong Kong and China, these foods should be readily available also. The prices generally are reasonable, but not cheap. In America, a Peking Duck dish could range from $20 to $30. The dishes we mention here are among the most popular in their own regions. When speaking of Peking, we recommend Peking Duck. For Cantonese cuisine, we suggest Lobsters in Black Bean sauce, or steamed fresh fish. These dishes are representative of each particular region.

We are giving you these banquet menus, so you can choose among these specialty items if you are dining with 10 to 12 people. Even if you are having a smaller dinner (4-6 people), some of these dishes are still available. Peking Duck must be ordered whole, but Skin Crisp Chicken, for example, can be ordered by halves or even quarters.

Just remember in each and every meal, a touch of green is important. Perhaps many of you who read this book thought that all-important touch of green would simply mean the olive in your martinis!

When ordering in a Chinese restaurant with varied dishes, it sometimes is difficult to figure out just how much will be enough, but not too much. For this reason, it is very acceptable and considered good manners to utilize the doggy bags available in all the Chinese restaurants, for your surplus dinner. So, hold your chin high and march out of the restaurant, doggy bag in hand and look forward to another delicious repast around midnight.

STEAMERS

Steamers are made out of bamboo or aluminum. A bamboo steamer may function as a container, even on the table. After purchase, the author recommends you boil the whole thing, submerged in water, for half an hour. This will kill any bugs, and prevent having stained-looking spots in the steamer.

Aluminum or metal steamers have strength for giving good steam and a deep-bottomed pot can be used for parboiling large amounts of vegetables in plenty of water. It is especially good for deep-frying because it is deep. One can deep-fry a whole chicken, a whole pressed duck or whole lemon chicken without worrying much about the overflow of oil creating a grease fire.

The bottom used along with the cover functions as a pot. You can do your stewing dishes in it, or use it to make soups such as oxtail soup. It also can be used as a container. After fried rice is made, you can put it in there and simply keep it warm by putting it on top of the stove over very low heat. Or you can use it to do American dishes such as your good old Southern Fried Chicken and Beef Stew, or Pot Roast. After the steamer is used for awhile, if the steam is escaping, you can simply cover it with a dampened towel.

STEAMING RACKS

Steaming racks or steaming plates may be used in the wok, but only with dishes that are small in quantity and simple in nature – for instance, steamed pork hash or steamed Lop Chong. For dishes that require stronger steam, such as steaming a whole fish or a crab, the author prefers that you use a steamer if you have one. A proper steaming device offers enough steam to cook the fish fast, and deliciously. Improper steaming may cause the fish meat to taste soggy and have an unappetizing effect. In the case of steaming Chinese Bao (with Char Sui or sweet paste inside), a proper steaming device offers a strong and proper steaming effect. The Bao looks white and firm. Otherwise, it turns to an embarrassing yellow color and is lumpy looking.

CHINESE CASSEROLES

Chinese clay casseroles may be purchased in various sizes and shapes in Chinatown. They are usually beige in color with a rough outside texture and a glazed inside, usually dark brown. The larger pot is usually fortified by wire.

There are three basic shapes. One is flared, with a hollow handle and a lid. The second is tall and bulbous, and is used mostly for soup, and Congee and Jok. There is another clay pot that is more flat and has two handles. These Chinese casseroles can be put directly over electric or gas heat. You can use medium-high heat, but don't place the casserole over the fire until some liquid has been added.

The whole casserole, once it is finished cooking, can be put on top of a round platter and served on the dining table. Chinese call it "Bo Jai Choy," and some specialty restaurants feature this kind of food and serving custom. In cold winter months it's a godsend.

### CHINESE FIREPOTS

The style of cooking in a Chinese firepot is called "Dar Bin Lo." It is mainly used in winter. The family or company gets together to drink hot soup and to eat thin meats and vegetables cooked in the broth in the firepot by each person. This is a leisurely way of enjoying a meal and keeping warm. This, although not such a basic tool as the wok, can add fun in cooking and dining.

Firepots come in two types: you can simply generate the heat by placing charcoal in the chimney, or there is another type that is electric.

### LONG WOODEN COOKING CHOPSTICKS

It may be handy to have these on hand, although they are not necessarily considered as basic cooking tools. If you were to deep-fry Chinese dumplings, such as Gin Doi (the round flour-based pastry that is deep-fried around New Year's Eve), or to deep-fry the tempura dishes, these chopsticks would come in handy. You can clean them up and use them again.

### CHINESE KNIVES

Although American people call these knives Chinese cleavers, to the Chinese they are simply knives. A Chinese knife that is for everyday use, for meat and vegetable cutting, should weigh from 14 ounces to 16 ounces. This way, when you chop a chicken or duck with bones, the weight helps the action so that the cut is clean and the bone doesn't fracture.

Chinese knives should be sharpened with a sharpening stone. It may be old-fashioned, but it can keep you from buying a new knife every year. To sharpen a Chinese knife, place a sharpening stone, the coarse side up, on a dampened towel. Add ½ teaspoon oil to the stone. Hold the knife in your right hand at a 15- to 20-degree angle, and rub over the stone 10 to 15 times, adding pressure from the palm or fingers of your left hand. Reverse to the finer side and repeat the same process. Wash, then it's ready for use.

A sharpening steel may be used, but it is only good while you are cooking. It sharpens for temporary relief only.

You may try your electrical sharpening device, but be careful because you lose so much of your blade that you have to buy a new knife more often.

Stainless steel Chinese knives seem to work better than the other type, which will rust, though the stainless ones cost somewhat more.

Another type of Chinese knife looks as if it were the same size and shape of the knife described above, but it is much lighter in weight (perhaps about 8 to 10 ounces) and is very much thinner. This is a good knife for vegetable cutting, especially for professional use because it doesn't tire your hand. It is good to thinly slice meat, or thinly shred meat. Northern or Mandarin cooking requires this type of knife more than Cantonese cuisine does. So for thinly cut meat and to filet a fish, this light knife functions better.

There are Chinese knives the same length as the knife described above, but only half the size in width. Perhaps the Western cook would prefer using this one, but it would not do the job of cutting through the bones of poultry.

To chop through bones of a fish head or spareribs, you need a Chinese cleaver. The cleaver at the top is nearly half an inch thick, and weighs about 1¼ pounds. To cut roast meat such as Peking duck, the professional chefs use heavier knives to ensure the bone is cut clean and no splinters hurt your palate.

Chinese knives are basic tools. In using this basic tool, we like to advise the reader to keep the cutting board as dry as possible, so that it doesn't create a slippery effect while you are chopping. A Chinese knife should be kept clean and sharp at all times. Be careful when chopping a chicken, the sauce may come out, thus creating a slippery effect on your cutting board. By the time you chop, you may actually be chopping at your finger instead of the chicken.

A sharp knife allows you to slice and chop as you intended. A dull knife creates much frustration.

## WOKS

A wok is no longer considered solely a Chinese cooking tool, although it is a basic cooking tool that has been used nearly since the beginning of Chinese civilization. Nowadays, wok cooking is not necessarily oriental cookery. Cooks in many countries like its energy-saving characteristics.

The author perhaps has more woks than his home can contain, as manufacturers have been constantly giving him their old and new creations. He has been exposed to woks costing $2 and to a wok costing over $300, and to a wok that can be folded up to look like a lawyer's brief case.

Some woks are round bottomed and others are flat. The round ones need a metal ring. Both are functional, and can be used on electric or gas stoves. Metal woks should be cleaned and wiped dry. In between dishes, a simple clean wash should be enough.

A wok should be accompanied by a cover that should be about 1 inch smaller than the diameter of the wok, so that it can rest inside the rim of the wok comfortably.

If the metal ring has holes, it should be covered with aluminum foil when used on an electric stove. It should not be covered when used for gas cooking.

## TOOLS FOR STIR-FRYING

The author is much in favor of the old-fashioned Chinese metal spatula and ladle that are designed primarily for the shape and the contour of the wok.

As a professional teacher and cooking chef in Chinese cuisine for over 15 years, the author appreciates only the proper tools to do the right job for Chinese cooking. You should use the long-handled stir-frying spatula with your right hand, and the ladle with the left hand. If you are left-handed, do the reverse.

## JOW LEE

A Jow Lee is a Chinese wire basket. It is a basic tool, as it is needed to take the vegetables out of hot boiling water when you are parboiling them. Or it can take the deep-fried Gau Gee or Won Ton quickly out of the deep oil when it reaches the perfect doneness. If you are to be placing the object to be deep-fried directly on the Jow Lee, you should put the Jow Lee in the hot oil 5 to 10 seconds first. After the Jow Lee is thoroughly hot, the object will not stick. It would be advisable for you to have two Jow Lees, one somewhat smaller than the other. One is strictly for oil and the other for water. This would prevent hot oil splattering. If you dip the Jow Lee that has been in water into the oil it may cause splattering. The Jow Lee made with a long bamboo handle is relatively inexpensive.

By using two Jow Lees, you can make a bird's nest by placing thinly shredded taro, potatoes or Mai Fun in the large one, and topping it with the smaller one. Deep-fry it in hot oil. It comes out a deep-fried basket of food resembling a bird's nest. Placing stir-fried succulent shrimp or green vegetables and straw mushrooms in the basket makes a classy dish that has a poetic name in Chinese. It is called "Jer Chow Chun Hui," meaning *beautiful songs sung by birds in the nest among the morning mist amid the spring flowers.*

# Chinese Cooking Utensils

14-inch steamer is recommended. Stainless steel is more functional. Bamboo steamer gives an Oriental touch.

A Chinese Fire Pot comes in various sizes and shapes. Perfect for cold weather get-togethers.

Chinese earthenware casserole for use on stove top for one-dish meals or fancy entertaining.

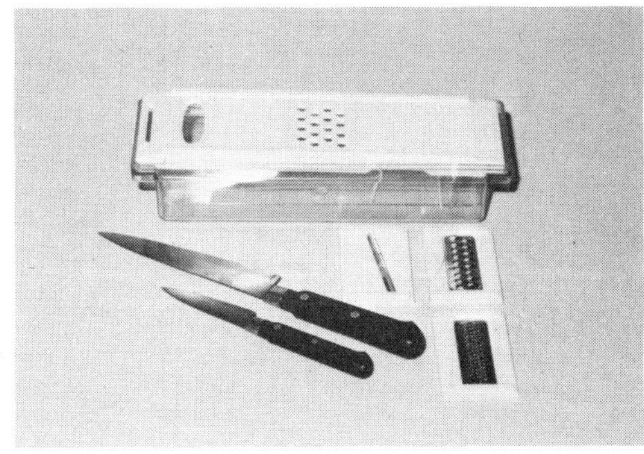

Vegetable carving tools can be simple. A paring knife, a sharp-pointed cutting knife and a vegetable slicer can create works of art.

A wok is the basic tool of Chinese cooking, especially for stir-frying. For electric stoves, one should wrap the ring in foil to keep the heat in. For gas cooking, leave the ring unwrapped, with the holes showing, for air.

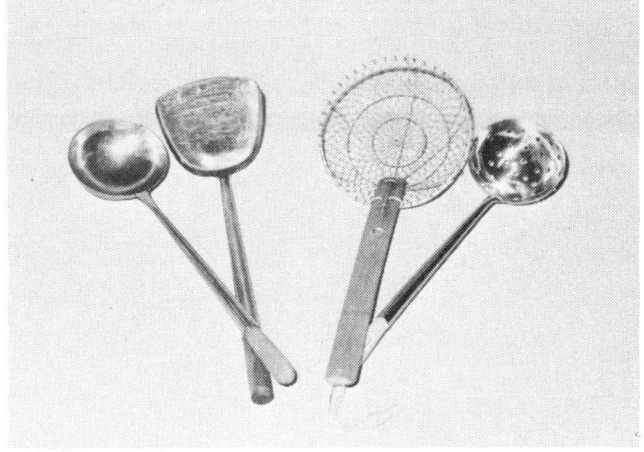

*Left:* A spatula and a ladle are the basic tools for stir frying. *Right:* A Chinese wire basket or a stainless steel perforated ladle is used for deep-frying or poaching.

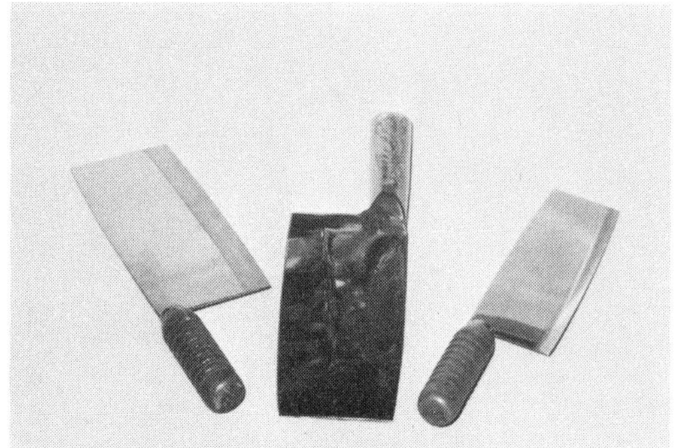

*Left:* Stainless steel Chinese all-purpose knife for meat and vegetables. *Middle:* Steel all-purpose knife. Proper weight should be about 16 ounces. *Right:* Thin, small knife of about 10 ounces for vegetables only.

A simple set of Chinese dinnerware. In the foreground is the serving platter. Behind is the individual dinner plate. The spoon and the small bowl may be used for soup or rice. The smallest dish is used for sauces.

The authentic Chinese cutting boards are made from blocks of pine, and are used mainly by Chinese restaurants. On top is the Chinese cleaver to chop spare ribs and fish heads. All other knives are referred to as knives and not cleavers.

# *Ingredients*



At times Chinese ingredients can be confusing – even to people who have been doing Chinese cooking for a long time. In this section the author will attempt to describe briefly some of these ingredients. If you cannot find all the ingredients of a recipe do not worry, some of them are used only for color or eye appeal. Even omitting 1 or 2 does not change the dish much in regard to eye appeal or aromatic effect. Thus, if you live where a few items are not available, do not let this stop you from trying the recipe.

YOUNG CORN. These are miniature ears of corn about 2 or 3 inches long, and canned in water. After the can is open it can be kept for a week or so, if you change the water every couple of days, and keep it refrigerated. The cooking time is simply a couple of minutes or you can eat it without even cooking at all. It can add interest to any vegetable or meat dish. And it adds attractiveness and convenience at a party when you want to serve it along with celery and carrot sticks as a pupu. Rinse before using.

BAMBOO SHOOTS. These are the young shoots of the bamboo tree when it is less than 2 feet high from the ground. The best time to harvest bamboo shoots is after a spring shower. Nowadays they are canned in water. Some are whole, some sliced and some are cut into thin strips. It depends on the kind you need. Once the can is open, it can be kept in the refrigerator for a couple of weeks, as long as you have the bamboo shoots completely submerged in water which you must change a couple of times a week. Bamboo can be used in many Chinese dishes. It adds a touch of yellow color. The shoots need only a couple of minutes to cook, simply heat them through.

TOFU. Tofu is made from pureed soybeans that are pressed into blocks about 3 or 4 inches in length and 2 inches in thickness. It is a popular dish among the Chinese, especially in respect to vegetarian cooking. It is very high in protein and inexpensive. Some people refer to it as "bean cake," or "fresh bean curd." It belongs to the "borrower" family. In other words, tofu by itself doesn't have a lot of taste. But it borrows the taste from other ingredients when you are cooking it. It needs only a couple of minutes of cooking time. Submerged in water and under refrigeration, it can be stored for a week. Be sure to change the water a couple of times a week. It can be steamed, stir-fried, french fried, or even used for dessert. One form is firm, one form is soft. The kind you use depends mostly on personal preference, and the recipe you are using.

RED BEAN CURD. This bean curd is seasoned with red color and salt. It is usually sold in a can or a jar and usually in the shape of a piece of cake approximately 1½ inch square by ½ inch thick. It is covered with red sauce and resembles cheese in markets in the Western world. Sometimes it is labeled as "bean cake." Chinese call it "Nom Yu," and is mostly used for roast meat, such as Peking Duck, Char Siu and Chinese Roast Pork.

FRIED BEAN CURD. Chinese call it "Doe Gawk." This is the type of bean curd that has been cubed and deep-fried. It is sold packaged or loose. It is one of the major ingredients for vegetarian dishes.

BEAN CURD STICKS. These are made of soy bean milk film that has been dried. About ½ inch in thickness and 1 to 1½ feet long, it has a licorice look. Chinese call it "Foo Jook." It is often used in soup and for vegetarian dishes. It must be soaked until softened before using.

BLACK BEANS. Sometimes people call it fermented black beans, or salted black beans. Chinese call it "Dau See." These beans have a pungent odor, and not everybody can fully appreciate them. They are sold in cellophane packages and look like raisins, but they are darker. Soak them in water for 15 or 20 minutes until they are softened. Pick them out with your fingers and place in another bowl, discard the water, because at the bottom of the water there may be sand. The beans can be stored under refrigeration for months. Combined with garlic and a little oil, they work wonders with Chinese classic dishes, such as Black Beans with Clams, or Lobster in Black Bean Sauce. Nowadays some markets have these finely ground beans all ready to use. For people who are not versed in this type of older cuisine, use it sparingly.

BLACK BEAN SAUCE. There is both sweet bean sauce and salty bean sauce; and they are the major ingredients in Mandarin cooking. They can be kept in the refrigerator for months.

BROWN BEAN SAUCE. It comes in two forms, usually in a jar. In one form you can identify the beans. The other form is completely ground into a paste, which is called "ground bean paste." It's a basic ingredient for roast meat, like Chinese spareribs, and for braising food, and is popularly used for Northern or Mandarin cooking. It can keep in the refrigerator for months. If it comes in a tin can, remove it from the can and put it in a jar.

WATER CHESTNUTS. Fresh water chestnuts can be bought in Chinatown when in season. After the black skin is peeled, the chestnuts are very sweet and crunchy. Chinese people eat them as if they were fruit. They come in whole pieces or in slices and can be used in many stir-fried dishes. They add a nice contrast in texture becaue they are round like a quarter, and they add a little crunchy effect to dishes. The canned variety of both bamboo shoots and water chestnuts is available in most supermarkets. Leftovers can be stored submerged in water in a plastic container. They will keep for a few weeks if the water is changed a couple of times a week.

CHILI OIL. This is a very hot liquid seasoning, red in color, and made from vegetable oil and chili peppers. It is mostly used in Northern cooking. Hot sauce can be substituted for Cantonese cooking.

CHILI PEPPERS. Fresh chili peppers add eye appeal as well as taste hotness. Dried red peppers are most popularly used in Northern cooking. They are available in whole or crushed form, and are about 1½ inches long. To eliminate some of the hotness, discard the seeds.

CHINESE PARSLEY. This is fresh coriander and is sometimes called cilantro, but the Chinese call it Chinese parsley. It has a very aromatic effect. Chinese use it more for toppings, to add a touch of green for eye appeal, especially in Cantonese cuisine. It is weak and wilts easily. Cut in 1½-inch lengths, and immerse in water. You can keep it in the refrigerator for a week. The roots, once washed, along with green onion roots and fresh ginger root, can be crushed to make a good ingredient for the water in which fish or chicken is poached. This creates an aromatic effect. The leaf of the Chinese parsley is very flat in comparison with the curly green leaf of American parsley. American parsley can be substituted if Chinese parsley is not available, but the taste and smell are completely different.

CHINESE FUNGUS. Chinese call it "Wun Yee." It means "cloud ear." In the market it is sold in a cellophane package and is labeled as black fungus. When it is in dry form, a tablespoon will be enough for dishes to serve 4 to 6 people, since after you soak it in 3 or 4 cups of water, it will expand. It takes about 20 minutes or so to soften. Pick it up with your fingers and discard the water, as the water may contain sand. Chop it coarsley, since it becomes rather large after it is soaked. It needs cooking only a few minutes. Dried fungus can be kept without refrigeration for months. It adds a touch of dark color and complements dishes involving the whole white water chestnuts and green vegetables.

FIVE SPICE POWDER. This is a combination of star anise, cloves, Szechwan pepper corns and cinnamon. It is brown looking and is available in most supermarkets. It may be replaced by star anise. Amazingly enough, everybody in the whole world knows Five Spice, but only a few dishes use it. It's mainly used for roast meat, such as Roast Peking Duck or Chinese Spareribs. It can be combined with hot stir-fried salt, or served as a dip for deep-fried chicken.

FRESH GINGER ROOT. This tropical plant is spicy and does more to neutralize fishy or gamey taste than to flavor a dish. It imparts a subtle fragrance to food. Peeled and finely chopped is the general way it is used. Stir-fry it in the wok and mix with meat or fish. For fast use, simply crush an inch or two and put it in soup or water. This way, it saves a lot of work but still yields its full function. Fresh ginger root, if used within a couple of weeks, should be placed in a ventilated area instead of in the refrigerator.

GUM JUM. These are dried tiger lily buds, and sometimes they are referred to as "dried lily flower." It resembles a needle, light golden brown in color, and some people call it "golden needle." Sold in cellophane packages, it can keep in a container at room temperature for months. Soak Gum Jum in cold or warm tap water for 20 minutes to soften. As in soaking black mushrooms, black fungus, black beans, etc., we recommend that you use either cold or warm water from the tap, but never hot water, as that would force out the natural taste. Once the Gum Jum is softened, if the base of a bud seems hard, nip it off by hand. It belongs to the "borrower" family. When it is cooked, it offers its own taste, yet absorbs the taste from the sauce that is being cooked. Tightly squeeze out the water before using. It is a great dried favorite among the oriental people, but it may not be appreciated fully by Westerners.

HOISIN SAUCE. It has a dark brown color, a thick paste look, and tastes sweetish. It comes in a jar or a can and is not to be confused with plum sauce. It serves as an excellent dip for roast meat such as Peking Duck or Chinese Roast Pork. It is also a basic sauce for roast meat. Cantonese people use this sauce more than the Northern people do.

LICHEE. Canned lichee are readily available and easy to use. In this book, we only call for canned lichee. It has whitish meat which has the texture of a peeled grape. It is not a difficult item to find, even in supermarkets. The canned variety has already been peeled and seeded. When it's fresh, it must be peeled and seeded. Dried lichees should also be peeled and seeded. For the few recipes we recommend in our book, canned lichee is sufficient.

BLACK MUSHROOMS. Sometimes we refer to dried mushrooms. There are so many varieties that one can write a book on mushrooms alone. In this book, for our recipes, we are very relaxed and we accept any mushroom that is dried, whether thick or thin, Chinese or Japanese. In recipes that have a long cooking period, such as Mushrooms with Abalone, the mushroom is stewed for an hour. Then we certainly recommend large and thick mushrooms, because they are in the "borrower" family. Thick meaty-looking mushrooms can certainly borrow more from the sauces and the ingredients that they are cooked with than the thin flat mushrooms. Mushrooms should be soaked in cold or warm tap water for 20 minutes until softened. Cut off the stems and discard. Don't ever forget to tightly squeeze off the water so it can borrow other tastes, and transform the mushroom to a juicy and tasty vegetable. In Japanese cooking, water that the mushrooms are soaked with is retained for cooking. We leave this option to your own discretion. Mushrooms are considered expensive. We recommend the least expensive type of mushrooms which are sufficient for our recipes at this time.

STRAW MUSHROOMS. These mushrooms look pretty much like French champignons. They come canned in water. They need to be cooked about 3 or 4 minutes because they are raw. The author prefers the type that are opened up, very much like a Japanese umbrella. But as far as the taste is concerned, the type that are opened up and the type that are buds are the same. For those that come up bigger than the thumb, you may cut them in half if you so wish. They are not an inexpensive item. Leftovers can be stored in water and under refrigeration. If you change the water several times a week, they will keep for weeks.

OYSTER SAUCE. Oyster sauce is very popular to use in Cantonese dishes. Less expensive brands can be used for general cooking. To serve as a dip on the table, you should select those sauces that are rather smooth-running and thin, which are a little more expensive. Some oyster sauce is labeled as "oyster-flavored sauce." Oyster sauce is made from oysters and has a full-bodied, rich and unique flavor. It also can add a touch of brown color to sauces, giving the dish more eye appeal. After it is opened, keep under refrigeration and it will keep for a few months. Unopened oyster sauce in the bottle can be kept for about 6 months from the day it is bottled. It makes a good sauce for marinating meat and poultry, but not seafood.

PLUM SAUCE. This is not to be confused with Hoisin sauce. It can be used as a condiment for roast meat such as Peking Duck. It is made of the fruit of the plum and other fruits. It is a Chinese chutney. If it comes in a can, after it is open, it should be put into a plastic or glass container and refrigerated. It can keep for 3 or 4 months.

Plum flowers are highly prized in the Chinese mind and frequently worn by girls in their hair to enhance their beauty. If a girl is wearing the flower to her right, she is married. If she is wearing the flower on the left; she is looking. If she is wearing the flower in the middle; she is married and still looking.

EGG ROLL WRAPPERS. Egg roll wrappers are like won ton wrappers, except they are 7 inches square, and won ton wrappers are about 3 inches square. These sheets of paper-thin dough are made from water, flour and eggs and are available frozen or fresh from oriental markets and some supermarkets. In the freezer, they can be kept frozen for up to 3 or 4 months. Thaw them out and throw away the few wrappers that are on the top and bottom. While you are wrapping, use a dampened towel to cover the bundle of wrappers to make it easier to do the wrapping. It is advisable to put the egg roll filling in the freezer for about 30 minutes to an hour so the juice will not soak through the wrapper and make holes in it.

GINGKO NUTS. These are the fruit of the Gingko tree. They are white-colored nuts with hard shells. We suggest you buy those that are in cans with water. They can be used for stir-fry or braised dishes. It is somewhat expensive, and it is optional. When used, the tiny egg-shaped nut adds a touch of yellow color and interesting shape contrasts to a dish.

ANGEL'S HAIR. Some call it "hair seaweed." Used mainly in vegetarian dishes, it has fine strands resembling hair. Chinese call it "Fat Choy." You must soak it in water to soften it. It is somewhat expensive. When dry, it can keep for months in the cupboard. Chinese believe that Fat Choy can help hair grow. In China, you can tell what kind of guy a man is by his hair line. If his hair is thin in the front, he is a thinker. If his hair is thin in the back, he is a lover. If his hair is thin in the middle, he thinks he is a lover.

DRIED SCALLOPS. This is a Chinese delicacy. It is rather expensive – about $35 to $40 per pound. These small round scallops are dried and packaged and most likely found in Chinatown. Put in a tightly covered jar or plastic container, they can keep for months and months outside the refrigerator. Mostly used for soup, they add a delicate flavor to vegetable dishes as well. Soak in warm tap water overnight and use that water for cooking. They should cook for an hour and a half.

RICE. The author suggests that uncooked long grain rice should be used for a Chinese dinner. Other types of rice may be too gooey and too sticky. The main requirement for making fried rice is that the rice should be separated and should not stick together. It is a good idea to use extra fancy long grain rice. One may want to wash the rice a few times before cooking. Generally speaking, one cup of raw rice will need 1¼ to 1½ cups of water. One cup of raw rice will yield 2 cups when it's cooked.

SALT. Low sodium is now the modern trend for healthy eating. In Chinese cookery, salt is not just a seasoning. Five-spice salt is an interesting condiment to serve as a dip for most deep-fried dishes. In some of the better restaurants, Spring Rolls, Deep-Fried Gau Gee, Crispy Won Ton and Deep-Fried Chicken are always served with the spicy salt as a dip. To make this, simply heat 4 tablespoons of salt in a skillet without oil, over medium heat, stirring it constantly until it is very hot. Remove from heat, drop in a pinch of five-spice powder and mix it up. If the powder does not burn and exude smoke, then for 4 tablespoons of salt you may add one teaspoon of five-spice powder. When it is cool you can store it in your cabinet in a plastic covered container for months. Salt-baked chicken is a specialty of Tong Kong (East River) style of cooking. The people simply bury a chicken wrapped in foil in a pot of coarse hot salt, making sure the salt completely covers the chicken. So in this case, salt in Chinese cooking is not a seasoning material, but a cooking agent. In this book, we suggest using "salt to taste."

SESAME SEED PASTE. This is a paste made from ground sesame seeds. It is mostly used in the Northern or Mandarin cooking. Tightly sealed in a jar, it can keep in the refrigerator for months.

SHARK'S FINS. This is actually the cartilage or gristle from the shark's fin. It's look is like transparent needles and it must be soaked overnight. It is mainly used for expensive banquets as soup or as an entree by itself. At room temperature it can keep for months. Caution: use only as directed.

BIRD'S NEST. These nests are made by birds like the sea swallow. When they have selected their mates, they both regurgitate the fish and seaweed they eat to make their nests. The nest looks somewhat ivory in color. The first nest is of the highest quality. Once people pick it, the birds will team up again to make the next one. By that time, they are somewhat exhausted, and the quality of the nest tastes inferior to the first one. After they lose a second one, the couples will do one more, the last one. Totally exhausted, instead of spitting out what they have eaten and digested, they will make do with a piece of feather, a fine grain of sand, or a fine chip of wood. And that is considered the least quality of birds' nest. Due to the fact that it is dangerous to gather these nests, it therefore becomes an expensive item, served mostly at elegant banquets. Soak in water overnight. Cook it a couple of hours in soup. Add a drop of egg white and a drop of Mui Kew Lu (a Chinese rose-flavored white wine). The taste is heavenly. A word to my Western reader, do try it in a classy Chinese restaurant.

DRIED SHRIMP. This dried shrimp comes in various sizes. It adds a delicate flavor to soup or to vegetables. Soften in water for an hour or overnight, using the water for cooking. Stored in a jar, it can keep outside of refrigeration for months.

SZECHWAN PEPPERCORNS. These have a subtle delicate smell and a somewhat hot taste. They are red looking, and somewhat like the head of a clove in size. They are commonly used in Northern or Mandarin cooking.

TANGERINE PEEL OR ORANGE PEEL. It has a sweet citrus smell. Soak it for 30 minutes to soften. It's good for soup and stewing dishes. Will keep indefinitely in a jar without refrigeration.

CHINESE HERBS FOR HERB SAUCE. This combination of herbs is used in soy sauce, water, and sugar to make big pots of sauce. Chinese call it "Low Sui." Some people refer to it as "Chinese spice sauce." One can use this sauce to cook a soyu chicken, soyu beef, or soyu beef tongue. It can be bought in Chinatown already packaged in a cellophane bag, or from herb stores in Chinatown. It is strong, therefore a tablespoon or so of the combined herbs can cook 3 or 4 soyu chickens. It can keep indefinitely in a jar outside of the refrigerator. Some people like to put it in an envelope and leave it in a drawer in the bedroom. The clothing comes out smelling herby and has a pleasant aroma.

SESAME OIL. Sesame oil, now in the markets, usually comes from China or Korea. A small amount will enhance the aromatic effect of a dish. Northern or

Mandarin cuisine uses it much more than the Cantonese. After it is open, it should be kept under refrigeration.

SHERRY. Straight sherry should be used for Chinese cooking. Cooking sherry is not very suitable. While doing Chinese cooking, you may have all the bottles open, such as the bottle of soy sauce and oyster sauce, but the bottle of sherry or wine and the sesame oil should be kept closed at all times, so as to keep the aromatic effect intact. If sherry is not on hand, you might substitute vodka. White wine or brandy are also good to use. To those who do not want to use liquor in cooking, simply omit this item from the recipe, since our recipes have taken this into consideration. And you can still turn out a very aromatic and tasty dish.

SOY SAUCE. Soy sauce is a basic seasoning for Chinese cooking. The proper amount will add taste, aromatic effect and coloring to a dish. Our recipes have taken into consideration moderate and proper amounts. It is good for people who want low-sodium diets.

STAR ANISE. This is a dried spice with pointed corners resembling a star. It has a licorice-like flavor. It is available in stores. It carries a strong aromatic effect, so use as directed in our recipes.

SUGAR. Sugar may enhance the flavor of a dish. In our recipes we have used just the right amount of sugar to enhance the taste of a dish, yet it will not cause any problem concerning calories. It can help to bring out the deep green color in green vegetables. Use sugar when parboiling broccoli or asparagus.

OIL FOR COOKING. While peanut oil may offer a strong aromatic effect, vegetable oil contains less fat content. We recommend that readers use any oil of their own descretion. Oil use is inevitable. You need to start the wok so the meat you place in the wok will not stick. Recommended, but not necessary for the finishing of a stir-fried dish, (after the thickening base is stirred in), a teaspoon or so of oil added will give a shiny effect to the dish. It's traditional, and it is eye appealing.

GLUTEN. One of the major ingredients of vegetarian food is called in Cantonese "Mein Gun." It is sold in cans, and is sometimes referred to as gluten balls, "Chai Pow Yu", or some would simply refer to it as an "American mock steak." Most likely you will find it in Chinatown. People cut into the shape of abolene, for mock abalone. Dying it red and roasting it, you have the Jai Char Siu (mock Chinese roast sweet pork). In certain recipes in which the gluten is not the main ingredient, it can be omitted.

VINEGAR. There are many varieties of vinegars in China. Black vinegar looks black, and at times it is used for medicinal purposes. When a woman gives birth, black vinegar is cooked with pig's feet and ginger roots for a long period of time, with a few hard-boiled eggs added. When it is served to the woman every day, she regains her strength rather rapidly. A bowl of black vinegar, pig's feet, ginger and hard-boiled eggs is served to guests to eat and drink when they come to admire the baby. It is an old tradition for the Chinese. White vinegars are frequently used. However, it is the red vinegar we use throughout this book. It gives so much flavor when it is used to make a salad.

PRESERVED VEGETABLES. Chinese preserved vegetables come in jars or cans, mostly with gingers, diakon, or cucumber. Once it is drained, it is very good to make Peking Duck Salad, or to be used as a topping for Sweet and Sour dishes such as Sweet and Sour Fish or Pork.

TOASTED SESAME SEEDS. Toasted sesame seeds are plain sesame seeds toasted in a pan without oil until they became golden brown. Cool and cover. They will keep out of the refrigerator for a month. You may also buy toasted sesame seeds.

LOTUS. Lotus is the Chinese water lily found plentifully in the pond of Summer Palace of Ching Dynasty (1644-1911) in Peking. The root can be bought fresh when in season, or in cans with water. The seeds must be soaked overnight until softened. The leaf can be used fresh or dried, to wrap a bundle of rice for steaming. It is one of the most versatile vegetables in China, as the flowers can be admired and the rest of the plant can be used for food. The Chinese herb doctor uses this plant freely for medicine. It is said that it can keep a person from catching a cold.

GLUTINOUS RICE. Chinese call it "Nor Mai." It's sticky and mostly used as a filling. It can be wrapped in a piece of caul fat or in lotus leaves. As the filling of Deep-Fried Crispy Rice Duck, it is terrific. When sweetened, it can be used as a dessert item. When cooked with dried shrimp and Lop Chong (Chinese sausage), it can be an entree for home cooking – as a welcome item.

CAUL FAT. Caul fat somewhat resembles a piece of netting, slightly reddish in color. It comes from the intestines of the pig, and it is clean and safe to use. Sometimes the Chinese use it as the wrapper of Spring Rolls, or for the Golden Brown Deep-Fried Taro Duck. It may be purchased in Chinatown at a meat stand.

CHINESE TARO. Chinese taro offers a good smell, and is soft and tasty. It can be cooked as a potato. Cut into a butterfly for decoration, it offers an unusual natural design, because it has fine red threads all over. If not available, any kind of taro can be substituted, but the Chinese is best. Taro may cause itching on the hands when handling. If so, wash your hands and put them over heat for a few minutes until itching disappears, then wash again with soap and water. At one time I called my doctor and told him my hands are itching because I cut taro. He told me to come into the office. I said it would cost me money to see a doctor, especially during the depressed economy. I asked for free advice. He told me simply to scratch it until good times return.

# Index




Abalone,
 Mock, in Oyster Sauce, 45
 with Black Mushrooms, 62
Almond,
 Chinese Cookies, 210
 Chinese Snow Cookies, 206
 Float, Low-Calorie, 205
 Slivered, Topped Chinese Cookies, 209
Appetizer,
 Deep-Fried Colorful Shrimp Chips, 10
 Deep-Fried Shrimp, 11
 Deep-Fried Shrimp Gau Gee, 13
 Golden Brown Sea Bass Fillet, 14
 Golden Brown Vegetarian Spring Rolls, 20
 Golden Brown Oyster Rolls, 22
 Old-Fashioned Oyster Rolls, 24
 Shanghai Drunken Chicken, 18
 Shrimp Toast, 12
 Szechwan Pan Pan Chicken, 15
 Szechwan Strange-Taste Chicken, 16
 Wonderful Taste Chicken, 17
Asparagus,
 Poached, 185
 Tender, 176
Assorted Vegetables in Turmeric Sauce, 189
Baked Fish in Red Cooked Sauce, 71
Baked Fish with Pineapple in Sweet and Sour Sauce, 72
Banana,
 Chinese Tea Muffins, 211
 Lichee Orange Dessert Topping, 207
Banquet for Chinese New Years, 234
Banquet for Christmas, 233
Barbecue, Red Chinese Sauce, 217
Barbecued Spareribs, 137
Basic Marinade, 216
Basic Marinade for Beef, 246
Basic Sweet and Sour Sauce, 216
Basic Tools, 257-260
Bean Curd Casserole, 178
Bean Curd Sticks, 264
Bean Sauce Pork, 140
Bean Sprout, Tofu and Salad, 38
Bean Thread, Vegetable and Soup, 31
Beef,
 Broccoli, 157
 Fresh Mushrooms with Boneless Chicken and, 158
 Grilled Short Ribs, 159
 Mongolian, 152
 on Deep-Fried Rice Sticks, 155
 Steamed, 159
 Tomato, 154
 with Oyster Sauce, 153
 White Turnips with, 172
Beijing – Feng Ze Yuan Restaurant, 239
Birthday Banquet for Ten Persons, 225
Black Mushrooms with Tofu, 166
Boiled Chicken in Oyster Sauce, 70
Bok Choy,
 Fresh, 175
 Poached, 194
 Soup, 26
Broccoli,
 Beef, 157
 Fresh, 176
 Poached Deluxe, 185
 Sauteed, in Mock Crab Meat Sauce, 43
 Stir-Fry Vegetables, and Carrots, 186
 Tofu and, 41
Buns, Chinese, 148
Cake, Butter, Steamed, 212
Cantonese,
 Banquet for All Special Occassions, 232
 Chicken in Oyster Sauce, 94
 Crab Meat Chow Mein, 199
 Lemon Chicken, 97
 Steamed Fish, 69
 Steamed Prawns, 81
 Style, Poached Fish, 66
Carrots,
 Stir-Fry Vegetables, Broccoli and, 186
 Young Corn with, 192
Cashew Nuts,
 Deep-Fried Chicken with, 113
 Toasted, Peking Duck with, 128
 Tofu with, 42
Casserole,
 Bean Curd, 178
 Chicken Hong Kong Style, 104
 Seafood, Hong Kong Style, 75
Celery, Stir-fried Peking Duck Meat with, and Young Corn, 121
Char Siu, Chinese Salad, 35
Chicken,
 Boiled, in Oyster Sauce, 90
 Boneless, Fresh Mushrooms and Beef, 158
 Broth, 252
 Cantonese in Oyster Sauce, 94
 Casserole, Hong Kong Style, 104
 Chinese Salad, 34
 Chow Mein, 96
 Cold, in Ginger-Onion Sauce, 92
 Cold with Dips, 95
 Deep-Fried, with Cashews, 113
 Fried Rice, 107
 How To Do a "Prepared Chicken," 90
 Kung Pao, 64
 Kung Pao, Peking Style, 102
 Lemon Cantonese, 97
 Mango in Hoisin Sauce, 99
 Phoenix Nest, 106
 Shanghai Drunken, 18
 Soyu, 100

Soyu with Vegetables, 101
Steamed with Black Mushrooms, 174
Szechwan Pan Pan, 15
Szechwan Red-Oil, 19
Szechwan Strange-Taste, 16
with Ham, Hong Kong Style, 93
Wonderful Taste, Hawaiian Style, 17
China, Titus Chan's, 2-8
Chinese,
Almond Cookies, 210
Almond Snow Cookies, 206
Banana Tea Muffins, 211
Broccoli, 175
Buns, 148
Char Siu Salad, 35
Chicken Salad, 34
Cooking Utensils (photographs), 261-262
Dinner, Proper Order for Serving a, 255-256
Food, How To Order, 220
Hot Mustard, 214
Red Barbecue Sauce, 217
Roast Pork Salad, 35
Slivered Almond Topped Cookies, 209
Stir-Fried Pea Pods, 187
Sweet Ginger Cookies, 207
Taro, 271
Chow Mein,
Cantonese Crab Meat, 199
Chicken, 96
Sparerib, 197
Choy Sum, Mock Abalone with, 44
Clams, Steamed in Black Bean Sauce, 88
Classic Peking Duck, 123
Cold Chicken in Ginger-Onion Sauce, 92
Cold Chicken with Dips, 95
Cookies,
Chinese Almond, 210
Chinese Almond Snow, 206
Sesame, 208
Slivered Almond-Topped Chinese, 209
Sweet Chinese Ginger, 207
Cooking Tips, 246-254
Corn,
Creamed Soup, 181
Stir-Fried Peking Duck Meat with Celery and Young, 121
Young, with Carrots, 192
Crab,
Ginger-Onion, 86
Meat, Cantonese, Chow Mein, 199
Meat, Tofu in Creamy White Sauce, 165
Shanghai Steamed, 87
Soup Supreme, 63
Creamed Corn Soup, 181
Crispy Walnuts with Diced Mushrooms, 51
Crunchy Peking Duck Salad, 120
Cubed Sweet and Sour Fish, 74
Curry, Singapore Noodles with, 201
Cutting Up Chicken (Photographs), 91
Dessert,
Chinese Almond Cookies, 210
Chinese Almond Snow Cookies, 206
Chinese Banana Tea Muffins, 211
Lichee Banana-Orange Topping, 207
Low-Calorie Almond Float, 205
Sesame Cookies, 208
Slivered Almond-Topped Chinese Cookies, 209
Steamed Butter Cake, 212
Strawberries with Tofu Dip, 204
Sweet Chinese Ginger Cookies, 207
Tofu with Fruit Cocktail, 204
Deep-Fried,
Beef on Rice Sticks, Peking Style, 155
Chicken with Cashews, 113
Golden-Brown Peking Duck in Sweet and Sour Sauce, 129
Shrimp, 11
Shrimp Gau Gee, 13
Dinner For A Romantic Occasion, 228
Dip, Sesame Lime Red Chili, 215
Dips, Cold Chicken with, 95
Dry Braised Shrimp Szechwan Style, 76
Duck,
Lichee Boneless, in Sweet and Sour Sauce, 110
Roast, Singapore Style, 111
Smoked Tea, 108
Szechwan Crispy, 112
E Mein,
Stir-Fry Vegetables, 202
With Ham, 198
Easy Chinese Pancakes, 144
Economical, Delicious Seafood Dinner, 237
Egg
Drop Soup, 179
Flower Soup, 180
Fu Young, 103
Roll Wrappers, 167
Eggplant,
With Pork in Bean Sauce, 141
Szechwan, 193
Elaborate Feast in Hong Kong, 244
Eleven-Course Peking Duck Feast, 117
Exotic Cantonese Dinner, 231
Fancy Pancakes for Peking Duck, 126
Fish and Seequar Soup, 29
Five Spice Powder, 265
Five Spice Salt, 214
Fresh Bok Choy, 175
Fresh Broccoli, 176
Fresh Mushrooms, 177
Fresh Mushrooms with Boneless Chicken and Beef, 157
Fresh Vegetable Soup, 27
Garlic Ginger Oil, 215
Gau Gee, Deep-Fried Shrimp, 13
Ginger,
Garlic Oil, 215
Onion Crab, 86
Cookies, Sweet Chinese, 207
Glutinous Rice, 271
Golden-Brown Oyster Rolls, 22
Golden-Brown Sea Bass Fillet Appetizer, 14
Golden-Brown Vegetarian Spring Rolls, 20
Grilled Short Ribs, 159

Guangzhon-Ban Xi Restaurant, 243
Guangzhon-Bei-Yuan Restaurant, 242
Ham,
Chicken with, Hong Kong Style 93
E Mein with, 198
Hangchow Fish Ball Soup, 28
Hash, Pork, 171
Hong Kong Style,
Chicken Casserole, 104
Chicken with Ham, 93
Fancy Floating Restaurant, Poached Fish, 67
Young Chow Fried Rice, 149
Hunan Shrimp, 78
Ingredients, 263-271
Introduction to Peking Duck, 116
Jai, Chinese Vegetarian Food, 49
Jow Lee, 260
Kau Yuk, 145
Kung Pao,
Chicken, 64
Chicken, Peking Style, 102
Fish, 73
Lemon Chicken Cantonese, 97
Lettuce, Poached Head, in Oyster Sauce, 127
Lichee,
Banana-Orange Dessert Topping, 207
Boneless Duck in Sweet and Sour Sauce, 110
Sweet and Sour Shrimp, 59
Light and Crispy Duck Spring Rolls, 118
Lion's Head, 170
Lobster,
in Black Bean Sauce, 61
in Creamy White Sauce, 85
Lotus, 271
Low-Calorie Almond Float, 205
Low Hon Jai, 47
Mango Chicken in Hoisin Sauce, 99
Marinade,
Basic, 216
Basic for Beef, 246
Meat and Vegetable Soup, 30
Menu for Dieters and Seafood Lovers, 236
Meal for Six Persons, 223
Menu for Special Holidays, 226
Meal for Ten Persons, 224
Menu for Tong Kong Specialty House, 235
Microwave
Bean Curd Casserole, 178
Chinese or American Broccoli, 175
Creamed Corn Soup, 181
Egg Drop Soup, 179
Egg Flower Soup, 179
Fresh Bok Choy, 175
Fresh Broccoli, 176
Fresh Mushrooms, 177
Mixed Fresh Vegetables, 177
Lion's Head, 170
Pork Hash, 171
Steamed Chicken with Black Mushrooms, 174
Steamed Eggs, 180
Steamed Fish in Black Bean Sauce, 173
Tender Asparagus, 176
White Turnips with Pork or Beef, 172
Mixed Fresh Vegetables, 177
Mixed Vegetables in Oyster Sauce, 188
Mixed Vegetables in White Sauce, 190
Mock Abalone in Oyster Sauce, 45
Mock Abalone with Choy Sum, 44
Mock Sweet and Sour Pork, 46
Mongolian Beef, 152
Monk's Food, 50
Mu Sai, Szechwan Pork, 142
Muffins, Chinese Banana Tea, 211
Mushrooms,
Black, Abalone with, 62
Black, Steamed Chicken with, 174
Black, with Tofu, 166
Crispy Walnuts with Diced, 51
Fresh, 177
Fresh, with Boneless Chicken and Beef, 158
Sea Bass Fillet with, 84
Tofu with, 167
Mustard, Chinese Hot, 214
Noodles,
Cantonese Crab Meat Chow Mein, 199
Chicken Chow Mein, 96
E Mein with Ham, 198
Pork with, 196
Sam See Gon Low Mein, 200
Singapore with Curry, 201
Stir-Fry Vegetables E Mein, 202
Oil, Garlic-Ginger, 215
Old-Fashioned Oyster Rolls, 21
Opakapaka with Ginger Sauce, 58
Ordering for Four to Ten Persons, 222
Oyster Rolls,
Golden Brown, 22
Old-Fashioned, 21
Soft, Steamed in Oyster Sauce, 23
Pancakes,
Easy Chinese, 144
Fancy, for Peking Duck, 126
Pea Pods, Stir-Fried Chinese, 187
Peas,
Green Scallops with, 83
Green, Shanghai Prawns with, 77
Peking Duck,
Classic, 123
Crunchy Salad, 120
Deep-Fried Golden Brown in Sweet and Sour Sauce, 129
Eleven-Course Feast, 117
Fancy Pancakes for, 126
Fried Rice, 131
Introduction to, 116
Light and Crunchy Spring Rolls, 118
Meat with Pickled Vegetables, 122
Soup, 132
Stir-Fried Meat with Celery and Young Corn, 121
"Strange-Taste," 119
with Toasted Cashew Nuts, 128
Peking Style,
Beef on Deep-Fried Sticks, 155

Kung Pao Chicken, 102
Poached Asparagus, 185
Poached Bok Choy, 194
Poached Broccoli, 185
Poached Fish Cantonese Style, 66
Poached Fish Hong Kong Fancy Floating Restaurant Style, 67
Poached Head Lettuce in Oyster Sauce, 127
Poached Watercress, 189
Phoenix Nest, 10
Pork,
Bean Sauce, 140
Chinese Char Siu Salad, 35
Roast, Chinese Salad, 36
Eggplant with, in Bean Sauce, 141
Hash, 171
Kau Yuk, 145
Steamed Ground, with Salt Fish, 147
Sweet and Sour, 134
Stir-Fried Diced, with Walnuts, 138
Szechwan Mu Sai, 142
Tofu, 162
with Noodles, 196
White Turnips with, 172
Prawns,
Cantonese Steamed, 81
Shanghai, with Green Peas, 77
Soochow Fried, 80
Spicy, 60
Preserved Vegetables with Rice Vermicelli, 52
Presidential Dinner in Peking, 221
Red Chinese Barbecue Sauce, 217
Red-Oil Szechwan Chicken, 19
Rice,
Chicken Fried, 107
Peking Duck Fried, 131
Vegetarian Fried, 53
Vermicelli, Preserved Vegetables with, 52
Young Chow Fried, Hong Kong Style, 149
Salad,
Chinese Char Siu
Chinese Chicken, 34
Chinese Roast Pork, 36
Crunchy Peking Duck, 120
Sam See, 37
Tofu and Bean Sprout, 38
Salt, Five Spice, 214
Sam See Gon Low Mein, 200
Sam See Salad, 37
Satay Sauce, 215
Sauce,
Sweet and Sour, 216
Red Chinese Barbecue, 217
Satay, 215
Spicy Fire, 215
Titus Chan's Mild Dipping, 214
Sauteed Broccoli in Mock Crab Meat Sauce, 43
Scallops with Green Peas, 83
Sea Bass,
Fillet with Mushrooms, 84
Golden Brown, Fillet, 14
With Aromatic Vegetables, 82
Seafood,
Baked Fish with Pineapple in Sweet and Sour Sauce, 72
Baked Fish in Red-Cooked Sauce, 71
Casserole, Hong Kong Style, 75
Cubed Sweet and Sour Fish, 74
Kung Pao Fish, 73
Poached Fish, Hong Kong Fancy Floating Restaurant Style, 67
Poached Fish Cantonese Style, 66
Shanghai Steamed Fish with Oyster Sauce, 70
Steamed Fish Cantonese Style, 69
Steamed Fish in Black Bean Sauce, 173
Seequar, Fish and Soup, 29
Sesame Cookies, 208
Sesame Lime Red Chili Dip, 215
Shanghai,
Drunken Chicken, 18
Luyang Tswun Restaurant, 240
Mansions, 241
Steamed Crab, 87
Steamed Fish with Oyster Sauce, 70
Prawns with Green Peas, 77
Short Ribs, Grilled, 159
Shrimp,
Colorful Chips Deep-Fried, 10
Deep-Fried, 11
Deep-Fried Gau Gee, 13
Dry-Braised Szechwan Style, 76
Hunan, 78
Sweet and Sour Lichee, 59
Toast, 12
Tofu with Dried, 164
with Pineapple, 79
Singapore,
Noodles with Curry, 201
Style Roast Duck, 111
Slivered Almond-Topped Chinese Cookies, 209
Smoked Tea Duck, 108
Soft, Steamed Oyster Rolls in Oyster Sauce, 23
Soochow Fried Prawns, 80
Soup,
Bok Choy, 26
Crab Supreme, 63
Creamed Corn, 181
Egg Drop, 179
Egg Flower, 180
Fish and Seequar, 29
Fresh Vegetable, 27
Hangchow Fish Ball, 28
Meat and Vegetable, 30
Peking Duck, 132
Tofu and Spinach, 32
Vegetable and Bean Thread, 31
Soyu Chicken, 100
Soyu Chicken with Vegetables, 101
Sparerib Chow Mein, 197
Spareribs,
Barbecued, 137
Sweet and Sour, 135
Spicy Fire Sauce, 215

Spicy Prawns, 60
Spring Rolls,
Golden Brown Vegetarian, 20
Light and Crispy Peking Duck, 118
Steamed Beef, 159
Steamed Butter Cake, 212
Steamed Chicken with Black Mushrooms, 174
Steamed Clams in Black Bean Sauce, 88
Steamed Eggs, 180
Steamed Fish Cantonese, 69
Steamed Fish in Black Bean Sauce, 173
Steamed Ground Pork with Salt Fish, 147
Stir-Fried Chinese Pea Pods, 187
Stir-Fried Diced Pork with Walnuts, 138
Stir-Fried Mixed Vegetables, 191
Stir-Fried Peking Duck with Celery and Young Corn, 121
Stir-Fried Vegetables, Broccoli and Carrots, 186
Stir-Fried Vegetables E Mein, 202
"Strange-Taste" Peking Duck, 119
Strawberries with Tofu Dip, 204
Sweet and Sour Sauce,
Basic Sauce, 216
Fish, Cubed, 74
Lichee Shrimp, 59
Mock Pork, 46
Pork, 134
Spareribs, 135
Sweet Chinese Ginger Cookies, 207
Szechwan,
Crispy Duck, 112
Cuisine Graduation Banquet, 230
Eggplant, 193
Mu Sai Pork, 142
Pan Pan Chicken, 15
Red-Oil Chicken, 19
Strange-Taste Chicken, 16
Style, Dried-Braised Shrimp, 76
Three Chinese Firepot Dinners, 238
Tofu,
and Bean Sprout Salad, 38
and Broccoli, 41
and Spinach Soup, 32
Black Mushrooms with 166
in Sweet and Sour Sauce, 168
Pork, 162
with Cashew Nuts, 42
with Crab Meat in Creamy White Sauce, 165
with Dried Shrimp, 164
with Fruit Cocktail, 204
with Ground Beef, 163
with Mushrooms, 167
Tofu Dip with Strawberries, 204
Turnips, White, with Pork or Beef, 172
Vegetable,
and Bean Thread Soup, 31
Cutting, 248
Meat and Soup, 30
Soup, Fresh, 27
Vegetable Main Dish,
Crispy Walnuts with Diced Mushrooms, 51
Jai, Chinese Vegetarian Food, 49
Mock Abalone in Oyster Sauce, 45
Mock Abalone with Choy Sum, 49
Mock Sweet and Sour Pork, 46
Monk's Food, 50
Preserved Vegetables with Rice Vermicelli, 52
Sauteed Broccoli in Mock Crab Meat Sauce, 43
Tofu and Broccoli, 41
Tofu with Cashew Nuts, 42
Vegetarian Fried Rice, 53
Vegetables,
Aromatic, Sea Bass with, 82
Assorted, in Turmeric Sauce, 189
Fresh Bok Choy, 175
Fresh Broccoli, 176
Fresh Mushrooms, 177
Mixed Fresh, 177
Mixed, in Oyster Sauce, 188
Mixed, in White Sauce, 190
Stir-Fried Mixed, 191
Poached Asparagus, 185
Poached Bok Choy, 194
Poached Broccoli Deluxe, 185
Poached Watercress, 184
Stir-Fried, Broccoli and Carrots, 186
Stir-Fry E Mein, 202
Tender Asparagus, 176
Young Corn with Carrots, 192
Vegetarian,
Fried Rice, 53
Spring Rolls, Golden Brown, 20
Thoughts on Food, 40
Walnuts,
Crispy with Diced Mushrooms, 51
Stir-Fried Diced Pork with, 138
Watercress, Poached, 189
White Turnips with Pork or Beef, 172
Wonderful Taste Chicken, Hawaiian Style, 17
Young Chow Fried Rice, Hong Kong Style, 149
Young Corn with Carrots, 192